Privacy and Human Rights 2000

An International Survey of Privacy Laws and Developments

David Banisar

Electronic Privacy Information Center
Washington, DC, USA

Privacy International
London, UK

About the Electronic Privacy Information Center

The Electronic Privacy Information Center (EPIC) is a public interest research center in Washington, D.C. It was established in 1994 to focus public attention on emerging civil liberties issues and to protect privacy, the First Amendment, and constitutional values. EPIC is a project of the Fund for Constitutional Government. EPIC is a member of the Transatlantic Consumer Dialog, Global Internet Liberty Campaign, the Internet Free Expression Alliance and the Internet Privacy Coalition.

The EPIC Bookstore provides a comprehensive selection of books and reports on computer security, cryptography, the First Amendment and free speech, open government, and privacy. Visit the EPIC Bookstore at www.epic.org/bookstore/.

About Privacy International

Privacy International (PI) is a human rights group formed in 1990 as a watchdog on surveillance by governments and corporations. PI is based in London, England, and has an office in Washington, D.C. PI has conducted campaigns throughout the world on issues ranging from wiretapping and national security activities, to ID cards, video surveillance, data matching, police information systems, and medical privacy.

An electronic version of this report and updates is available from the Privacy International web page at http://www.privacyinternational.org/

EPIC Staff

Marc Rotenberg, Executive Director
David L. Sobel, General Counsel
Andrew Shen, Policy Analyst
Sarah Andrews, Policy Analyst
David Banisar, Senior Fellow
Wayne Madsen, Senior Fellow

Acknowledgments

This study was written by David Banisar, Deputy Director of Privacy International and a Senior Fellow at the Electronic Privacy Information Center. Substantial writing and research assistance for this edition was provided by Sarah Andrews, Policy Analyst at EPIC, Colleen Chien, of the Boalt Hall Law School, University of California, Berkeley and Pablo Palazzi of Fordham University Law School. Simon Davies, Director General of Privacy International, contributed to the introductory material.

To gather information for this study and previous editions, knowledgeable individuals from academia, government, human rights groups and other fields were asked to submit reports and information. Their reports were supplemented with information gathered from Constitutions, laws, international and national government documents, news reports, human rights reports and other sources.

EPIC and Privacy International would like to thank the following people for providing invaluable reports, information and advice: Jason Abrams, EPIC; Andrzej Adamski, Nicolas Copernicus University, Poland; Yaman Akdeniz, Cyber-Rights & Cyber-Liberties; Andrej D. Bartosiewicz, Citizen's Initiative for a Good Law on Access To Information, Slovakia; Diana Alonso Blas, Registratiekamer, Netherlands; Mads Bryde Andersen, University of Copenhagen, Denmark; Jacques Berleur, Facultes Universitaires N.D. de la Paix, Belgium; Colin Bennett, University of Victoria, Canada; Mark Berthold, Office of the Ombudsman, New Zealand; Herbert Burkert, GMD, Germany; Lee Bygrave, Norwegian Research Centre for Computers & Law; Rafael Fernandez Calvo, CLI, Spain; Anne Carblanc, OECD, France; Pavel Cerny, EPS, Czech Republic; Dmitry Chereshkin, Russian Academy of Natural Sciences; Tyng-Ruey Chuang, Taiwan Association of Human Rights; Dr. Richard Claude,

Washington, D.C.; Tracy Cohen, Link Centre, University of the Witwatersrand, South Africa; Ulrich Dammann, Bundesbeauftragte für den Datenschutz, Germany; Alexander Dix, Commissioner for Data Protection and Access to Information, Brandenburg, Germany; Ronnie Downes, Irish Data Protection Agency; Jón Erlendsson, Iceland; William G. Ferroggiard, National Security Archive, USA; Maurice Frankel, Campaign for Freedom of Information, UK; Miguel Angel Garcia, Estudios de Consumo, Spain; Marie Georges, CNIL, France; Rishab Aiyer Ghosh, India; Eric Goldstein, Human Rights Watch Middle East/North Africa; Graham Greenleaf, University of New South Wales, Australia; Marina Gromova, Russia; Alex Hamilton, Liberty, United Kingdom; Pétur Hauksson, Mannvernd, Iceland; Bénédicte Havelange, Commission de la Protection de la Vie Privée, Belgium; Jan Holvast, Holvast and Partners, Netherlands; Gus Hosein, Privacy International; Deborah Hurley, Harvard Information Infrastructure Project; Pavol Husar, Commissioner for the Protection of Personal Data in Information Systems, Slovak Republic; Joel Jaakkola, Finland; Ms. Ona Jakstaite, State Data Protection Inspection, Lithuania; Sigrún Jóhannesdóttir, The Iclandic Data Protection Commission; Marina Karakonova, Access to Information Programme, Bulgaria; Michael Kassner, EPIC; Yeoh Beng Keat, Ministry of Energy, Communications and Multimedia, Malaysia; Maija Kleemola, Office of Data Protection Ombudsman, Finland; Dieter Kronegger, Arge Daten, Austria; Jorma Kuopus, Office of the Parliamentary Ombudsman, Finland; Margarita Lacabe, Derechos Human Rights; Anne-Christine Lacoste, Belgian Privacy Data Protection Commission; Steven Lau, Hong Kong Privacy Commissioner; Pippa Lawson, Public Interest Advocacy Centre, Canada; Georg Lechner, Austrian Data Protection Commission; Wayne Madsen, EPIC; László Majtényi, Hungarian Information and Privacy Commissioner; Veni Markovski, Internet Society Bulgaria; Viktor Mayer-Schönberger, Harvard University; Jay McKinnon, EPIC; Robin McLeish, Hong Kong; Erich Moechel, quintessenz, Austria; Andrea Monti, Studio Legale Monti, Italy; Dinesh Nair; Victor Naumov, St.Petersburg Institute for Informatics, Russia; Dr. Karel Neuwirt, Office for Personal Data Protection, Czech Republic; Detlef Nogala, Max-Planck-Institut, Germany; Nelly Ognyanova, Bulgarian Institute for Legal Development; Kaidi Oone, Estonian State Chancellery, Department of State Information Systems; Maxim Otstavnov, Computerra, Russia; Hugues Parasie, Commission de la Protection de la Vie Privée, Belgium; Andriy Pazyuk, Privacy Ukraine; Charlotte Edholm Petersen, Datatilsynet, Denmark; Yves Poullet, Centre de Recherches Informatique et Droit, Belgium; Andrei Pribylov, Human Rights Network, Russia; Joel Reidenberg, Fordham University Law School, USA; Dovota Rowicka, Bureau of Inspector General for the Protection of Personal Data, Poland; Felipe Rodriquez, Electronic Frontiers Australia; Roman Romanov, Sebastopol Group for Human Rights Protection,

Ukraine; Anneliese Roos, University of South Africa; Dr Paul Roth, University of Otago, New Zealand; Dag Wiese Schartum, University of Oslo, Norway; Anat Scolnicov, Association for Civil Rights in Israel; Jin Wan Seo, Department of Public Administration, University of Inchon, South Korea; Antonino Serra Cambaceres, Consumers International; Justyna Seweryoska, Bureau of the Inspector General for the Protection of Personal Data, Poland; Bernard Silva, Office of the Federal Privacy Commissioner, Australia; Andrew Shen, EPIC; Sergei Smirnov, Human Rights Network, Russia; Robert Ellis Smith, Privacy Journal; Christoph Sobotta, University of Frankfurt, Germany; Barry Steinhardt, ACLU; Blair Stewart, New Zealand Privacy Commission; Bettina Stomper, quintessenz, Austria; Ivan Szekely, Central European University, Hungary; Kosmas Tsiraktsopulos, Swiss Data Protection Commission; Marie Vallée, Videotron, Canada; Shauna Van Dongen, Privacy Journal, USA; Nigel Waters, Australia; Raymond Wacks, The University of Hong Kong; Elisabeth Wallin, The Data Inspection Board, Sweden; Maurice Wessling, Bits of Freedom, Netherlands; Ingrid Wilson; Australian Privacy Commission; Bobson Wong, Digital Freedom Network; Ko Youngkyoung, Social Information Networking Group, South Korea.

Financial assistance was provided by the Open Society Institute and the EPIC Trust.

Privacy and Human Rights 2000

Executive Summary

This report reviews the state of privacy in over fifty countries around the world. It outlines the constitutional and legal conditions of privacy protection, and summarizes important issues and events relating to privacy and surveillance. Among the key findings:

Privacy is a fundamental human right recognized in all major international treaties and agreements on human rights. Nearly every country in the world recognizes privacy as a fundamental human right in its constitution, either explicitly or implicitly. The most recently drafted constitutions include specific rights to access and control one's personal information.

Nearly all industrialized countries support comprehensive privacy and data protection acts and nearly fifty countries and jurisdictions have, or are in the process of, enacting such laws. In the past year, over a dozen countries have enacted new laws or updated previous acts. Countries are adopting these laws in many cases to address past governmental abuses, to promote electronic commerce, or to ensure compatibility with international standards developed by the European Union, the Council of Europe, and the Organization for Economic Cooperation and Development.

New technologies are increasingly eroding privacy rights. The technologies frequently are moving ahead of the legal protections. These include video surveillance cameras, identity cards and genetic databases.

Surveillance authority is regularly abused, even in many of the most democratic countries. The main targets are political opponents, journalists, and human rights activists. The U.S. government is leading efforts to relax legal and technical barriers to electronic surveillance, especially for Internet and satellite communications.

There is an increased right of access to public records. Nearly 40 countries now provide a legal right of access to government records through Freedom of Information Acts or Codes of Access.

Table of Contents

OVERVIEW..1

  DEFINING PRIVACY 1

    Aspects of Privacy..3

  MODELS OF PRIVACY PROTECTION 3

    Comprehensive laws...3

    Sectoral Laws...4

    Self- Regulation...4

    Technologies of Privacy 4

  THE RIGHT TO PRIVACY 5

  THE EVOLUTION OF DATA PROTECTION 8

    Rationales for Adopting Comprehensive Laws 9

    The European Union Data Protection Directives...................................9

  OVERSIGHT AND PRIVACY AND DATA PROTECTION COMMISSIONERS 11

  TRANSBORDER DATA FLOWS AND DATA HAVENS.....................................13

    EU-U.S. "Safe Harbor" Negotiations 15

THREATS TO PRIVACY..17

    Trends..18

    Technology transfer and policy convergence 18

  IDENTITY SYSTEMS...20

    Identity (ID) cards 20

    Biometrics 21

  SURVEILLANCE OF COMMUNICATIONS...22

    CALEA, ENFOPOL and Building in Surveillance................................23

    Internet Surveillance and Black Boxes 25

    Cyber-crime 27

    National Security and the "Echelon system" 29

    Tools for fighting surveillance 34

  ELECTRONIC COMMERCE...35

  SPY TV: INTERACTIVE TELEVISION & "T-COMMERCE".............................39

  AUDIO BUGGING 41

  VIDEO SURVEILLANCE 41

  SATELLITE SURVEILLANCE..44

  WORKPLACE PRIVACY 45

    Legal Background..46

    Performance Monitoring 48

    Telephone Monitoring 49

    E-mail and Internet Use Monitoring..*50*

    Drug Testing *52*

COUNTRY REPORTS..**57**

  ARGENTINE REPUBLIC 57

  COMMONWEALTH OF AUSTRALIA 62

  REPUBLIC OF AUSTRIA...68

  KINGDOM OF BELGIUM 70

  FEDERATIVE REPUBLIC OF BRAZIL..73

  REPUBLIC OF BULGARIA 75

  CANADA 79

  REPUBLIC OF CHILE..85

  PEOPLE'S REPUBLIC OF CHINA 87

    Special Administrative Region of Hong Kong *92*

  CZECH REPUBLIC 95

  KINGDOM OF DENMARK 98

    Greenland..*101*

  REPUBLIC OF ESTONIA 101

  REPUBLIC OF FINLAND..105

    Aland Islands *107*

  FRENCH REPUBLIC 108

  FEDERAL REPUBLIC OF GERMANY 112

  HELLENIC REPUBLIC (GREECE)..116

  REPUBLIC OF HUNGARY..119

  REPUBLIC OF ICELAND 122

  REPUBLIC OF INDIA 124

  IRELAND 127

  STATE OF ISRAEL..131

  ITALIAN REPUBLIC 134

  JAPAN 137

  REPUBLIC OF KOREA (SOUTH KOREA)...142

  REPUBLIC OF LATVIA..146

  REPUBLIC OF LITHUANIA 147

  GRAND DUCHY OF LUXEMBOURG..150

  MALAYSIA..153

  UNITED MEXICAN STATES...155

  KINGDOM OF THE NETHERLANDS..158

  NEW ZEALAND...162

    Self-governing territories *167*

  KINGDOM OF NORWAY 167

REPUBLIC OF PERU 170

REPUBLIC OF THE PHILIPPINES 173

REPUBLIC OF POLAND 176

REPUBLIC OF PORTUGAL 181

RUSSIAN FEDERATION 184

    Autonomous Russian Republics *187*

REPUBLIC OF SAN MARINO 188

REPUBLIC OF SINGAPORE 189

SLOVAK REPUBLIC 193

REPUBLIC OF SLOVENIA 195

REPUBLIC OF SOUTH AFRICA 197

KINGDOM OF SPAIN 201

KINGDOM OF SWEDEN 203

SWISS CONFEDERATION (SWITZERLAND) 207

REPUBLIC OF CHINA (TAIWAN) 211

KINGDOM OF THAILAND 213

REPUBLIC OF TURKEY 216

REPUBLIC OF UKRAINE 219

UNITED KINGDOM OF GREAT BRITAIN AND NORTHERN IRELAND 224

    Territories *229*

UNITED STATES OF AMERICA 229

Overview

Privacy is a fundamental human right. It underpins human dignity and other values such as freedom of association and freedom of speech. It has become one of the most important human rights issues of the modern age.

Privacy is recognized around the world in diverse regions and cultures. It is protected in the Universal Declaration of Human Rights, the International Covenant on Civil and Political Rights, and in many other international and regional human rights treaties. Nearly every country in the world includes a right of privacy in its constitution. At a minimum, these provisions include rights of inviolability of the home and secrecy of communications. Most recently written constitutions include specific rights to access and control one's personal information. In many of the countries where privacy is not explicitly recognized in the constitution, the courts have found that right in other provisions. In many countries, international agreements that recognize privacy rights such as the International Covenant on Civil and Political Rights or the European Convention on Human Rights have been adopted into law.

Defining Privacy

Of all the human rights in the international catalogue, privacy is perhaps the most difficult to define.[1] Definitions of privacy vary widely according to context and environment. In many countries, the concept has been fused with data protection, which interprets privacy in terms of management of personal information. Outside this rather strict context, privacy protection is frequently seen as a way of drawing the line at how far society can intrude into a person's affairs.[2] The lack of a single definition should not imply that the issue lacks importance. As one writer observed, "in one sense, all human rights are aspects of the right to privacy."[3]

Some viewpoints on privacy:

---

[1] James Michael, Privacy and Human Rights (UNESCO 1994) p.1.

[2] Simon Davies, Big Brother: Britain's web of surveillance and the new technological order (Pan, London, 1996) p. 23.

[3] Volio, Fernando, "Legal personality, privacy and the family" in Henkin (ed), The International Bill of Rights,(New York: Columbia University Press 1981).

In the 1890s, future U.S. Supreme Court Justice Louis Brandeis articulated a concept of privacy that urged that it was the individual's "right to be left alone." Brandeis argued that privacy was the most cherished of freedoms in a democracy, and he was concerned that it should be reflected in the Constitution.[4]

Alan Westin, author of the seminal 1967 work "Privacy and Freedom," defined privacy as the desire of people to choose freely under what circumstances and to what extent they will expose themselves, their attitudes and their behavior to others.[5]

According to Edward Bloustein, privacy is an interest of the human personality. It protects the inviolate personality, the individual's independence, dignity and integrity.[6]

According to Ruth Gavison, there are three elements in privacy: secrecy, anonymity and solitude. It is a state which can be lost, whether through the choice of the person in that state or through the action of another person.[7]

The Calcutt Committee in the UK said that, "nowhere have we found a wholly satisfactory statutory definition of privacy." But the committee was satisfied that it would be possible to define it legally and adopted this definition in its first report on privacy:

> The right of the individual to be protected against intrusion into his personal life or affairs, or those of his family, by direct physical means or by publication of information.[8]

The Preamble to the Australian Privacy Charter provides that, "A free and democratic society requires respect for the autonomy of individuals, and limits on the power of both state and private organizations to intrude on that autonomy . . . Privacy is a key value which underpins human dignity and other key values such as freedom of association and freedom

---

[4] Samuel Warren and Louis Brandeis, "The right to privacy," Harvard Law Review 4, 1890 pp 193 - 220.

[5] Alan F Westin, Privacy and Freedom, (New York: Atheneum: 1967) p. 7.

[6] "Privacy as an Aspect of Human Dignity," 39 New York University Law Review, p. 971 (1964).

[7] "Privacy and the Limits of Law," 89 Yale Law Journal 421, at 428 (1980).

[8] Report of the Committee on Privacy and Related Matters, Chairman David Calcutt QC, 1990, Cmnd. 1102, London: HMSO, page 7.

---

of speech. . . . Privacy is a basic human right and the reasonable expectation of every person."[9]

Aspects of Privacy

Privacy can be divided into the following separate but related concepts:

Information privacy, which involves the establishment of rules governing the collection and handling of personal data such as credit information, and medical and government records. It is also known as "data protection";

Bodily privacy, which concerns the protection of people's physical selves against invasive procedures such as genetic tests, drug testing and cavity searches;

Privacy of communications, which covers the security and privacy of mail, telephones, e-mail and other forms of communication; and

Territorial privacy, which concerns the setting of limits on intrusion into the domestic and other environments such as the workplace or public space. This includes searches, video surveillance and ID checks.

Models of Privacy Protection

There are four major models for privacy protection. Depending on their application, these models can be complimentary or contradictory. In most countries reviewed in the survey, several are used simultaneously. In the countries that protect privacy most effectively, all of the models work together to ensure privacy protection.

Comprehensive laws

In many countries around the world, there is a general law that governs the collection, use and dissemination of personal information by both the public and private sectors. An oversight body then ensures compliance. This is the preferred

---

[9] "The Australian Privacy Charter," published by the Australian Privacy Charter Group, Law School, University of New South Wales, Sydney 1994.

model for most countries adopting data protection laws and was adopted by the EU to ensure compliance with its data protection regime. A variation of these laws, which is described as a *co-regulatory model*, was adopted in Canada and is pending in Australia. Under this approach, industry develops rules for the protection of privacy which are enforced by the industry and overseen by the privacy agency.

Sectoral Laws

Some countries, such as the United States, have avoided enacting general data protection rules in favor of specific sectoral laws governing, for example, video rental records and financial privacy. In such cases, enforcement is achieved through a range of mechanisms. A major drawback with this approach is that it requires that new legislation be introduced with each new technology so protections frequently lag behind. The lack of legal protections for medical and genetic information in the U.S. is a striking example of its limitations. There is also the problem of a lack of an oversight agency. In many countries, sectoral laws are used to complement comprehensive legislation by providing more detailed protections for certain categories of information, such as telecommunications, police files or consumer credit records.

Self- Regulation

Data protection can also be achieved - at least in theory - through various forms of self-regulation, in which companies and industry bodies establish codes of practice and engage in self-policing. However, in many countries, especially the U.S., these efforts have been disappointing, with little evidence that the aims of the codes are regularly fulfilled. Adequacy and enforcement are the major problem with these approaches. Industry codes in many countries have tended to provide only weak protections and lack enforcement. This is currently the policy promoted by the governments of the United States, Japan, and Singapore.

Technologies of Privacy

With the recent development of commercially available technology-based systems, privacy protection has also moved into the hands of individual users. Users of the Internet and of some physical applications can employ a range of programs and systems that provide varying degrees of privacy and security of communications. These include encryption, anonymous remailers, proxy servers, digital cash and smart cards. Questions remain about security and trustworthiness of these systems.

The Right to Privacy

The recognition of privacy is deeply rooted in history. The Bible has numerous references to privacy.[10] Jewish law has long recognized the concept of being free from being watched.[11] There were also protections in Classical Greece and ancient China.[12]

Western countries have had protections for hundreds of years. In 1361, the Justices of the Peace Act in England provided for the arrest of peeping toms and eavesdroppers.[13] In 1765, British Lord Camden, striking down a warrant to enter a house and seize papers wrote, "We can safely say there is no law in this country to justify the defendants in what they have done; if there was, it would destroy all the comforts of society, for papers are often the dearest property any man can have."[14] Parliamentarian William Pitt wrote, "The poorest man may in his cottage bid defiance to all the force of the Crown. It may be frail; its roof may shake; the wind may blow though it; the storms may enter; the rain may enter – but the King of England cannot enter; all his forces dare not cross the threshold of the ruined tenement."[15]

Various countries developed specific protections for privacy in the centuries that followed. In 1776, the Swedish Parliament enacted the Access to Public Records Act which required that all government-held information be used for legitimate purposes. France prohibited the publication of private facts and set stiff fines for violators in 1858.[16] The Norwegian criminal code prohibited the publication of information relating to "personal or domestic affairs" in 1889.[17]

---

[10] Richard Hixson, Privacy in a Public Society: Human Rights in Conflict, p. 3 (1987). See Barrington Moore, Privacy: Studies in Social and Cultural History (1984).

[11] See Jeffrey Rose, The Unwanted Gaze (Random House, 2000).

[12] Ibid. at 5.

[13] Infra James Michael, p. 15. Justices of the Peace Act, 1361 (Eng.), 34 Edw. 3, c. 1.

[14] Entick v. Carrington, 1558-1774 All E.R. Rep. 45.

[15] Speech on the Excise Bill, 1763.

[16] The Rachel affaire. Judgment of June 16, 1858, Trib. pr. inst. de la Seine, 1858 D.P. III 62. See Jeanne M. Hauch, Protecting Private Facts in France: The Warren & Brandeis Tort is Alive and Well and Flourishing in Paris, 68 Tul. L. Rev. 1219 (May 1994).

[17] See prof. dr. juris Jon Bing, Data Protection in Norway, 1996.
<http://www.jus.uio.no/iri/rettsinfo/lib/papers/dp_norway/dp_norway.html>.

In 1890, American lawyers Samuel Warren and Louis Brandeis wrote a seminal piece on the right to privacy as a tort action, describing privacy as "the right to be left alone."[18] Following the publication, this concept of the privacy tort was gradually picked up across the U.S. as part of the common law.

The modern privacy benchmark at an international level can be found in the 1948 Universal Declaration of Human Rights, which specifically protects territorial and communications privacy. Article 12 states:

> No one should be subjected to arbitrary interference with his privacy, family, home or correspondence, nor to attacks on his honour or reputation. Everyone has the right to the protection of the law against such interferences or attacks.[19]

Numerous international human rights treaties specifically recognize privacy as a right. The International Covenant on Civil and Political Rights (ICCPR), the UN Convention on Migrant Workers[20] and the UN Convention on Protection of the Child[21] adopt the same language.[22]

On the regional level, various treaties make these rights legally enforceable. Article 8 of the 1950 Convention for the Protection of Human Rights and Fundamental Freedoms[23] states:

> (1) Everyone has the right to respect for his private and family life, his home and his correspondence. (2) There shall be no interference by a public authority with the exercise of this right except as in accordance with the law and is necessary in a democratic society in the interests of national security, public safety or the economic well-being of the country, for the prevention of disorder or crime, for the protection of health of morals, or for the protection of the rights and freedoms of others.

---

[18] Warren and Brandeis, The Right to Privacy, 4 Harvard Law Review 193 (1890).

[19] Universal Declaration of Human Rights, <http://www.hrweb.org/legal/udhr.html>.

[20] A/RES/45/158 25 February 1991, Article 14.

[21] UNGA Doc A/RES/44/25 (12 December 1989) with Annex, Article 16.

[22] International Covenant on Civil and Political Rights, <http://www.hrweb.org/legal/cpr.html>.

[23] Convention for the Protection of Human Rights and Fundamental Freedoms Rome, 4.XI.1950. <http://www.coe.fr/eng/legaltxt/5e.htm>.

The Convention created the European Commission of Human Rights and the European Court of Human Rights to oversee enforcement. Both have been active in the enforcement of privacy rights and have consistently viewed Article 8's protections expansively and interpreted the restrictions narrowly.[24] The Commission found in 1976:

> For numerous Anglo-Saxon and French authors, the right to respect "private life" is the right to privacy, the right to live, as far as one wishes, protected from publicity . . . In the opinion of the Commission, however, the right to respect for private life does not end there. It comprises also, to a certain degree, the right to establish and develop relationships with other human beings, especially in the emotional field for the development and fulfillment of one's own personality.[25]

The Court has reviewed member states' laws and imposed sanctions on numerous countries for failing to regulate wiretapping by governments and private individuals.[26] It has also reviewed cases of individuals' access to their personal information in government files to ensure that adequate procedures exist.[27] It has expanded the protections of Article 8 beyond government actions to those of private persons where it appears that the government should have prohibited those actions.[28]

Other regional treaties are also beginning to be used to protect privacy. Article 11 of the American Convention on Human Rights sets out the right to privacy in terms similar to the Universal Declaration.[29] In 1965, the Organization of American States proclaimed the American Declaration of the Rights and Duties of Man, which called for the protection of numerous human rights, including privacy.[30] The Inter-American Court of Human Rights has begun to address privacy issues in its cases.

---

[24] Nadine Strossen, "Recent U.S. and Intl. Judicial Protection of Individual Rights: A comparative Legal Process Analysis and Proposed Synthesis," 41 Hastings Law Journal 805 (1990).

[25] X v. Iceland, 5 Eur. Comm'n H.R. 86.87 (1976).

[26] European Court of Human Rights, Case of Klass and Others: Judgement of 6 September 1978, Series A No. 28 (1979). Malone v. Commissioner of Police, 2 All E.R. 620 (1979). See Note, "Secret Surveillance and the European Convention on Human Rights," 33 Stanford Law Review 1113, 1122 (1981).

[27] Judgement of 26 March 1987 (Leander Case).

[28] Id. at 848, 849.

[29] Signed Nov. 22, 1969, entered into force July 18, 1978, O.A.S. Treaty Series No. 36, at 1, O.A.S. Off. Rec. OEA/Ser. L/V/II.23 dec rev. 2.

[30] O.A.S. Res XXX, adopted by the Ninth Conference of American States, 1948 OEA/Ser/. L./V/I.4 Rev (1965).

The Evolution of Data Protection

Interest in the right of privacy increased in the 1960s and 1970s with the advent of information technology. The surveillance potential of powerful computer systems prompted demands for specific rules governing the collection and handling of personal information. The genesis of modern legislation in this area can be traced to the first data protection law in the world enacted in the Land of Hesse in Germany in 1970. This was followed by national laws in Sweden (1973), the United States (1974), Germany (1977), and France (1978).[31]

Two crucial international instruments evolved from these laws. The Council of Europe's 1981 Convention for the Protection of Individuals with regard to the Automatic Processing of Personal Data[32] and the Organization for Economic Cooperation and Development's (OECD) Guidelines Governing the Protection of Privacy and Transborder Data Flows of Personal Data[33] set out specific rules covering the handling of electronic data. These rules describe personal information as data that are afforded protection at every step from collection to storage and dissemination.

The expression of data protection in various declarations and laws varies. All require that personal information must be:

- obtained fairly and lawfully;
- used only for the original specified purpose;
- adequate, relevant and not excessive to purpose;
- accurate and up to date;
- accessible to the subject;
- kept secure; and
- destroyed after its purpose is completed.

These two agreements have had a profound effect on the enactment of laws around the world. Nearly thirty countries have signed the COE convention and several others are planning to do so shortly.[34] The OECD guidelines have also

---

[31] An excellent analysis of these laws is found in David Flaherty, Protecting Privacy in Surveillance Societies (University of North Carolina Press 1989).

[32] Convention fn the Protection of Individuals with regard to the Automatic Processing of Personal Data Convention, ETS No. 108, Strasbourg, 1981. <http://www.coe.fr/eng/legaltxt/108e.htm>.

[33] OECD, "Guidelines Governing the Protection of Privacy and Transborder Data Flows of Personal Data" Paris, 1981. <http://www.oecd.org/dsti/sti/it/secur/prod/PRIV-EN.HTM>.

[34] Council of Europe <http://conventions.coe.int/>.

---

been widely used in national legislation, even outside the OECD member countries.

Rationales for Adopting Comprehensive Laws

There are three major reasons for the movement towards comprehensive privacy and data protection laws. Many countries are adopting these laws for one or more reasons.

> **To remedy past injustices.** Many countries, especially in Central Europe, South America and South Africa, are adopting laws to remedy privacy violations that occurred under previous authoritarian regimes.

> **To promote electronic commerce.** Many countries, especially in Asia, have developed or are currently developing laws in an effort to promote electronic commerce. These countries recognize consumers are uneasy with their personal information being sent worldwide. Privacy laws are being introduced as part of a package of laws intended to facilitate electronic commerce by setting up uniform rules.

> **To ensure laws are consistent with Pan-European laws.** Most countries in Central and Eastern Europe are adopting new laws based on the Council of Europe Convention and the European Union Data Protection Directive. Many of these countries hope to join the European Union in the near future. Countries in other regions, such as Canada, are adopting new laws to ensure that trade will not be affected by the requirements of the EU Directive.

The European Union Data Protection Directives

In 1995 and 1997, the European Union enacted two directives to harmonize laws throughout the EU to ensure consistent levels of protections for citizens and to allow for the free flow of personal information throughout the EU.

The Directives set a baseline common level of privacy which not only reinforces current data protection law, but extended it to establish a range of new rights. The 1995 Data Protection Directive sets a benchmark for national law for processing personal information in electronic and manual files.[35] The 1997 Telecommunications Directive[36] establishes specific protections covering telephone, digital television, mobile networks and other telecommunications systems. Each EU member country was required to enact implementing legislation by October 1998, though as of the Summer of 2000, several are still pending.

Several principles of data protection are strengthened under the Directives: the right to know where the data originated, the right to have inaccurate data rectified, a right of recourse in the event of unlawful processing and the right to withhold permission to use data in some circumstances. For example, individuals have the right to opt-out free of charge from being sent direct marketing material. The Data Protection Directive contains strengthened protections over the use of sensitive personal data relating, for example, to health or finances. In the future, the commercial and government use of such information will generally require "explicit and unambiguous" consent of the data subject.

A key concept in the European model is "enforceability." The European Union is concerned that data subjects have rights that are enshrined in explicit rules, and that they can go to a person or an authority empowered to act on their behalf. Every EU country has a Data Protection Commissioner or agency that enforces the rules. It is expected that the countries with which Europe does business will need to provide a similar level of oversight.

The Directive imposes an obligation on member States to ensure that the personal information relating to European citizens has the same level of protection when it is exported to, and processed in, countries outside the EU. This requirement has resulted in growing pressure outside Europe for the passage of privacy laws. Those countries that refuse to adopt meaningful privacy laws may find themselves unable to conduct certain types of information flows with Europe, particularly if they involve sensitive data. (See below)

The Telecommunications Directive imposes wide-ranging obligations on carriers and service providers to ensure the privacy of users' communications, including Internet-related activities. The new rules will cover areas that until now have

---

[35] Directive 95/46/EC of the European Parliament and of the Council of 24 October 1995 on the protection of individuals with regard to the processing of personal data and on the free movement of such data, <http://europa.eu.int/comm/internal_market/en/media/dataprot/law/index.htm>.

[36] Directive Concerning the Processing of Personal Data and the Protection of Privacy in the Telecommunications Sector (Directive 97/66/EC of the European Parliament and of the Council of 15 December 1997), <http://www.ispo.cec.be/legal/en/dataprot/protection.html>.

fallen between the cracks of data protection laws. Access to billing data will be severely restricted, as will marketing activity. Caller ID technology must incorporate an option for per-line blocking of number transmission. Information collected in the delivery of a communication must be purged once the call is completed.

In July 2000, the European Commission, issued a proposal for a new directive on "the processing of personal data and the protection of privacy in the electronic communications sector."[37] The proposed directive was introduced as a part of a larger package aimed at strengthening competition within the European electronic communications markets. It will replace the existing 1997 Telecommunications Directive by extending the existing protections for an individual's "telecommunications" to a broader, more technology neutral category of "electronic communications." The proposed directive replaces existing definitions of telecommunications services and networks with new definitions of "electronic communications services and networks." In addition, it adds new definitions and protections for "calls," "communications," "traffic data" and "location data" in order to enhance the consumer's right to privacy and control in all kinds of data processing. These new provisions would, for example, ensure the protection of all information ("traffic") transmitted across the Internet, prohibit unsolicited commercial marketing by e-mail (spam) without opt-in consent, and protect mobile phone users from precise location tracking and surveillance. The directive also gives subscribers to all electronic communications services (such as GSM and e-mail) the right to chose whether they are listed in a public directory. As before, member states could restrict provisions of the Directive in the interests of law enforcement and public security.

Oversight and Privacy and Data Protection Commissioners

An essential aspect of any privacy protection regime is oversight. In most countries with an omnibus data protection or privacy act, there is also an official or agency that oversees enforcement of the act. The powers of these officials - Commissioner, Ombudsman or Registrar - vary widely by country. A number of countries including Germany and Canada also have officials or offices on a state or provincial level.

---

[37] European Commission, 'Proposal for a directive of the European Parliament and of the Council concerning the processing of personal data and the protection of privacy in the electronic communications sector' <http://europa.eu.int/comm/information_society/policy/framework/pdf/com2000385_en.pdf>.

Under Article 28 of the EU Data Protection Directive, all EU countries must have an independent enforcement body. Under the Directive, these agencies are given considerable power: governments must consult the body when the government draws up legislation relating to the processing of personal information; the bodies also have the power to conduct investigations and have a right to access information relevant to their investigations; impose remedies such as ordering the destruction of information or ban processing, and start legal proceedings, hear complaints and issue reports. The official is also generally responsible for public education and international liaison in data protection and data transfer. Many authorities also maintain the register of data controllers and data bases. They must approve licensing for data controllers.

A number of countries that do not have a comprehensive act still have a commissioner. These include Australia, Thailand and Canada. A major power of these officials is to focus public attention on problem areas, even when they do not have any authority to fix the problem. They can do this by promoting codes of practice and encouraging industry associations to adopt them. They also can use their annual reports to point out problems. For example, in Canada, the Federal Privacy Commissioner announced in his 2000 report the existence of an extensive database maintained by the federal government. Once the issue became public, the Ministry disbanded the database.

In a number of countries, the official also serves as the enforcer of the jurisdiction's Freedom of Information Act. These include Hungary and Thailand. The pending U.K. Freedom of Information Bill will make the Data Protection Commissioner also the Information Commissioner. On the sub-national level, many of the German Lund Commissioners have recently been given the power of information commissioner and most of the Canadian provincial agencies handle both data protection and freedom of information.

A major problem with many agencies around the world is a lack of resources to adequately conduct oversight and enforcement. Many are burdened with licensing systems which use much of their resources. Others have large backlogs of complaints or are unable to conduct significant number of investigations. Many that started out with adequate funding find their budgets cut a few years later. The Australian Privacy Commission had its budget severely cut in 1997 even as it was given more duties.

Independence is also a problem. In many countries, the agency is under the control of the political arm of the government or part of the Ministry of Justice and lacks the power or will to advance privacy or criticize privacy invasive proposals. In the U.S., the Office of Management and Budget is part of the Executive Office of the President. In Japan and Thailand, the oversight agency is under the control of the Prime Ministers Office. In Thailand, the director was transferred in 2000 after conflicts with the Prime Ministers' Office.

Finally, in some countries that do not have a separate office, the role of investigating and enforcing the laws is done by a human rights ombudsman or by a parliamentary official.

Transborder Data Flows and Data Havens

The ease with which electronic data flows across borders led to a concern that data protection laws could be circumvented by simply transferring personal information to a third countries, where the law didn't apply. This data could then be processed in those countries, frequently called a "data havens," without any limitations.

For this reason, most data protection laws include restrictions on the transfer of information to third countries unless the information is protected in the destination country. For example, Article 12 of the Council of Europe's 1981 Convention places restrictions on the transborder flows of personal data.[38] Similarly, Article 25 of the European Directive imposes an obligation on member States to ensure that any personal information relating to European citizens is protected by law when it is exported to, and processed in, countries outside Europe. It states:

> The Member States shall provide that the transfer to a third country of personal data which are undergoing processing or are intended for processing after transfer may take place only if . . . the third country in question ensures an adequate level of protection.

This requirement has resulted in growing pressure outside Europe for the passage of strong data protection laws. Those countries that refuse to adopt meaningful privacy laws may find themselves unable to conduct certain types of information flows with Europe, particularly if they involve sensitive data. Determination of a third country's system for protecting privacy is made by the European Commission. The overarching principle in this determination process is that the

---

[38] Council of Europe, Convention for the Protection of Individuals with regard to the Automatic Processing of Personal Data, 1981. <http://www.coe.fr/eng/legaltxt/108e.htm>.

level of protection in the receiving country must be "adequate" rather than "equivalent." Therefore, a reasonably high standard of protection is expected from the third party, although the precise dictates of the Directive need not be followed.

On July 26, 2000 the European Commission ruled that both Switzerland and Hungary provide "adequate" protection for personal information and therefore that all transfers of personal data to these countries could continue. The Commission is currently looking into the privacy protection schemes in several other non-EU countries, including New Zealand, Australia, Canada and Japan.[39]

Another possible way to protect the privacy of information transferred to countries that do not provide "adequate protection" is to rely on a private contract containing standard data protection clauses. This kind of contract would bind the data processor to respect fair information practices such as the right to notice, consent, access and legal remedies. In the case of data transferred from the European Union, the contract would have to meet the standard "adequacy" test, in order to satisfy the Data Protection Directive.[40] A number of model clauses that could be included in such a contract were outlined in a 1992 joint study by the Council of Europe, the European Commission and the International Chamber of Commerce.[41] In a June 2000 report (see below), the European Parliament accused the European Commission of a "serious omission" in failing to draft standard contractual clauses that European citizens could invoke in the courts of third countries before the Data Directive came into force. [42] It recommended that they do so before September 30, 2000. [43]

---

[39] See European Commission Press Release, 'Data protection: Commission adopts decisions recognising adequacy of regimes in US, Switzerland and Hungary', July 27, 2000.
<http://europa.eu.int/comm/internal_market/en/media/dataprot/news/safeharbor.htm>.

[40] See European Union, Internal Market Directorate, Background Information: Transfer of data to non-EU countries – FAQ. <http://europa.eu.int/comm/internal_market/en/media/dataprot/backinfo/info.htm>.

[41] Study Made Jointly by the Council of Europe, the Commission of the European Communities (1992). <http://www.coe.fr/dataprotection/Etudes_Rapports/ectype.htm>.

[42] European Parliament resolution on the Draft Commission Decision on the adequacy of the protection provided by the Safe Harbour Privacy Principles and related Frequently Asked Questions issued by the US Department of Commerce. <http://www.epic.org/privacy/intl/EP_SH_resolution_0700.html>.

[43] The article 29 data protection working group of the European Commission has issued documents giving guidance on the role of contracts generally. See 'Transfers of personal data to third countries: Applying Articles 25 and 26 of the EU data protection directive' 24 July 1998.
<http://europa.eu.int/comm/internal_market/en/media/dataprot/wpdocs/wp12en.htm>.

EU-U.S. "Safe Harbor" Negotiations

Although it was never formally ruled upon by the Commission, there were serious doubts whether the United States' sectoral and self-regulatory approach to privacy protection would pass the adequacy test laid down by the Directive. The EU commissioned two prominent U.S. law professors, who wrote a detailed report on the state of U.S. privacy protections and pointed out the many gaps in U.S. protection.[44]

The U.S. strongly lobbied the EU and members countries to find the U.S. system adequate. In 1998, the U.S. began negotiating a "Safe Harbor" agreement with the EU in order to ensure the continued transborder flows of personal data. The idea of the "Safe Harbor" was that U.S. companies would voluntarily self-certify to adhere to a set of privacy principles worked out by the U.S. Department of Commerce and the Internal Market Directorate of the European Commission. These companies would then have a presumption of adequacy and they could continue to receive personal data from the European Union. Negotiations on the drafting of the principles lasted nearly two years and were the subject of bitter criticism by privacy and consumer advocates.[45] In early July, the European Parliament approved a forceful resolution that the agreement needed to be re-negotiated in order to provide adequate protection.[46]

On July 26, 2000, the Commission approved the agreement.[47] The Commission did, however, promise to re-open negotiations on the arrangement if the remedies available to European citizens prove inadequate. EU member states were given 90 days to put the Commission's decision into effect and U.S. companies may join Safe Harbor starting in November. There is an open-ended grace period for U.S. signatory companies to implement the principles.

The principles require all signatory organizations to provide individuals with "clear and conspicuous" notice of the kind of information they collect, the purposes for which it may be used, and any third parties to whom it may be

---

[44] Paul M. Schwartz and Joel R. Reindenberg, Data Privacy Law, (Michie) (1996).

[45] See e.g., Public Comments Received by the US Department of Commerce in Response to the Safe Harbor Documents April 5, 2000, <http://www.ita.doc.gov/td/ecom/Comments400/publiccomments0400.html>.

[46] European Parliament resolution on the Draft Commission Decision on the adequacy of the protection provided by the Safe Harbour Privacy Principles and related Frequently Asked Questions issued by the US Department of Commerce. <http://www.epic.org/privacy/intl/EP_SH_resolution_0700.html>.

[47] Commission Decision on the adequacy of the protection provided by theSafe Harbour Privacy Principles and related Frequently Asked Questions issued by the US Department of Commerce. <http://europa.eu.int/comm/internal_market/en/media/dataprot/news/decision.pdf>.

---

disclosed. This notice must be given at the time of the collection of any personal information or "as soon thereafter as is practicable." Individuals must be given the ability to choose (opt-out of) the collection of data where the information is either going to be disclosed to a third party or used for an incompatible purpose. In the case of sensitive information, individuals must expressly consent (opt-in) to the collection. Organizations wishing to transfer data to a third party may do so if the third party subscribes to Safe Harbor or if that third party signs an agreement to protect the data. Organizations must take reasonable precautions to protect the security of information against loss, misuse and unauthorized access, disclosure, alteration and destruction. Organizations must provide individuals with access to any personal information held about them, and with the opportunity to correct, amend, or delete that information where it is inaccurate. This right is to be granted only if the burden or expense of providing access would not be disproportionate to the risks to the individual's privacy or where the rights of persons other than the individual would not be violated. In terms of enforcement, organizations must provide access to readily available and affordable independent recourse mechanisms which may investigate complaints and award damages. They must issue follow up compliance procedures and must adhere to sanctions for failing to comply with the Principles.

Privacy advocates and consumer groups both in the U.S. and Europe are highly critical of the European Commission's decision to approve the agreement, which they say will fail to provide European citizens with adequate protection for their personal data.[48] The agreement rests on a self-regulatory system whereby companies merely promise not to violate their declared privacy practices. There is little enforcement or systematic review of compliance. The Safe Harbor status is granted at the time of self-certification. There is no individual right to appeal or right to compensation for privacy infringements. There is an open ended grace period for U.S. signatory companies to implement the principles. The agreement will only apply to companies overseen by the Federal Trade Commission and Department of Transportation (excluding the financial and telecommunications sectors) and there are special exceptions granted for public records information protected by EU law.

---

[48] See for example the earlier Statement of the Transatlantic Consumer Protection Dialogue on U.S. Department of Commerce Draft International Safe Harbor Privacy Principles and FAQs March 30, 2000, <http://www.tacd.org/ecommercef.html#usdraft>.

Threats to Privacy

Even with the adoption of legal and other protections, violations of privacy remain a concern. In many countries, laws have not kept up with the technology, leaving significant gaps in protections. In other countries, law enforcement and intelligence agencies have been given significant exemptions. Finally, without adequate oversight and enforcement, the mere presence of a law may not provide adequate protection.

There are widespread violations of laws relating to surveillance of communications, even in the most democratic of countries. The U.S. State Department's annual review of human rights violations finds that over 90 countries illegally monitor the communications of political opponents, human rights workers, journalists and labor organizers. In 1996, a French government commission estimated that there were over 100,000 illegal wiretaps conducted by private parties, many on behalf of government agencies. There were protests in Ireland after it was revealed that the UK was monitoring all UK/Ireland communications from a base in Northern England. In Japan, police were fined 2.5 million yen for illegally wiretapping members of the Communist Party. The Echelon system is used by the United States, UK, Australia, Canada and New Zealand to monitor communications worldwide. (See below)

Police services, even in countries with strong privacy laws, still maintain extensive files on citizens for political purposes not accused or even suspected of any crime. Recently, investigations were held in Denmark, Sweden and Norway, countries with long histories of privacy protection, to investigate illegal spying by intelligence and police officials. In Switzerland, a scandal over secret police spying led to the enactment of a data protection act. In many former Eastern Bloc countries, there are still controversies over the disposition of the files of the secret police.

Companies regularly flaunt the laws, collecting and disseminating personal information. In the United States, even with the long-standing existence of a law on consumer credit information, companies still make extensive use of such information for marketing purposes and banks sell customer information to marketers. In many countries, inadequate security has resulted in the accidental disclosure of thousands of customers' records.

Trends

It is now common wisdom that the power, capacity and speed of information technology is accelerating rapidly. The extent of privacy invasion – or certainly the potential to invade privacy – increases correspondingly.

The increasing sophistication of information technology with its capacity to collect, analyze and disseminate information on individuals has introduced a sense of urgency to the demand for privacy legislation. Furthermore, new developments in medical research and care, telecommunications, advanced transportation systems and financial transfers have dramatically increased the level of information generated by each individual. Computers linked together by high-speed networks with advanced processing systems can create comprehensive dossiers on any person without the need for a single central computer system. New technologies developed by the defense industry are spreading into law enforcement, civilian agencies, and private companies.

Beyond these obvious aspects of capacity and cost, there are a number of important trends that contribute to privacy invasion:

> GLOBALISATION removes geographical limitations to the flow of data. The development of the Internet is perhaps the best known example of a global technology.

> CONVERGENCE is leading to the elimination of technological barriers between systems. Modern information systems are increasingly inter-operable with other systems, and can mutually exchange and process different forms of data.

> MULTI-MEDIA fuses many forms of transmission and expression of data and images so that information gathered in a certain form can be easily translated into other forms.

Technology transfer and policy convergence

The macro-trends outlined above have had particular effect on surveillance in developing nations. In the field of information and communications technology, the speed of policy convergence is compressed. Across the surveillance spectrum – wiretapping, personal ID systems, data mining, censorship or encryption

---

controls – it is the industrialized countries that invariably set the rules for the rest of the world.[49]

Human rights groups are concerned that much of this technology is being exported to developing countries that lack adequate protections. Currently, there are few barriers to the trade in surveillance technologies. Governments of developing nations rely on First World countries to supply them with technologies of surveillance such as digital wiretapping equipment, deciphering equipment, scanners, bugs, tracking equipment and computer intercept systems. The transfer of surveillance technology from first to third world is now a lucrative sideline for the arms industry.[50]

According to a 1997 report, *Assessing the Technologies of Political Control,* commissioned by the European Parliament's Civil Liberties Committee and undertaken by the European Commission's Science and Technology Options Assessment Office (STOA),[51] much of this technology is used to track the activities of dissidents, human rights activists, journalists, student leaders, minorities, trade union leaders, and political opponents. The report concludes that such technology (which it describes as "new surveillance technology") can exert a powerful "chilling effect" on those who "might wish to take a dissenting view and few will risk exercising their right to democratic protest." Large-scale ID systems are also useful for monitoring larger sectors of the population. In the absence of meaningful legal or constitutional protections, such technology is inimical to democratic reform. It can certainly prove fatal to anyone "of interest" to a regime.

Government and citizen alike may benefit from the plethora of IT schemes being implemented by the private and public sectors. New "smart card" projects in which client information is placed on a chip in a card may streamline complex transactions. The Internet will revolutionize access to basic information on government services. Encryption can provide security and privacy for all parties.

However, these initiatives will require a bold, forward looking legislative framework. Whether governments can deliver this framework will depend on their willingness to listen to the pulse of the emerging global digital economy and to recognize the need for strong protection of privacy.

---

[49] Simon Davies and Ian Hosein, "Liberty on the Line" in Liberating Cyberspace (Pluto Press, London, 1998)

[50] Big Brother Incorporated, Privacy International site: <http://www.privacy.org/pi/reports/.

[51] Science and Technology Options Assessment (STOA). Ref : project no. IV/STOA/RSCH/LP/politicon.1 <http://cryptome.org/stoa-atpc.htm>.

Identity systems

Identity (ID) cards

Identity (ID) cards are in use in one form or another in virtually all countries of the world. The type of card, its function, and its integrity vary enormously. While a majority of countries have official, compulsory, national IDs that are used for a variety of purposes, many developed countries do not. Amongst these are the United States, Canada, New Zealand, Australia, the United Kingdom, Ireland, and the Nordic countries. Those that do have such a card include Germany, France, Belgium, Greece, Luxembourg, Portugal and Spain.

ID cards are established for a variety of reasons. Race, politics and religion were often at the heart of older ID systems. The threat of insurgence, religious discrimination, or political extremism have been all too common motivators for the establishment of ID systems which would force enemies of the State into registration, or make them vulnerable in the open without proper documents.

In recent years, ID cards have been linked to national registration systems, which in turn form the basis of government administration. In such systems – for example Spain, Malaysia, Thailand and Singapore – the ID card becomes merely one visible component of a much larger system. With the advent of microprocessor technology, these cards can also become an interface for receipt of government services. Thus the cards become a fusion of a service technology and a means of identification. At the heart of such plans is a parallel increase in police powers. Even in democratic nations, police retain the right to demand ID on pain of detention.

In a number of countries, these systems have been successfully challenged on constitutional privacy grounds. In 1998, the Philippine Supreme Court ruled that a national ID system violated the constitutional right to privacy.[52] In 1991, the Hungarian Constitutional Court ruled that a law creating a multi-use personal identification number violated the constitutional right of privacy.[53] The 1997 Portuguese Constitution states "Citizens shall not be given an all-purpose national identity number."

---

[52] Philippine Supreme Court Decision of the National ID System, July 23, 1998, G.R. 127685. <http://bknet.org/laws/nationalid.html>.

[53] Constitutional Court Decision No. 15-AB of 13 April 1991, <http://www.privacy.org/pi/countries/hungary/hungarian_id_decision_1991.html>.

In other countries, opposition to the cards combined with the high economic cost of implementing the systems has led to their withdrawal. Massive protests against the Australia Card in 1987 resulted in the near collapse of the government. In the last year, cards projects in South Korea and Taiwan were stopped after protests. In the United States, government agencies and members of Congress received thousands of letters of protest against a regulation to make state drivers' licenses into uniform ID cards nationwide.

Biometrics

Biometrics is the process of collecting, processing and storing details of a person's physical characteristics for the purpose of identification and authentication. The most popular forms of biometric ID are retina scans, hand geometry, thumb scans, fingerprints, voice recognition, and digitized (electronically stored) photographs. The technology has gained the interest of governments and companies because, unlike other forms of ID such as cards or papers, it has the capacity to accurately and intimately identify the target subject.

Biometrics schemes are being implemented across the world. The technology is being used in retail outlets, government agencies, childcare centers, police forces and automated-teller machines. Spain has commenced a national fingerprint system for unemployment benefits and healthcare entitlements. Russia has announced plans for a national electronic fingerprint system for banks. Jamaicans are required to scan their thumbs into a database before qualifying to vote in elections. In France and Germany, tests are under way with equipment that puts fingerprint information onto credit cards. In Mexico, the Federal Election Institute funded a facial recognition system to use in the 2000 elections. In the US and Germany, some air travelers are now subject to scans of their iris before boarding airplanes.[54] Many computer manufacturers are proposing including biometric readers on their systems for security purposes.

An automated immigration system developed by the U.S. Immigration and Naturalization Service (INS) uses hand geometry.[55] In this project, frequent travelers have their hand geometry stored in a "smart" computer chip card. The traveler places a hand onto a scanner, and places the card into a slot. The system is open to all citizens in the visa waiver countries. The scheme may ultimately

---

[54] Iris scans take off at airports, ComputerWorld, July 17, 2000.

[55] See INS INSPASS Pages <http://www.ins.usdoj.gov/graphics/Howdoi/iNSpass.htm>.

result in a worldwide identification system for travelers. 80,000 travelers had signed up by December 1998.

The most controversial form of biometrics – DNA identification – is benefiting from new scanning technology that can automatically match DNA samples against a large database in minutes. Police forces in several countries including the United States, Germany and Canada have created national DNA databases. Samples are being routinely taken from a larger and larger groups of people. Initially, it was only individuals convicted of sexual crimes. Then it was expanded to people convicted of other violent crimes and then to arrests. Now, many jurisdictions are collecting samples from all individuals arrested, even for the most minor offenses. New York City Mayor Rudolf Giuliani even proposed that all children have a DNA sample collected at birth. In the United Kingdom, Australia, and the U.S., police have been demanding that all individuals in a particular area voluntarily provide samples or face being considered a suspect.

Surveillance of Communications

Nearly every country in the world has established some form of eavesdropping capability over telephone, fax and telex communications. In most countries, these intercepts are initiated and authorized by law enforcement or intelligence agencies. However, wiretapping abuses have been revealed in most countries, sometimes occurring on a vast scale involving thousands of illegal taps. The abuses invariably affect anyone "of interest" to a government. Targets include political opponents, student leaders and human rights workers.[56]

Law enforcement agencies have traditionally worked closely with telecommunications companies – many until recently controlled by government telecommunications agencies – to formulate arrangements that would make phone systems "wiretap friendly." These agreements range from allowing police physical access to telephone exchanges, to installing equipment to automate the interception.

The U.S. government has led a worldwide effort to limit individual privacy and enhance the capability of its police and intelligence services to eavesdrop on personal conversations. The campaign has had two strategies. The first is to promote laws that make it mandatory for all companies that develop digital telephone switches, cellular and satellite phones and all developing

---

[56] U.S. Department of State Country Report on Human Rights Practices for 1997, January 30, 1998.

communication technologies to build in surveillance capabilities; the second is to seek limits on the development and dissemination of products, both in hardware and software, that provide encryption, a technique that allows people to scramble their communications and files to prevent others from reading them.[57]

At the same time, the United States has been promoting greater use of electronic surveillance. FBI Director Louis Freeh has traveled extensively around the world, promoting the use of wiretapping in recently free countries such as Hungary and the Czech Republic. The U.S. pressured countries such as Japan in adopting their first ever laws allowing for wiretapping. The U.S. has also been working through international groups such as the OECD, G-8 and the Council of Europe to promote surveillance.

CALEA, ENFOPOL and Building in Surveillance

In the early 1990s, U.S. law enforcement agencies, led by the Federal Bureau of Investigation, began demanding that all current and future telecommunications systems be designed to ensure that they would be able to conduct wiretaps. After several years of lobbying, the U.S. Congress approved the Communications Assistance for Law Enforcement Act (CALEA) in 1994.[58] The act sets out legal requirements for telecommunications providers and equipment manufacturers on the surveillance capabilities that must be built into all telephone systems used in the United States. However, due to lobbying by the computer industry, the Internet was exempted from the requirements.

While the FBI was lobbying for CALEA in the United States, it also began working with the Justice and Interior Ministers of the European Union towards creating international technical standards for wiretapping.[59] In 1993, the FBI began hosting meetings at its research facility in Quantico, Virginia called the "International Law Enforcement Telecommunications Seminar" (ILETS). The meetings included representatives from Canada, Hong Kong, Australia and the EU. At these meetings, an international technical standard for surveillance, based on the FBI's CALEA demands, was adopted as the "International Requirements for Interception."

---

[57] See David Banisar and Simon Davies, "The Code War," Index on Censorship, January 1998.

[58] See EPIC Wiretap Pages: http://www.epic.org/privacy/wiretap/

[59] See ENFOPOL Timeline 1991-1999, <http://www.telepolis.de/tp/english/special/enfo/6382/1.html >.

In January 1995, the Council of the European Union approved a secret resolution adopting the ILETS standards.[60] The resolution was not formally debated and was not made public until late 1996. Following this, many countries adopted the resolution into their domestic laws without revealing the role of the FBI in developing the standard. Following the adoption, the EU and the U.S. offered a Memorandum of Understanding for other countries to sign to commit to the standards. A number of countries including Canada and Australia immediately signed the MOU. Others were encouraged to adopt the standards to ensure trade. International standards organizations, including the International Telecommunications Union and the European Telecommunication Standardisation Institute (ETSI), were then successfully approached to adopt the standards.

The ILETS group continued to meet. A number of committees were formed and developed a more detailed standard extending the scope of the interception standards. The new standards were designed to apply to a wide range of communications technologies, including the Internet and satellite communications. It also set more detailed criteria for surveillance across all technologies. The result was a 42-page document called ENFOPOL 98 (the EU designation for documents created by the EU Police Cooperation Working Group).[61]

In 1998, the document became public and generated considerable criticism. The committees responded by removing most of the controversial details and putting them into a secret operations manual that has not been made publicly available. The new document, now called ENFOPOL 19, expanded the type of surveillance now to include "IP address (electronic address assigned to a party connected to the Internet), credit card number and E-mail address."[62] In April 1999, the Council proposed the new draft council resolution to adopt the ENFOPOL 19 standards into law in the EU.

In May 1999, the European Parliament approved the ENFOPOL 19 resolution.[63] However, the vote was criticized for being taken late on a Friday with only 20 percent of the delegates present, and was reversed by the Council of Ministers.

---

[60] Council Resolution of 17 January 1995 on the lawful interception of telecommunications, Official Journal of the European Communities November 4, 1996 <http://europa.eu.int/eur-lex/en/lif/dat/1996/en_496Y1104_01.html>.

[61] ENFOPOL 98. <http://www.telepolis.de/tp/deutsch/special/enfo/6326/1.html>.

[62] Draft COUNCIL RESOLUTION of on the lawful interception of telecommunications in relation to new technologies ENFOLPOL 19, 15 March 1999 (22.03 <http://www.fipr.org/polarch/enfopol19.html>.

[63] See http://futurezone.orf.at/futurezone.orf?read=detail&id=994

The rejection has not stopped the ETSI from continuing their work on developing wiretapping standards.[64]

Internet Surveillance and Black Boxes

Following closely on the success of forcing telecommunications equipment manufacturers and companies to build in surveillance capabilities, intelligence and law enforcement agencies have turned their attention to force Internet Service Providers to facilitate surveillance of their users. A number of countries are demanding that ISPs install "black boxes" on their systems that can monitor the traffic of their users.

The actual workings of these black boxes are unknown to the public. What little information has been made public has revealed that many of the systems are based on "packet sniffers" typically employed by computer network operators for security and maintenance purposes. These are specialized software programs running in a computer that is hooked into the network at a location where it can monitor traffic flowing in and out of systems. These sniffers can monitor the entire data stream searching for key words, phrases or strings such as net addresses or e-mail accounts. It can then record or retransmit for further review anything that fits its search criteria. In many of the systems, the boxes are connected to government agencies by high speed connections. The U.S. FBI has developed a system called "Carnivore" that places a PC running Windows NT at an Internet Service Provider's offices and can monitor all traffic about a user including e-mail and browsing.[65] According to press reports, Carnivore "can scan millions of e-mails a second" and "would give the government, at least theoretically, the ability to eavesdrop on all customers' digital communications, from e-mail to online banking and Web surfing."[66] In response to the public uproar over Carnivore, Attorney General Janet Reno announced that the technical specifications of the system would be disclosed to a "group of experts" to allay

---

[64] See e.g. ETSI, Security Techniques Advisory Group (STAG), Definition of user requirements for lawful interception of telecommunications; Requirements of the law enforcement agencies, ETR 331, December 1996. ETSI, Telecommunications and Internet Protocol Harmonization Over Networks (TIPHON); Security; Studies into the Impact of lawful interception, ETSI TR 101 750 V1.1.1 (1999-11), November 1999; Intelligent Networks (IN); Lawful interception, ETSI EG 201 781 V1.1.1 (2000-07).

65 Testimony of Robert Corn-Revere, before the Subcommittee on the Constitution of the Committee on the Judiciary, United States House of Representatives, The Fourth Amendment and the Internet, April 6, 2000. <http://www.house.gov/judiciary/corn0406.htm>.

66 "FBI's System to Covertly Search E-Mail Raises Privacy," Legal Issues, Wall Street Journal, July 11, 2000.

---

public concerns.[67] EPIC has filed suit demanding access to all relevant information, including the sourcecode for the system.

In some countries, there have been laws or decrees enacted to require the systems to facilitate surveillance. Russia has been the leading country in this effort, but according to Russian computer experts, the U.S. government advised them on implementation. In 1998, the Russian Federal Security Service (FSB) issued a decree on the System for Operational Research Actions on the Documentary Telecommunication Networks (SORM-2) that would require Internet Service Providers to install surveillance devices and high speed links to the FSB which would allow the FSB direct access to the communications of Internet users without a warrant.[68] ISPs are required to pay for the costs of installing and maintaining the devices. When an ISP based in Volgograd challenged FSB's demand to install the system, the local FSB and Ministry of Communication attempted to have its license revoked. The agencies were forced to back off after the ISP challenged the decision in court. In a separate case, the Supreme Court ruled in May 2000 that SORM-2 was not a valid ministerial act because it failed several procedural requirements.

Following the Russian lead, in September 1999, Ukrainian President Leonid Kuchma proposed requiring that Internet Service Providers install surveillance devices on their systems based on the Russian SORM system. The rules and a subsequent bill were attacked by the Parliament and withdrawn. However, in August 1999, the security service visited a number of the large ISP who were reported to have installed the boxes.

In the Netherlands, a new Telecommunications Act was approved in December 1998 which requires that Internet Service Providers have the capability by August 2000 to intercept all traffic with a court order and maintain users logs for three months.[69] The bill was enacted after XS4ALL, a Dutch ISP, refused to conduct a broad wiretap of electronic communications of one of its subscribers. The Dutch Forensics Institute[70] has developed a "black-box" that is used to intercept Internet traffic at an ISP. The black box is under control of the ISP and is turned on after receiving a court order. The box is believed to look at

---

[67] "Reno to double-check Carnivore's bite," Reuters, July 13, 2000.

[68] Russia Prepares To Police Internet, The Moscow Times, July 29, 1998. More information in English and Russian is available from the Moscow Libertarium Forum <http://www.libertarium.ru/libertarium/sorm/>.

[69] Telecommunications Act <http://www.minvenw.nl/dgtp/data/tweng.doc>. Rules pertaining to telecommunications (Telecommunications Act), December 1998, <http://www.minvenw.nl/hdtp/hdtp2/wetsite/engels/index.html>.

[70] Dutch Forensics Institute Homepage: <http://www.holmes.nl/>.

authentication traffic of the person to wiretap and divert the person's traffic to law enforcement if the person is online.

More recently, the UK Parliament approved the Regulation of Investigatory Powers Act in July 2000. It requires that ISPs provide a "reasonable interception capability" in their networks. The intercepted traffic will be forwarded to a Government Technical Assistance Centre based in the headquarters of a branch of British Intelligence. While the legislation itself does not mention a black box, a government-sponsored report raised the likelihood that they would be necessary.

Not satisfied with national efforts based on laws, governments have begun demanding that computer and networking companies build in these capabilities. In 1999, the FBI approached the Internet Engineering Task Force, an Internet standards body, and asked that it facilitate net surveillance by designing communications protocols to facilitate surveillance.[71] The initiative was strongly opposed. The group held a meeting in November 1999 and found that the consensus was against the proposal. In April 2000, the group came out with an official position opposing the recommendation.[72]

Cyber-crime

A related effort for enhancing government control of the Internet and promoting surveillance is also being conducted in the name of preventing "cyber-crime," "information warfare" or "protecting critical infrastructures." Under these efforts, proposals to limit online privacy of net users are being introduced as a way to prevent computer hackers from attacking systems.

The lead bodies internationally are the European Union, the Council of Europe and the G-8, a high level organization made up of eight major industrialized countries.[73] The United States has been active behind the scenes in developing and promoting these efforts.[74] After meeting secretly for years, the organizations recently made public proposals that would place restrictions on online privacy, anonymity and encryption in the name of preventing cyber-crime.

---

[71] "Net Wiretapping: Yes or No?" Wired News, October 13, 1999.

[72] See RFC 2804, IETF Policy on Wiretapping <http://www.faqs.org/rfcs/rfc2804.html>.

[73] Dr Paul Norman, "Policing 'high tech crime' in the global context: the role of transnational policy networks," <http://www.bileta.ac.uk/99papers/norman.htm>.

[74] See http://www.privacyinternational.org/issues/cybercrime/ for details.

Since 1997, the Council of Europe's Committee of Experts on Crime in Cyber-space (PC-CY) has been meeting and drafting an international treaty. In April 2000, the Council of Europe released the "Draft Convention on Cyber-crime."[75] According to the COE, the U.S. was "very active" in its development.

The draft treaty requires countries to pass laws on cyber-crime and agree to promote mutual assistance in enforcing laws and conducting investigations. Among the provisions, it requires that countries enact laws guaranteeing that users provide access to all files on a system under penalty of jail including their encryption keys. It bans security tools that probe systems for known problems, and requires that ISPs keep detailed logs of their users for an undefined period of time, said to be somewhere between 40 days and a year. To make it more difficult politically to oppose, copyright and child porn provisions have also been included. After working on this for three years, the COE left blank in the public document two sections on interception of communications. It is expected that these sections will facilitate cross-border wiretaps and are likely to include the ILETS/ENFOPOL requirements.

The draft is expected to be completed by December 2000 and will be open for signature by the member countries by September 2001. The Convention is open to the 52 members of the Council of Europe and to countries that were involved in the development, which includes the United States, Canada, Japan and South Africa. At the G-8 meeting in Paris in July 2000, the French Government, which will be the Presidency of the EU, recommended that the convention be opened to all countries.

The proposal has already been criticized by privacy experts on a number of grounds and a group of prominent security experts for the limitations on security software.[76] The EU's Data Protection Working Group has expressed concern about efforts to require ISPs to preserve information for law enforcement purposes.[77]

The G-8 has been meeting since 1996 on the issue. At the Birmingham, England meeting on May 18, 1998, the G8 adopted a recommendation on ten principles

---

[75] COE, Draft Treaty on Cybercrime <http://conventions.coe.int/treaty/en/projets/cybercrime.htm>.

[76] Statement of Concerns, July 20, 2000. <http://www.cerias.purdue.edu/homes/spaf/coe/index.html>.

[77] European Commission Data Protection Working Group, Recommendation 3/99 on the preservation of traffic data by Internet Service Providers for law enforcement purposes, Adopted on 7 September 1999. <http://europa.eu.int/comm/internal_market/en/media/dataprot/wpdocs/wp25en.htm>.

and a ten-point action plan on high-tech crime. The ministers announced, "We call for close cooperation with industry to reach agreement on a legal framework for obtaining, presenting and preserving electronic data as evidence, while maintaining appropriate privacy protection, and agreements on sharing evidence of those crimes with international partners. This will help us combat a wide range of crime, including abuse of the Internet and other new technologies." In July 2000, the Group of 8 met in Paris to discuss responses to cyber-crime.

The Council of Ministers of the European Union reached a Common Position on the convention in May 1999.[78] In July 2000, the Commission announced that it is planning a new directive for fighting cyber-crime.[79]

National Security and the "Echelon system"

In the past several years, there has been considerable attention given to mass surveillance by intelligence agencies of international and national communications. Investigations have been opened and hearings held in parliaments around the world about the "Echelon" system coordinated by the United States.

Immediately following the Second World War, in 1947, the governments of the United States, the United Kingdom, Canada, Australia and New Zealand signed a National Security pact known as the "Quadripartite," or "United Kingdom - United States" (UKUSA) agreement. Its intention was to seal an intelligence bond in which a common national security objective was created. Under the terms of the agreement, the five nations carved up the earth into five spheres of influence, and each country was assigned particular signals intelligence (SIGINT) targets.

The UKUSA Agreement standardized terminology, code words, intercept handling procedures, arrangements for cooperation, sharing of information, Sensitive Compartmented Information (SCI) clearances, and access to facilities. One important component of the agreement was the exchange of data and personnel.

---

[78] Common position 99/364/JAI, of 27 May 1999, of the Council on negotiations relating to the Draft Convention on Cyber Crime held in the Council of Europe.
<http://europa.eu.int/scadplus/leg/en/lvb/l33084.htm>.

[79] "European Union Ministers Vow Cyber Crime Crackdown," Reuters, July 29, 2000.

The strongest alliance within the UKUSA relationship is the one between the U.S. National Security Agency (NSA), and Britain's Government Communications Headquarters (GCHQ). The NSA operates under a 1952 presidential mandate, National Security Council Intelligence Directive (NSCID) Number 6, to eavesdrop on the world's communications networks for intelligence and military purposes. In doing so, it has built a vast spying operation that can reach into the telecommunications systems of every country on earth. Its operations are so secret that this activity, outside the U.S., occurs without any legislative or judicial oversight. The most important facility in the alliance is Menwith Hill, an Air Force base in the north of England. With over two dozen radomes and a vast computer operations facility, the base has the capacity to eavesdrop on vast chunks of the communications spectrum. With the creation of Intelsat and digital telecommunications, Menwith Hill and other stations developed the capability to eavesdrop on an extensive scale on fax, telex and voice messages.

The current debate over NSA activities has erupted because of two recent European Parliament (EP) studies that confirm the existence in Britain of a network of signals intelligence bases operated by the NSA. The publication in 1997 of the first EP report, "An Appraisal of the Technologies of Political Control,"[80] stated that the NSA had established an integrated communications surveillance capability in Europe.

It also described a communications intelligence sharing sub-system known as "Echelon," which is said to be capable of scanning particular communications to detect information of interest. The Echelon sub-system also catalogues intelligence for sharing with various consumers in the UKUSA countries based on clearance and need-to-know. According to informed sources that served within the National Security Council, the Echelon sub-system was greatly expanded in the 1980s to include new functions in order to keep pace with technological advances in telecommunications and data networking.

What is more important about Echelon is what the sub-system is not. First, Echelon is not a worldwide communications surveillance system. The system by which the United States conducts communications intelligence gathering is known as the United States Signals Intelligence System (USSS). The collection of intelligence that involves "U.S. persons" (U.S. citizens, legal residents, and foreign residents visiting the United States) is governed by United States Signals

---

[80] Published by STOA (Science and Technology Options Assessment). Ref : project no. IV/STOA/RSCH/LP/politicon.1

Intelligence Directive 18 (USSID 18), which is titled "Limitations and Procedures in Signals intelligence Operations of the USSS." The Australian Defense Signals Directorate operates under a similar regulation known as "Rules on SIGINT and Australian Persons." Other directives cover other aspects of signals intelligence gathering by the five SIGINT agencies individually and jointly.

In a 1999 report, the oversight Commissioner for the Canadian Communications Security Establishment (CSE), Claude Bisson, stated that his "review and analysis indicates that CSE is not using its technology to target Canadian communications . . . in keeping with the policy of the government, CSE goes to considerable effort to avoid collecting Canadian communications." Bisson cited regulations that govern the collection of intelligence on Canadians, "CSE has policies and practices to address the safeguarding and proper handling of inadvertently collected Canadian communications in accordance with the laws of Canada, including the Privacy Act, the Criminal Code, and the Canadian Charter of Rights and Freedoms."[81] Following New Zealand parliamentary protests over the SIGINT base at Waihopai near Blenheim on the South Island, Prime Minister Helen Clark also referred to the intelligence relationship between New Zealand's SIGINT agency, the Government Communications Security Bureau (GCSB) and the NSA. She stated that the GCSB is aware of all communications intelligence sent to NSA from the Waihopai satellite communications intercept facility and that the station does not intercept economic intelligence.

Second, contrary to media reports, no intelligence official has ever confirmed that Echelon is the name of NSA's worldwide SIGINT system. For example, the Director of Australia's Defense Signals Directorate, Martin Brady, in a letter sent to Australia Nine Network's "Sunday" program, stated, "DSD does cooperate with counterpart signals intelligence organizations overseas under the UKUSA relationship." This was widely reported as a confirmation of Echelon's role as a stand-alone international surveillance system. In fact, Echelon is one system of hundreds of similarly named cover term systems that make up the USSS. In his 1999 Report, CSE Commissioner Bisson also referred to the UKUSA system. He stated, "CSE is both a collector of foreign communications intercepts and a recipient of communications intercepts collected by Second Parties," which he went on to identify by name: Australia, New Zealand, United Kingdom, United States.[82]

---

[81] Annual Report of the CSE Commissioner 1998-1999,
<http://www.dnd.ca/menu/press/Reports/A_Report/CDS_Annual_Report_e.htm>.

[82] ibid.

In 1999, a second EP report, "Interception Capabilities 2000"[83] set out the technical specifications of the interception system. The report describes the merger of Echelon and the International Law Enforcement Telecommunications Seminar (ILETS). In time, two vast systems - one designed for national security and one for law enforcement - will merge, and in the process will compromise national control over surveillance activities.

Of particular interest to the European Parliament were allegations that the NSA was beefing up its commercial espionage activities. Although the NSA and other U.S. intelligence officials deny that the U.S. SIGINT System is used for commercial espionage, they do admit that intercepted intelligence that indicates bribery and other unfair trade practices is brought to the attention of senior U.S. policymakers, and, in some cases, is briefed in a sanitized form to the U.S. companies threatened by the unfair trade practices.

However, the U.S. SIGINT base at Bad Aibling in the Bavarian Alps of Germany may have a more expanded mission than countering bribery and unfair trade deals. According to intelligence expert Erich Schmidt-Eenboom, the Bad Aibling base, while not actually committing economic espionage (confirmed by a German parliamentary delegation that visited the base in June 2000), does conduct financial intelligence gathering. Schmidt-Eenboom said, "the antannae and satellites in Bad Aibling are now directed at Switzerland and Liechtenstein where there is more to be uncovered about secret bank accounts and money laundering."[84] These reports of financial network snooping by NSA and its allies, along with similar reports that the NSA illegally penetrated bank computers and networks in Switzerland, Liechtenstein, Cyprus, Russia, Greece, South Africa, and South Africa looking for accounts of Serb President Slobodon Milosevic and his family and associates in order to loot them, indicates that NSA's protestations that it does not conduct economic espionage are both misleading and inaccurate.

Parliamentarians in Germany, Norway, France, Italy, Denmark, Finland, the Netherlands, and Sweden subsequently raised concerns. A plenary session of the European Parliament took the unprecedented step of openly debating the

---

[83] Report to the Director General for Research of the European Parliament (Scientific and Technical Options Assessment programme office) on the development of surveillance technology and risk of abuse of economic information. This study considers the state of the art in Communications intelligence (Comint) of automated processing for intelligence purposes of intercepted broadband multi-language leased or common carrier systems, and its applicability to Comint targeting and selection, including speech recognition. <http://cryptome.org/dst-1.htm>.

[84] "Germany voices concerns over Echelon and wonders who is listening." ZDNet Germany, June 30, 2000.

activities of the NSA. In a Consensus Resolution of all major parties, the Parliament signaled its concern by calling for more openness and accountability of this once hidden activity. However, in April 2000, the Parliament agreed to appoint a Temporary Committee to look into the so-called Echelon system. The Greens and other small leftist and right-wing parties claimed that instead of establishing a full Committee of Inquiry, the large parties -- Conservatives, Socialists, and Liberals -- were attempting to weaken the investigation of Echelon by only appointing a Temporary Committee which, under EP rules, lacks the subpoena power of a Committee of Inquiry.

In June 1999, the U.S. House of Representatives Permanent Select Committee on Intelligence ordered the NSA to hand over documents relating to Echelon. The NSA, for the first time in the Committee's history, refused to do so, claiming attorney/client privilege.[85] In May 1999, Representative Bob Barr, worried by the potential breach of constitutional privacy rights, introduced an amendment to the fiscal 2000 Intelligence Authorization Act requiring the Director of Central Intelligence, the director of NSA, and the Attorney General to submit a report outlining the legal standards being employed within project Echelon to safeguard the privacy of American citizens.

Reacting to pressure from House Permanent Select Committee on Intelligence Chairman Port Goss, the NSA turned over the documents Congress previously requested. Following a lawsuit brought under the Freedom of Information Act, NSA provided redacted copies of these documents to EPIC. Among other things, they indicate that the level of authority for NSA to provide SIGINT reports to other agencies of the federal government has been delegated to lower levels within NSA. They also indicate special NSA rules for handling intercepted communications of or about First Lady Hillary Rodham Clinton and former President Jimmy Carter.[86]

These recent events have left observers contemplating two profound conclusions. First, as long as the UKUSA SIGINT partners police and govern their own operations outside of actual effective parliamentary and judicial oversight, there is good reason to believe that SIGINT can be turned against individuals and groups exercising civil and political rights. There is ample evidence that the activities of Greenpeace, Christian Aid, Amnesty International, the International Committee to Ban Landmines, the Tibetan government-in-exile, and the International Committee of the Red Cross have been targeted by UKUSA

---

[85] "Congress, NSA butt heads over Echelon", Federal Computer Week, June 3, 1999.

[86] Documents available at: http://www.epic.org/privacy/nsa/documents.html

agencies. Second, there is an increasing blurring between the activities of intelligence agencies and law enforcement. The creation of a seamless international intelligence and law enforcement surveillance system has resulted in the potential for a huge international network that may, in practice, negate current rules and regulations prohibiting domestic communications surveillance by national intelligence agencies.

Tools for fighting surveillance

The law enforcement efforts to demand greater powers for surveillance has also resulted in a greater interest in tools that prevent eavesdropping. These tools are generally written by users concerned about their privacy in the U.S. and Europe.

Encryption has become the most important tool for protection against surveillance. A message is scrambled so that only the intended recipient will be able to unscramble, and subsequently read, the contents. Pretty Good Privacy (PGP) is the best-known encryption program and has hundreds of thousands of users, including human rights groups.[87] An open source program called GNU Privacy Guard is being developed as a free replacement that will allow anyone to view the full source of the system to ensure that it does not allow for secret surveillance.[88]

"Anonymous remailers" strip identifying information from e-mails and can stop traffic analysis. They have also generated opposition from police and intelligence services. In Finland, a popular anonymous remailer had to be shut down due to legal challenges that forced the operator to reveal the name of one of the users.

More advanced tools that merge the functions of anonymous remailers and encryption have also been developed. The Mixmaster anonymous remailers used encryption links between anonymous remailers to hide the identity of the original sender by sending the message randomly through a series of remailers before delivering it to the final destination. Freedom.net provides a fully encrypted link between the user and secure servers run by the company to prevent wiretapping and encrypted headers so that users can receive email without even the company knowing who is using the system.

---

[87] PGP International Page: http:/www.pgpi.com/

[88] Homepage: http://www.gnupg.org/

Users should be aware that not all tools are effective as protecting privacy. Some are poorly designed while others may be designed to facilitate law enforcement access.[89]

Electronic Commerce

Surveillance by law enforcement is not the only concern users should have about their online privacy. The growth of the Internet and electronic commerce has dramatically increased the amount of personal information that is collected about individuals by corporations. As consumers surf the net and engage in routine online transactions, they leave behind a trail of personal details, often without any idea that they are doing so. Much of this information is routinely captured by the computers that log all activities on their systems.

Most on-line companies keep track of users' purchases. This information ranges from the trivial to the most sensitive and, unless adequately protected, can be used for purposes that seriously harm the interests of the consumer. Other companies gather personal information from visitors by offering personalized services such as news searches, free email and stock portfolios. They then sell, trade or share that information among third party companies without the consumer's express knowledge or consent. The perceived value of this kind of information is behind the stock-market valuations of many dotcom companies.

Many on-line companies, for example, provide lists of their customers' e-mail addresses to companies that specialize in sending unsolicited commercial e-mail (spam). Other companies mine e-mail address from sources such as messages posted on mailing lists, from newsgroups, or from domain name registration data. This results in consumers being barraged by advertisements and "once-off" deals by companies or people they have never even heard of. Studies show that consumers resent spam both for the time it takes to process and for the loss of privacy resulting from their e-mail address circulating freely on countless directories.[90]

Probably even more worrying is the increasing practice of "online profiling" Internet users. Companies, including Internet Service Providers, web site hosts and others, monitor users as they travel across the Internet, collecting information

---

[89] EPIC maintains a list of tools at http://www.epic.org/privacy/

[90] For more information on SPAM generally and how to reduce it see, http://www.junkbusters.com, http://www.cauce.org/

---

on what sites they visit, the time and length of these visits, search terms they enter, purchases they make or even "click-through" responses to banner ads. In the off-line world this would be comparable to, for example, having someone follow you through a shopping mall, scanning each page of every magazine you browse though, every pair of shoes that you looked at and every menu entry you read at the restaurant. When collected and combined with other data such as demographic or "psychographic" data, these diffuse pieces of information create highly detailed profiles of net users. These profiles have become a major currency in electronic commerce where they are used by advertisers and marketers to predict a user's preferences, interests, needs and possible future purchases. Most of these profiles are currently stored in anonymous form. However, there is a distinct likelihood that they will soon be linked with information, such as names and addresses, gathered from other sources, making them 100 percent personally identifiable.

The most pervasive tracking technology is the cookie. The cookie is a small file containing an ID number that is placed on a user's hard drive by a website. Cookies were developed to improve websites' ability to track users over a session. The cookie can also notify the site that the user has returned and can allow the site to track the user's activities across many different visits. The use of cookies expanded greatly when it was realized that a single cookie could be used across many different sites. This led to the development of advertising network companies that can track users across thousands of sites. The largest ad service is DoubleClick, which has agreements with over 11,000 websites and maintains cookies on 100 million users, each linking to hundreds of pieces of information about the user's browsing habits. A more secretive manner of tracking Internet users takes place through the use of web bugs, invisible images that also place cookies on users' computers. As of July 2000, DoubleClick had placed web bugs on over 60,000 different web pages.[91]

The line between online tracking and offline databases has also become blurred in the U.S. In 1999, DoubleClick announced that it was buying Abacus, owner of the largest direct marketing lists in the country, with information on the purchasing habits of 90 percent of all U.S. households, and that DoubleClick was going to merge information from the purchasing databases with information from online browsing. Following a public outcry, the company suspended its plan to merge personal data with profiles.[92] However, in July 2000 the Federal Trade

---

[91] To find the number of web bugs used on pages by Internet advertisers, see http://www.tiac.net/users/smiths/privacy/wbfind.htm.

[92] For more background information on this deal see http://www.epic.org/doubletrouble/.

Commission reached an agreement with the Network Advertisers Initiative, a group consisting of the largest online advertisers including DoubleClick, which will allow for online profiling and any future merger of such databases to occur with only "opt-out" consent.[93]

Not satisfied with cookies, which can be rejected or deleted by a user, the industry is also now developing more permanent methods of identifying users. In 1999, Intel announced that it was including a serial number in each new Pentium III chip that could be accessed by websites and internal corporate networks.[94] Most of the manufacturers suppressed the number after a consumer boycott was announced, and Intel announced in 2000 that it is dropping the serial number in future chips. Meanwhile, a number of companies, including, Microsoft and RealAudio, have been discovered using the internal networking number found in most computers as another identifier.[95] The Internet Engineering Task Force has developed specifications for the next version of the Internet's underlying protocols called IPv6 that will assign a unique permanent ID number to every device hooked into the net, which could one day include refrigerators and VCRs.[96]

As noted above, there are tools available that can be used to protect the privacy of users in many cases. These technologies are known as "Privacy Enhancing Technologies" (PETs). Ones that can be useful include anonymous web browsers, remailers and encryption. There are also many that are offered by industry that are not privacy protective. Many of these systems, such as Microsoft's Passport and the World Wide Web Consortium's (W3C) Platform for Privacy Preferences (P3P), are designed more to facilitate data sharing than to protect users.[97] They are also frequently used by US industry as justification for not passing laws. The European Commission in 1998 looked as some PETs and stated that the tools would not replace a legal framework but could be used to compliment existing laws.[98]

---

[93] Electronic Privacy Information Center (EPIC) and Junkbusters. 'Network Advertising Initiative: Principles not Privacy', July 28, 2000. <http://www.epic.org/privacy/internet/NAI_analysis.html>.

[94] See http://www.bigbrotherinside.org/

[95] See Richard Smith, Internet Privacy Issues. <http://www.tiac.net/users/smiths/privacy/index.htm>.

[96] See http://www.junkbusters.com/ht/en/new.html#IPv6

[97] EPIC and Junkbusters, 'Pretty Poor Privacy: An Assessment of P3P and Internet Privacy', June 2000, <http://www.epic.org/reports/prettypoorprivacy.html>.

[98] Opinion 1/98: Platform for Privacy Preferences (P3P) and the Open Profiling Standard (OPS), <http://europa.eu.int/comm/internal_market/en/media/dataprot/wpdocs/wp11en.htm>.

Other companies are trying a different approach, offering to become "information brokers." Under many of these systems, users provide information to the company, which then provides it to a third-party website with the consent of the user. These sites raise a question of trust. Given that many of them are run by the same Internet companies that are also major privacy invaders, the user must wonder why they should volunteer providing information to these companies. They are also frequently used by U.S. industry as justification for not passing laws.

A common practice among online companies is to sign on to a "seal" program in order to provide consumers with a sense of security that their personal information is being protected. These programs follow the traditional seal programs in laying down certain eligibility standards which participant companies must respect in order to get a compliance seal. The better seal programs conduct monitoring and compliance checks, provide educational information, offer consumer dispute resolution, and enforce sanctions against errant companies. There are many disadvantages of seal programs operating within a self-regulatory system. All too often, seal program operators have been shown to be ineffective and reluctant to take enforcement measures against their members including companies such as Microsoft. A 1999 Forrester research report found that, "because independent privacy groups like TRUSTe and BBBOnline earn their money from e-commerce organizations, they become more of a privacy advocate for the industry -- rather than for consumers."[99]

Finally, Internet security also raises serious problems for privacy. Many web sites are poorly secured against accidental releases or deliberate attacks.[100] In March 2000, De Beers lost 35,000 names, addresses, phone numbers and e-mail addresses of people inquiring about buying diamonds following a security breach. In April 2000, it was revealed that an unknown Microsoft engineer had included a backdoor into its webserver software. If someone typed "Netscape engineers are weenies!" backwards, they would have access to the websites and associated data. In August 2000, Kaiser Permanente, a top U.S. health insurer, admitted that it had compromised the confidentiality and privacy of its members when it sent over 800 e-mail messages, many containing sensitive information, to the wrong members.[101]

---

[99] Forrester Research Inc, "Privacy Wake-Up Call," September 1, 1999.

[100] See eg. Eric Murray, SSL Server Security Survey, July 31, 2000 showing that encryption on most e-commerce sites is inadequate. <http://www.meer.net/~ericm/papers/ssl_servers.html>.

[101] See, "Sensitive Kaiser E-Mails Go Astray," Washington Post, August 10, 2000.

Spy TV: Interactive Television & "T-Commerce"

The convergence of communications networks, computers and mass media into an interactive network combining television and the Internet is the next progression of the technology currently being developed. Already, the new boxes are replacing the traditional cable TV set-top box with an interactive device that also includes the functions of a limited personal computer and video recorder. At the same time, personal computers are regularly equipped with TV tuner cards to handle advanced video operations.

The designers of these new appliances paint a pleasant picture of the conveniences that will be available with these new systems. They anticipate that viewers will be able to make spur of the moment purchases over their boxes, based on what their favorite star is wearing or on an individually tailored ad that appears between shows. Communities will be formed as people chat live about the plots of their favorite shows or sporting events. Vast libraries of movies and shows will be available for renting on demand by just pressing a button on the remote control. The industry calls this "T-Commerce" for Television Commerce. Millions of users are expected to be using these in just the next few years, and the ad revenue to justify the new expensive boxes is expected to hit $5 billion by 2004.

Interactiveness has been the dream of the television industry since the invention of the TV. For several decades, there have been a series of expensive tests that have failed because the technology has been crude and expensive.[102] The change that now makes ITV possible is the evolution of the Internet and its underlying protocols and the advancement of digital television. These protocols are now being used to allow for interactive high-speed access to the Internet over existing cable lines. Slowly, intelligent cable TV boxes which can use broadband and interactive cable systems are being deployed in some places.

A number of companies have jumped into this new market in the last few years. The largest players are America Online and Microsoft. Microsoft purchased WebTV in 1998 and has also been including interactive television abilities in their operating systems for several years. Thus far, because of poor service, little interactive programming, and relatively high prices, the number of users has not significantly grown. They also are hampered by needing to use telephone lines to

---

[102] See L. J. Davis, The Billionaire Shell Game: How Cable Baron John Malone and Assorted Corporate Titans Invented a Future Nobody Wanted (1998) for a review of the early failures of the industry.

---

communicate with the service in most areas as cable lines are slowing becoming converted to interactive communications. America Online has announced that it will start deploying AOL TV in the United States in 2000. When its merger with media giant Time-Warner is complete, it will have control over a significant portion of the cable television lines and television shows in the U.S. It is expected that AOL will use that market power to force the development of more interactive television and the deployment of interactive boxes that will be capable of tracking users even if they do not wish to use the functions.

Meanwhile, there are other companies that have developed devices that will automatically record television shows for viewers and make recommendations for new shows based on viewers' previous behavior. These systems also send some information on the viewers' habits back to the central offices. TiVO and ReplayTV are two of the major manufacturers of such systems. Many of these features will be included in future WebTV and AOL TV boxes.

Behind the hype, the technical details are a more chilling. The new systems are being designed, like their Internet predecessors, to track every activity of users as they surf the net through the boxes. They also are being designed to track the shows and commercials users watch and to use that information to tailor advertising for the greatest effect.[103] Rupert Murdoch said in the NewsCorp annual report, "It will tell us not only who our customers are, but what they buy, what they watch, what they read and what they want."[104] George Orwell's vision of the television that watches you will soon be a standard consumer appliance.

Unlike personal computers that give users control over their actions and choices, the new ITV systems are generally based on a sealed "black box" controlled by the company which gives the user little or no control. In the WebTV box, users are not able to refuse cookies or delete them afterwards. The systems are closed and it is difficult, if not impossible, for even advanced users to identify what the system is doing. It will also prevent users from being able to use their own software.

There are other significant differences in that the media is more top-down, and corporatized than the Internet, which is decentralized and allows nearly any user to set up his own web site and become a content producer. Many of the ITV providers describe their systems as "closed gardens" that will only show content

---

[103] See David Burke, Spy TV (Slab-O-Concrete Press, 1999).
<http://www.spyinteractive.com/spyinteractive/>.

[104] Cited in Privacy Journal, October 1999.

that the providers have a financial interest in. Other information will either be banned or be slower or more difficult to locate and view.

Audio Bugging

Advances in technology are also making it easier and cheaper to conduct covert audio surveillance. Bugs come in many shapes and sizes. They range from micro engineered transmitters the size of an office staple, to devices no bigger than a cigarette packet that are capable of transmitting video and sound signals for miles. Many of the bugs are cleverly camouflaged. They are hidden in everything from umbrella stands to light shades. Sometimes, the infiltrator will hide them in a business or sports trophy where they will stay indefinitely. The latest bugs remain active with their own power supply for around ten years.

Laws restricting the use of covert audio devices vary widely across the world. Many countries have provisions in their general wiretap laws that also cover the use of bugs. The European Court of Human Rights has ruled several times that all signatories of the Convention must enact laws governing their use. While it is illegal in most circumstances in the U.S. to use or sell such devices, the British market had no restrictions whatever until recently. As one private investigator told the London Daily Telegraph, "It's a game anyone can play." Millions of bugs are sold every year in Asian countries such as Hong Kong and Japan.

The devices are used for a variety of reasons. In many Asian countries, use of the devices for industrial espionage is widespread. They are also frequently used in the workplace or in homes. Law enforcement and intelligence agencies also use the devices but according to government records in the U.S., Canada and other countries, they are used much less frequently than traditional wiretaps for law enforcement purposes.

Video Surveillance

In recent years, the use of video surveillance cameras (also called Closed Circuit Television, or CCTV) to monitor public and private spaces throughout the world has grown to unprecedented levels. The leader in this trend is the United Kingdom, where it is estimated that between 150 and 300 million pounds per year is now spent on a surveillance industry involving an estimated 200,000 cameras monitoring public spaces.[105] Most towns and cities are moving to CCTV surveillance of public areas, housing estates, car parks and public facilities. Growth in the market is estimated at fifteen to twenty per cent annually. Many Central Business Districts in Britain are now covered by surveillance camera systems involving a linked system of cameras with full pan, tilt, zoom and infrared capacity. Their use on private property is also becoming popular.[106]

The CCTV trend is not confined to Britain. CCTV activity in Norway has prompted specific inclusion of such surveillance in the data protection act. Meanwhile, CCTV activity has grown markedly in North America and Australia to monitor public squares. In New York City, the NYCLU Surveillance Camera Project identified 2,397 cameras in Manhattan.[107] In Singapore, they are widely employed for traffic enforcement and to prevent littering.

These systems involve increasingly sophisticated technology. Features include night vision, computer-assisted operation, and motion detection facilities that allow the operator to instruct the system to go on red alert when anything moves in view of the cameras. Camera systems increasingly employ bulletproof casing and automated self-defense mechanisms. The clarity of the pictures is usually excellent, with many systems being able to read a cigarette packet at a hundred meters. The systems can often work in pitch black, bringing images up to daylight level. The technologies are converging with sophisticated software programs that are capable of automated recognition of faces, crowd behavior analysis, and in certain environments, intimate scanning of the area between skin surface and clothes. In Newham, UK, a facial recognition system that can scan faces against a database of millions of photographs in seconds is already in place to identify people "of interest." The U.S. government is funding "passive millimeter wave technology" that allows police to peer under clothing to see if a person is carrying contraband or weapons. The power and capabilities of cameras will continually increase, while the cost and size will decrease. It is reasonable to assume that covert visual surveillance will in some environments be ubiquitous.

Some observers believe this phenomenon is dramatically changing the nature of cities. The technology has been described as the "fifth utility."[108] CCTV is being

---

[105] House of Lords, Science and Technology Committee, Fifth report, "Digital images as evidence", 3 February 1998, London.

[106] Stephen Graham, John Brooks, and Dan Heery "Towns on the Television : Closed Circuit TV in British Towns and Cities"; Centre for Urban Technology, University of Newcastle upon Tyne.

[107] NYCLU Surveillance Camera Project <http://www.nyclu.org/surveillance.html>.

[108] Stephen Graham, The Fifty Utility, Index on Censorship, issue 3, 2000. <http://www.indexoncensorship.org/300/gra.htm>.

integrated into the urban environment in much the same way as the electricity supply and the telephone network in the first half of the century. CCTV is profoundly changing the nature of the urban environment, and is now an important part of the core management of cities. Visual surveillance is becoming a fixed component in the design of modern urban centers, new housing areas, public buildings and even the road system. CCTV images may in the future be viewed as just one more type of necessary data, and considered a "value added" product.

Their use has come under greater criticism recently and recent research by the Scottish Centre for Criminology found that the cameras did not reduce crime, nor did they improve public perception of crime problems.[109] Researchers at the University of Hull, UK found that the cameras were frequently used for other reasons:

- 40 percent of people were targeted for "no obvious reason," mainly "on the basis of belonging to a particular or subcultural group." "Black people were between one-and-a-half and two-and-a-half times more likely to be surveilled than one would expect from their presence in the population." 30 percent of targeted surveillances on black people were protracted, lasting nine minutes or more, compared with just 10 percent on white people.
- People were selected primarily on the basis of "the operators' negative attitudes towards male youth in general and black male youth in particular. ... [I]f a youth was categorised as a 'scrote' they were subject to prolonged and intensive surveillance."
- Those deemed to be "out of time and out of place" with the commercial image of city centre streets were subjected to prolonged surveillance. "Thus drunks, beggars, the homeless, street traders were all subject to intense surveillance."
- "Finally, anyone who directly challenged, by gesture or deed, the right of the cameras to monitor them was especially subject to targeting."[110]

Campaigns have been started in several countries to stop their spread.[111] In 1997 and 1999, the city of Oakland, California voted to reject their use.[112]

---

[109] Home Page: <http://www.scotcrim.u-net.com/researchc.htm>.

[110] Dr Clive Norris and Gary Armstrong, "The unforgiving Eye: CCTV surveillance in public space," Centre for Criminology and Criminal Justice at Hull University.
<http://merlin.legend.org.uk/~brs/archive/stories97/Suspects.html>.

[111] see Privacy International, CCTV Pages, <http://www.privacyinternational.org/issues/cctv/index.html>.
Watching Them, Watching Us - UK CCTV Surveillance Regulation Campaign <http://www.spy.org.uk/>.

[112] ACLU, Second Attempt Fails to Install Spy Cams on Oakland Streets,

There has also been greater activity by data protection commissioners as the technology merges with information systems and contains information on identifiable individuals. In July 2000, the UK Data Protection Commissioner issued a code of practice on the use of CCTV. The code sets out guidelines for the operators of CCTV systems and makes clear their obligations under the recently implemented Data Protection Act 1998.[113]

Satellite Surveillance

Developments in satellite surveillance (also called "remote sensing") are also occurring at a fast pace, and embrace features similar to those of more conventional visual surveillance. Satellite resolution has constantly improved over the past decade. Since the end of the Cold War, companies such as EarthWatch, Motorola and Boeing have invested billions of dollars to create satellites capable of mapping the most minute detail on the face of the earth.

A commercial satellite capable of recognizing objects the size of a student's desk was launched from the U.S. in September 1999 and began releasing images in October 2000.[114] The Ikonos is most powerful commercial imaging satellite ever built. Its parabolic lens can recognize objects as small as one meter anywhere on earth and the according to the company, viewers can see individual trees, automobiles, road networks, and houses. The satellite, owned by Denver company Space Imaging, will be the first of a new generation of high resolution satellites using technology formerly restricted to government security agencies. Another ten companies have received licenses to launch equally powerful satellites and several are expected to launch shortly.[115]

The technology is already being used for a vast range of purposes from media reporting of war and natural disasters, to detecting unlicensed building work and even illegal swimming pools. Public interest groups are using the information to show images of nuclear testing by countries and even images of secret U.S. bases such as Area 51 in Nevada.[116]

<http://www.aclunc.org/aclunews/news499/oakland-cams.html?video#first_hit>.

[113] See http://wood.ccta.gov.uk/dpr/dpdoc.nsf

[114] See http://www.spaceimaging.com/

[115] CBS, "Satellites Change How We See the Earth," <http://cbsnews.cbs.com/now/story/0,1597,34059-412,00.shtml>.

[116] See eg, Federation of American Scientists, Dimona Photographic Interpretation Report <http://www.fas.org/nuke/guide/israel/facility/dimona_pir.html>.

While industry looks for the opportunity to exploit current spy satellite technology, a great deal of effort is being made to integrate the existing images with ground-based Geographic Information System (GIS) databases than can provide detailed data on human activity. Double clicking on a satellite image of an urban area can reveal precise details of the occupants of a target house. The "Open Skies" policy accepted worldwide means that there are few restrictions of the use of the technology.[117]

But the companies have a distance to go before they catch up with governments. It is estimated that the current generation of secret spy satellites such as the Ikon/Keyhole-12 can recognize objects as small as 10cm across and some analysts say that it can image a license plate.[118] Boeing recently landed a 10-year contract from the U.S. Government for a Future Imagery Architecture (FIA) to replace the KH satellites and the ground infrastructure.[119] The FIA is based on a constellation of new satellites that are smaller, less expensive, and placed in orbit to allow for real-time surveillance of battlefields and other targets.

Workplace Privacy

Workers around the world are frequently subject to some kind of monitoring by their employers. Employers supervise work processes for quality control and performance purposes. They collect personal information from employees for a variety of reasons, such as health care, tax, and background checks.

Traditionally this monitoring and information gathering involved some form of human intervention and either the consent, or at least the knowledge, of employees. The changing structure and nature of the workplace, however, has led to more invasive and often, covert, monitoring practices which call into question employee's most basic right to privacy and dignity within the workplace. The progress in technology has facilitated an increasing level of automated surveillance. Now the supervision of employee's performance, behavior and communications can be carried out by technological means, with increased ease and efficiency. The technology currently being developed is extremely powerful and can extend to every aspect of a workers life. Software programs can record keystrokes on computers and monitor exact screen images, telephone

---

[117] ibid

[118] "Spy Satellites: the Next Leap Forward," International Defense Review, January 1, 1997.

[119] "Boeing to build new US satellites," Jane's Defence Weekly, September 15, 1999.

management systems (TMS) can analyze the pattern of telephone use and the destination of calls, and miniature cameras and "Smart" ID badges can monitor an employee's behavior and movements.

Advances in science have also pushed the boundaries of what personal details and information an employer can acquire from an employee. Psychological tests, general intelligence tests, performance tests, personality tests, honesty and background checks, drug tests, and medical tests are routinely used in workplace recruitment and evaluation methods. A recent report by the American Management Association found that 43 percent of companies carry out basic skills testing, 69 percent test for specific skills and 46 percent used some kind psychological evaluation.[120] Since the discovery of DNA there has also been an increased use of genetic testing, allowing employers to access the most intimate details of a person's body in order to predict susceptibility to diseases, medical or even behavioral conditions. The success of the Human Genome Project will likely make this kind of testing more prevalent.

Employers' collection of personal information and use of surveillance technology is often justified on the grounds of health and safety, customer relations or legal obligation. However, in many cases workplace monitoring can seriously compromise the privacy and dignity of employees. Surveillance techniques can be used to harass, discriminate and to create unhealthy dynamics in the workplace.

Legal Background

Privacy advocates have long maintained that providing notice of a monitoring or surveillance policy should, as a bare minimum, be required before employers can engage in such invasive activities. They support strong privacy principles in the workplace such as the International Labor Office's "Code of Practice on the Protection of Workers' Personal Data," which protect employees' personal data and fundamental right to privacy in the technological era.[121] These guidelines were issued by the ILO in 1997, following three comprehensive studies on international workers' privacy laws.[122] The general principles of the code are:

---

[120] AMA, 'Workplace Testing: Basic Skills, Job Skills, Psychological Measurement', 2000 . <http://www.amanet.org/research/stats.htm>.

[121] 'Protection of workers' personal data', An ILO Code of Practice, Geneva, International Labour Office, 1997.

[122] International Laobour Office, Conditions of Work Digest: Worker's Privacy Part I: Protection of Personal Data, (1991)10 (2); Worker's Privacy Part II: Monitoring and Surveillance in the Workplace,(1993) 12(1); and Worker's Privacy Part III: Testing in the Workplace, (1993) 12(2).

- personal data should be used lawfully and fairly; only for reasons directly relevant to the employment of the worker and only for the purposes for which they were originally collected;
- employers should not collect sensitive personal data (e.g., concerning a worker's sex life, political, religious or other beliefs, trade union membership or criminal convictions) unless that information is directly relevant to an employment decision and in conformity with national legislation;
- polygraphs, truth-verification equipment or any other similar testing procedure should not be used;
- medical data should only be collected in conformity with national legislation and principles of medical confidentiality; genetic screening should be prohibited or limited to cases explicitly authorized by national legislation; and drug testing should only be undertaken in conformity with national law and practice or international standards;
- workers should be informed in advance of any advance monitoring and any data collected by such monitoring should not be the only factors in evaluating performance;
- employers should ensure the security of personal data against loss, unauthorized access, use, alteration or disclosure; and
- employees should be informed regularly of any data held about them and be given access to that data.

The code does not form international law and is not of binding effect. It was intended to be used "in the development of legislation, regulations, collective agreements, work rules, policies and practical measures." Unfortunately, however, the laws differ greatly from country to country and in some there are few legal constraints on workplace surveillance. In the U.S., for example, the courts have typically been slow to recognize employees' rights to privacy. There have not yet been any satisfactory and uniform determination of what level of privacy employees are entitled to and how that privacy should be protected. Many believe that since employers have ownership or "control" over the working premises, its contents and facilities, that employees give up all rights and expectations to privacy and freedom from invasion. Others simply avoid the question by making employees consent to surveillance, monitoring and testing as a condition of employment. Legislation has recently been introduced, however, which would prevent employers from secretly monitoring the communications and computer use of their employees.[123]

---

[123] The "Notice of Electronic Monitoring Act" (S.2898 and H.R.4908), introduced July 20, 2000.

In European countries, the collection and processing of personal information is uniformly protected by the Data Protection Directive. The 1997 Telecommunication directive, however, which provides for the confidentiality of communications is aimed at "public" systems and so would not cover privately owned systems in the workplace.[124] Nonetheless, many European countries, such as Austria, Germany, Norway and Sweden have strong labor codes and privacy laws which directly or indirectly prohibit or restrict this kind of surveillance.[125] In July 2000, the UK Data Protection Commissioner also issued a new draft code of guidance for employer/employee relationships.[126] The code states the obligations of employers under the Data Protection Act, and also takes into account the presumed requirements of the soon to be implemented Human Rights Act 1998. It lays down strong principles of data protection, prohibits the making of decisions solely on basis of automated data, requires employers to notify employees of surveillance policies and places limits on the extent of monitoring which can take place. It requires the explicit consent of employees before sensitive data such as medical or information can be collected and places strict limitations on drug, alcohol, genetic, aptitude and psychometric testing within the workplace.

Performance Monitoring

Automated workplace monitoring has become increasingly common in recent years. Even in workplaces staffed by highly skilled information technology specialists, bosses demand the right to spy on every detail of a workers performance. Modern networked systems can interrogate computers to determine which software in being run, how often, and in what manner. A comprehensive audit trail gives managers a profile of each user, and a panorama of how the workers are interacting with their machines. Software programs can also gives managers total central control individual PCs. A manager can now remotely modify or suspend programs on any machine, while at the same time reading and analyzing email traffic and Internet activity.

An employer can monitor the level of use of a computer through monitoring the number of keystrokes a word processing employee enters in a specified period of

---

[124] Directive Concerning the Processing of Personal Data and the Protection of Privacy in the Telecommunications Sector (Directive 97/66/EC of the European Parliament and of the Council of 15 December 1997), <http://www2.echo.lu/legal/en/dataprot/protection.html>.

[125] For a review of these laws see International Labour Office, Conditions of Work Digest, Op Cit.

126 Issued under section 51 (3) (b) of the UK Data Protection Act 1998. Available at <http://www.dataprotection.gov.uk>.

time or the amount of time a computer is idle during the workday. Numerous technologies are available which monitor and analyze the performance of IT workers. Some allow network administrators to observe an employee's screen in real time, scan data files and e-mail, analyze keystroke performance, and even overwrite passwords. Once this information is collected, it can be analyzed by standard processing programs to determine a worker's performance profile. These monitoring products are sold at very low prices and have infiltrated the market. A recent study by the American Management Association report found that forty-five percent of major U.S. firms record and review employee communications and activities on the job and that one of four companies said they had fired employees for misuse of telecommunication equipment.[127] These snooping programs have also become popular not just among employers but also law enforcement agencies, private attorneys and investigators and suspicious lovers.

In the workplace, the use of CCTV is usually limited to environments where the workers are confined to an office. Where staff are more mobile, companies are now using a range of technologies to track geographic movements.[128] Advances in this area now allow carrier companies to place an electronic mechanism (described as a geostationary satellite-based. mobile communications system)[129] on trucks that then sends back to a main terminal the exact position of the vehicle at all times. In this way, carrier companies can ensure that no side trips nor other deviations are taken from the prescribed route.[130] Wide area systems such as Trackback are in use throughout the UK.

Telephone Monitoring

Telephone surveillance has become endemic throughout the private and public sector. In the U.S., employers have broad discretion to monitor employees' calls for "business purposes." Companies are extensively using telephone analysis technology. Call center workers for British Telecom are regularly presented with a comprehensive analysis sheet, showing their performance relative to other

---

127 American Management Association, "Workplace Monitoring and Surveillance," 1999. <
http://www.amanet.org/research/monit/index.htm

128 Laura Pincus Hartman, "The Economic and Ethical Implications of New Technology on
Privacy in the Workplace," Business and Society Review, March 22, 1999.

129 "Bulkmatic Equips Fleet with OmniTRACS System," Qualcomm Press release, December 19, 1996.
<http://www.qualcomm.com/Press/pr961219c.html>.

130 Qualcomm Press release, December 19, 1996.

---

workers. Airline reservations clerks in the U.S. and elsewhere wear telephonic headsets that monitor the length and content of all telephone calls, as well as the duration of their bathroom and lunch breaks.[131] In one instance, telephone calls received by airline reservation agents were electronically monitored on a second-by-second basis: agents were allowed only 11 seconds between each call and 12 minutes of break time each day.[132] Other airline reservationists have complained that they are evaluated based on how many times they use a customer's name during a call or how often they try to overcome a customer's initial objections to buying a ticket.

The level of sophistication of telephone surveillance systems can be astonishing. Some systems can record all transactional activity on a phone, together with destination numbers and times. Other technology can then process and analyze this data. A British program called "Watcall," produced by the Harlequin company, can analyze telephone calls and group them into "friendship networks" to determine patterns of use.[133] Voice mail systems are also subject to systematic or random monitoring by managers. Most new systems have default pass codes for administrators, and these can open all message boxes.

E-mail and Internet Use Monitoring

Computers and networks are particularly conducive to surveillance. Employers can monitor e-mail by randomly reviewing e-mail transmissions, by specifically reviewing transmissions of certain employees, or by selecting key terms to flag e-mail. In the latter case software analyses a company's entire e-mail traffic phrase by phrase, and draws conclusions about whether a message is legitimate company business. It can be instructed to search for specific keywords and "damaging" phrases. Some programs can even use algorithms to analyze communications patterns and turn them into images. Monitors can then look at these images to follow traffic patterns and detect whether sensitive data is at risk. Many employers rely on software for remote monitoring of e-mail messages. With a few clicks they can see every e-mail message that employees send or receive and determine whether they are "legitimate" or not. Managers give a variety of reasons for installing such software. Some say it is to protect trade secrets or preventing sexual harassment incidents. Others want to prevent oversized-mails clogging networks and using too much bandwidth. Others simply

---

131 Laura Pincus Hartman, "The Economic and Ethical Implications of New Technology on Privacy in the Workplace," Business and Society Review, March 22, 1999.

132 Charles Pillar, "Bosses with X-Ray Eyes," MacWorld., July 1993.

133 Simon Davies, "Watch out for the Old Bill", Daily Telegraph, April 29, 1997.

don't want employees "wasting" company time by using the systems for personal activities. In an ideal world, this monitoring should follow the conventional format, i.e., identical to the quality check that has applied to correspondence sent out on company letterhead. However, the speed and efficiency of e-mail means that digital communication involves a vast intersection with personal correspondence. It also has features more in common with an internal memo, for which there has always been less monitoring and management.

In July of this year, Dow Chemical Company in the U.S. fired 50 employees and threatened 200 others with suspension after they found "offensive" material in their e-mail. The company opened the personal e-mail of more than 7,000 employees.[134] Similarly, the New York Times fired 23 employees last year for sending "obscene" messages. These cases raise complex legal and ethical questions concerning an employee's fundamental right to privacy and due process. What if employees are sent "offensive" e-mails by accident or maliciously? The e-mail cannot simply be deleted. It remains logged on the company server, threatening the relationship of trust between employee and management. Or what if an employee is dismissed on the grounds of sensitive personal information (for example relating to sexual preferences, a medial condition, etc.) gathered through a system? This problem also arises when companies monitor all Internet activity looking for visits to "inappropriate" sites. At first sight, such surveillance has elements in common with traditional surveillance for hard copy pornography, but there are significant dangers to workers in the realm of electronic surveillance. The use of spam e-mail to advertise X rated sites results in workers entering sites that appear to be quite benign. Or websites may be accidentally visited when displayed as a "hit" in response to a perfectly innocent search query. The surveillance technology does not, however, distinguish between an innocent mistake and an intentional visit.

The monitoring of chat room visits has also created some distress in the workplace. There is an increasing trend among companies to dismiss and/or sue employees for divulging company "trade secrets" or defaming the company in chat rooms. These have become known as "John Doe" cases. As most people log on to chat rooms anonymously or using an alias, once a company observes a certain party in a chat room engaging in "illegitimate" speech, they must subpoena the message-board services such as Yahoo or America Online, to obtain the identify the specific author. The service providers often turn over identifying information when presented with a subpoena without any notice to

---

[134] 'Dow Chemical Fires Employees Over Inappropriate E-mails', ABCNEWS.com, July 27, 2000.

the individual. The number of these cases is rapidly increasing and threatens not only the privacy of employees but also their rights to anonymity and free speech.

Drug Testing

There is also an increasing amount of drug testing in many countries. The number of companies using these tests has risen proportionately with the decreasing costs of the tests. For many employees, drug testing is now a standard part of working life. Companies routinely administer tests in the recruitment stage or at intermittent periods during employment even where there is no evidence of misconduct, poor performance or any other reason to suspect drug use. There are thousands of easy to use kits, which can detect traces of drugs within minutes and without the need for a laboratory, available on the market today. Most of these tests analyze hair or urine samples to detect traces of drugs such as amphetamines, marijuana, cocaine, opiates and methamphetamines

The issue of widescale "preventative" drug testing raises a whole host of questions concerning privacy, bodily integrity, freedom and the presumption of innocence. The process of testing itself can be hugely invasive. Observers are often present to prevent employees tampering with samples. In the case of urine testing this can be particularly offensive. Consider the case of one employee who wrote:

> I waited for the attendant to turn her back before pulling down my pants, but she told me she had to watch everything I did. I am a 40-year-old mother of three: nothing I have ever done in my life equals or deserves the humiliation, degradation and mortification I felt.[135]

This type of test can quickly turn from a necessary evil needed to protect lives and reputations to intimidation and harassment. It raises questions about whether the benefits to employers really outweigh the rights and dignity of workers. Manufacturing companies wishing to sell their products obviously claim they can. They extol the advantages of drug tests, claiming they can save employers thousands by reducing incidences of absenteeism, low productivity, accidents, injuries, compensation and health care claims. Governments generally have also encouraged testing as part of a larger war on drugs. What employers are not told,

---

[135] From a letter to the American Civil Liberties Union describing a workplace drug test. See, ACLU, Drug Testing: A Bad Investment, September 1999. <http://www.aclu.org/issues/worker/drugtesting1999.pdf>.

however, is that there are also numerous ethical and economic disadvantages to drug testing.

Drug testing fosters a climate of negativity based on suspicion and secrecy rather than trust, openness and respect. Low morale or resentment among workers may consequently lead to low productivity or profits. In addition, even though individual tests may no longer be expensive, because they are so sweepingly administered among employees, they may be costing employers far more than they are saving them. Catching one or two light drug users for every few thousand people tested is hardly an economical justification for the initial outlay. Even if tests do reveal traces of drugs there is no clear evidence to suggest that mild drug use has a greater effect on productivity than, for example, alcohol. Dismissing workers on grounds of policy and suspicion rather than performance and proof, may result in the loss of valuable employees to the employer. Testing does not involve good management policy. Evidence has not shown that drug testing can deter future use, and it is in no way a substitute for proper guidance, support and counseling. In fact, in an ironic twist, routine testing may even encourage more serious drug usage among employees. As one commentator says:

> If one wants to get inebriated on a Friday night and still pass a urine test Monday, smoking a joint would be foolish. Cocaine and alcohol would represent the "safer" choices of intoxicants because alcohol is "legal" and cocaine cannot be detected in the body as long.[136]

Finally, drug testing is inaccurate and can often lead to false and misleading results. A report by the Ontario Information and Privacy Commissioners' Office says up to 40 per cent of tests are inaccurate.[137] Highly sensitive tests can be positive even when the drug sought is not present. Some say positive reactions may result from a carry-over following a strongly positive earlier or from human error, such as contamination due to failure to cleanse equipment.[138] Others note that certain legal substances can also result in positive tests for illegal drugs. For example, there have been reports of Vicks inhalers resulting in positive tests for amphetamines and metamphetamines, standard anti-inflammatory drugs like

---

[136] Ethan A. Nadelmann. "Drawing the Line on Drug Testing". IntellectualCapital.Com. October 14, 1999. <http://www.lindesmith.org/library/ethan_drugtesting2.html>.

[137] Information and Privacy Commissioner/Ontario, Workplace Privacy: The Need for a Safety-Net, November 1993. <http://www.ipc.on.ca/english/pubpres/sum_pap/papers/safnet-e.htm>.

[138] Morgan, John P. "Problems of Mass Urine Screening for Misused Drugs." Journal of Psychoactive Drugs. Vol. 16(4) (1984): 305-317. available at The Lindesmith Center - Drug Policy Foundation <http://www.lindesmith.org/library/grmorg2.html>.

Ibuprofen showing up positive on marijuana tests, and even traces of morphine being detected from poppy seeds. [139]

Genetic Testing

As DNA and genetic databases become more common world-wide, there has been a concurrent rise in the use of testing by employers. Although there are legitimate uses of genetic testing, such as the prevention of occupational diseases, there is also a serious danger that employers will use these tests to discriminate against current or potential employees. Without legal intervention, information indicating, for example, whether someone is prone to a debilitating illness or even an "undesirable" condition (such as laziness or depression) may be used by employers to discriminate against employees.

Genetic testing is a particularly intrusive invasion of privacy involving as it does the very "core" or "make-up" of an individual. Moreover, this testing may have implications not only for the individual but also one's family, gender, community or race. The ACLU notes that "some genetic conditions are associated (sometimes inappropriately) with certain racial or ethnic groups. For example, sickle cell anemia is associated with African-Americans, and predisposition for breast cancer ... with Ashkenazi Jews." [140]

Although genetic testing is still not as common as, for example, drug testing within the workplace, there are strong indications that it becoming an increasing practice for employers. In 1982, a U.S. federal government survey found that 1.6 percent of companies were using genetic testing for employment purposes.[141] A follow up survey in 1989 found that number increased to 5 percent. A recent American Management Association study now finds that 15 percent of major U.S. firms are conducting some kind of genetic testing or "testing for susceptibility to workplace hazards."[142]

[139] National Academy of Sciences, "Under the Influence? Drugs and the American Work Force", 1994. Also, ACLU, Drug Testing: A Bad Investment, September 1999.
<http://www.aclu.org/issues/worker/drugtesting1999.pdf>.

[140] American Civil Liberties Union: Genetic Discrimination in the Workplace Fact Sheet.
<http://www.aclu.org/issues/worker/gdfactsheet.html>.

[141] United States Congress, Office of Technology Assessment, The Role of Genetic Testing in the Prevention of Occupational Diseases 33-35 (1983); United States Congress, Office of Technology Assessment, Genetic Monitoring and Screening in the Workplace 173-177 (1990).

[142] See American Management Association, "Workplace Testing Medical Testing", 2000.
<http://www.amanet.org/research/stats.htm>.

Recognizing this danger, a number of international bodies have recommended that the use of genetic testing within the workplace should be carefully circumscribed by law. In 1989, the European Parliament issued a resolution recommending legislation to prohibit genetic testing for the purposes of selecting workers or examining employees without their consent. It advised that employees must be informed of any analysis and implications of genetic data before tests are carried out and allowed withdraw from testing at any time.[143] The Council of Europe has also recommended that "the admission to, or the continued exercise of . . . employment, should not be made dependent on the undergoing of tests or screening."[144] Similarly, the World Medical Association (WMA) has issued statements to this effect. In 1992, issuing a Declaration on the Human Genome Project, it recommended the adoption of laws similar to those which prohibit "the use of race discrimination in employment or insurance."[145] In May 2000, it announced that it will draw up guidelines on the development of centralized health storage databases which will address "the issues of privacy, consent, individual access and accountability."[146]

Perhaps because it is still a relatively new phenomenon, few countries around the world have yet to adopt specific laws on genetic testing. In many cases this kind of testing may be indirectly prohibited by existing labor codes.[147] It is also possible that the use of genetic data by employers to discriminate against workers

[143] European Parliament, "Resolution on the Ethical and Legal Problems of Genetic Engineering", OJ, No. C.96, April 17, 1989.

[144] Council of Europe, Committee if Ministers: Recommendation No. R(92)3 on genetic testing and screening for heath care purposes, Principle 6 (a).

[145] See ILO, Condtion of Work Digest,Part II,

[146] WMA To Draw Up Health Database Guidelines, WMA Press Release, 8 May 2000. <http://www.wma.net/e/press/00_5.html>.

[147] See generally, ILO, Conditions of Work Digest: Part III: Testing in the Workplace.

may violate equal-opportunity or anti-discrimination laws. In the U.S., for example, it has been suggested that genetic testing could violate the 1964 Civil Rights Act which prohibits discrimination in employment on the basis of "race, sex, national origin, and religion," or the Americans with Disabilities Act of 1990, which prohibits discrimination in employment against a "qualified individual with a disability."[148] However, these protections are no substitute for clear and meaningful guidelines and there is ample evidence to suggest that discrimination in the workplace is already occurring.[149]

---

[148] Hebert, Employee Privacy Law, Volume 2, Chapter 12, (West Group 2000).

[149] See for example cases described by Senate Democratic Leader Tom Daschle, in his Remarks To The Committee On Health, Education, Labor, And Pensions U.S. Senate on Genetic Information in the Workplace July 20, 2000. Available at: < http://www.senate.gov/~labor/hearings/july00hrg/072000wt/072000wt.htm>.

Country Reports

Argentine Republic

Articles 18 and 19 of the Argentine Constitution provide (in part), "The home is inviolable as is personal correspondence and private papers; the law will determine what cases and what justifications may be relevant to their search or confiscation. The private actions of men that in no way offend order nor public morals, nor prejudice a third party, are reserved only to God's judgment, and are free from judicial authority. No inhabitant of the Nation will be obligated to do that which is not required by law, nor be deprived of what is not prohibited." Article 43, enacted in 1994, provides a right of habeas data: "Every person may file an action to obtain knowledge of the data about them and its purpose, whether contained in public or private registries or databases intended to provide information; and in the case of false data or discrimination, to suppress, rectify, make confidential, or update the data. The privacy of news information sources may not be affected."[150] Habeas data is also included in the constitutions of many provinces of Argentina. Several cases of habeas data have dealt with correction of commercial information.

In 1999, the Supreme Court of Argentina ruled in two important cases on the scope of habeas data. The leading case is *Urteaga v. Estado Nacional*.[151] There, the Supreme Court allowed an individual access to personal information about his brother, who had disappeared during the military government, presumably in an armed conflict.[152] The lower courts dismissed the action of habeas data for lack of standing. The Court of Appeals reasoned that habeas data grants access only to personal information, and the claimant was trying to access data related to a third person. However, the Supreme Court reversed. The core of the judgment indicated an expanding approach to the interpretation of habeas data, granting a

---

[150] Constitucion de la Nacion Argentina (1994), <http://www.constitution.org/cons/argentin.htm>.

[151] Supreme Court of Argentina, Urteaga c. Estado Nacional (October 15, 1998), in Derecho y Nuevas Tecnologias No. 1-2 (2000), at 193.

[152] This case was decided one month after a case where the Supreme Court denied a mother the right to access to information about her daughter, who had also disappeared during the military regime. In "Aguiar de Lapaco," the Court based its opinion in the principle of non bis in idem or guarantee against double prosecution (double jeopardy) because the right of access was used being claimed criminal proceedings and the defendants were benefited by a Presidential pardon. But the Court opinion was the object of strong political and scholarly criticism, and the high tribunal distinguished "Aguiar de Lapaco" from "Urteaga" since the last one was a civil case. Justice Boggiano's dissidence in "Aguiar de Lapaco" stated that habeas data could be used in the case to access to any kind of information held by government.

---

wide right of access to personal information. The other case is *Ganora v. Estado Nacional*,[153] where the Supreme Court of Argentina established that habeas data can be used against any kind of public database. The claim was initiated by two lawyers who were defending Adolfo Scilingo, an ex-navy official who confessed his participation in crimes during the military regime. Arguing investigation and surveillance from the Government, the lawyers requested access to data in official databases about them. The district court judge and the Court of Appeals refused access, even without hearing the government's arguments based on a national security exception. The Supreme Court of Argentina restated its holding in *Urteaga* and the need to interpret habeas data in light of the international and foreign legislation.[154] They cited the European Human Rights case *Leander*[155] and also made a reference to *Nixon v. US*,[156] where the U.S. Supreme Court rejected the arguments of President Nixon, who alleged a confidential privilege over information. Finally they concluded that habeas data allowed access to government databases, and that an exception based on public interest should be subject to judicial review. This case shows the expanding interpretation of habeas data by the Supreme Court of Argentina.

In April 1999, the Civil Court of Appeals of Buenos Aires ruled that processing of personal information was unlawful unless the data subject has given "consent" or he has been notified. The Supreme Court is currently reviewing this case. Another case decided that credit report agencies must place limits on the duration of storage of personal information. This is the first case in Argentina to recognize the "right to forget."

In November 1998, the Senate approved a Law for the Protection of Personal Data.[157] It is in conformance with Article 43 of the Constitution and based on the E.U. Data Protection Directive. The bill covers electronic and manual records. It requires express consent before information can be collected, stored, processed, or transferred. Collection of sensitive data is given additional protections and is prohibited unless authorized by law. International transfer of personal information is prohibited to countries without adequate protection. Individuals

---

[153] Ganora, Mario c/ Estado Nacional y otrs s/habeas corpus y habeas data (Supreme Court of Argentina, September 16 1999), 1-2 Derecho y Nuevas Tecnologías, at 229 (2000).

[154] The Habeas Data clause in the Spanish, Peruvian and Brazilian constitutions and the U.S. Freedom of Information Act were cited.

[155] Leander Case, 116 Eur. Ct. H.R. (ser. A) at 9 (1987). Digest of Strasbourg case law relating to the European Court of Human Rights, section 8.1.2.2.1.(a) and (b).

[156] 418 U.S. 683 (1974).

[157] S. 577/98, Ley de Protección de los Datos Personales, 26 November 1998. Also see S.0684/98, S.1582/98, S.1094/98, S. 277/98.

---

have an express right of habeas data to access information about themselves held by government or private entities. The bill sets up an independent commission within the Ministry of Justice to enforce the law. In July 2000, the bill was approved by two committees of the House of Representatives. It is expected that the Bill will be approved by the House of Representatives at the end of 2000.

The U.S. Direct Marketing Association launched a lobbying effort against the bill in December 1998 urging Argentinean companies to oppose the efforts to enact the law.[158] Previously, in December 1996, the Congress approved a data protection law.[159] However, upon request of the Central Bank, the law was subsequently vetoed by the President.[160]

Under the Code of Penal Procedure, "A judge may arrange, for the purposes of building a case, the intervention of telephone communications or whatever other means of communication." The Penal Code provides penalties for publishing private communications.[161] The National Defense Law prohibits domestic surveillance by military personnel. In April 1999, the Criminal Court of Appeals in Buenos Aires recognized a right to privacy in electronic mail communications applying a section of the Penal Code related to the protection of secrets. Although the criminal provision was drafted in 1921, the Court had an open approach to the interpretation of the statute.[162] Under this case, data such as stored files and e-mail, is not to be examined by anyone else without the user's permission.

The UN Human Rights Committee in 1995 expressed concern that the judicial authorization for wiretaps was too broad.[163] In Argentina the Penal Code, dating from the year 1921, does not punish wiretapping. Several cases of wiretapping were dismissed because of the lack of a criminal statute. Two Army colonels and two non-commissioned officers were relieved of duty in May 1999 after testifying that they conducted domestic surveillance on "orders from above" to

---

[158] Argentina wars on the direct practice, Precision Marketing, January 11, 1999. See also See Damian Kantor, Habeas Data:Traba en Diputados, in Clarin, June 25, 2000.

[159] Law No. 24.745 of December 23, 1996, <http://www.privacyexchange.org/legal/ppl/nat/argpending.html>.

[160] Decree No. 1616/96, Comment by Supreme Court of Argentina Comparative Law Research and Library Secretary.

[161] Código Penal de la República Argentina, Art 153-157, <http://www.codigos.com.ar/penal/indice.htm>.

[162] Criminal Court of Appeals in Buenos Aires (Sixth chamber), 4.3.99 "Lanata c. Dufau", in El Derecho, (E.D.) 17.5.99.

[163] United Nations, 19th Annual Report of the Human Rights Committee, A/50/40, 3 October 1995.

---

interfere with investigations into human rights abuses during the dictatorship.[164] Illegal wiretapping has been common since the transition to civilian rule. In 1990, the entire telephone switchboard of the President's official residence was extensively bugged and a major government scandal ensued.[165] In 1996, the telephones of the Archdiocese of Formosa were found to be wiretapped.[166] Also that year, former Economy Minister Domingo Cavallo accused Interior Minister Carlos Corach of ordering the telephone bugging of a federal prosecutor.[167] In 1998, the Mayor of Buenos Aires and 1999 presidential candidate Fernando de la Rua lodged a criminal complaint against two city councilors and another party member, accusing them of tapping his family's telephone for years and recording 3000 hours of conversation.[168] He also accused the secret police, known as SIDE, of complicity with the wiretaps.[169] The same two city councilors have been wiretapping the Prosecutor Attorney of the Criminal Chamber of Appeals in 1996.

The Civil Code prohibits "that which arbitrarily interferes in another person's life: publishing photos, divulging correspondence, mortifying another's customs or sentiments or disturbing his privacy by whatever means."[170] This article has been applied widely to protect the privacy of the home, private letters and a number of situations involving intrusive telephone calls, and neighbor's intrusions into one's private life.

In 1998, the Argentine Congress enacted the Credit Card Act.[171] The object of this bill is to regulate credit card contracts between consumers and financial institutions and specifically the interest rates that banks charge to consumer credit cards. Article 53 restricts the possibility of transferring information from banks or credit card companies to credit reporting agencies.[172] There is also a

---

[164] "Two army officers, others relieved of duty over intelligence scandal," BBC Summary of World Broadcasts, May 1999.

[165] Reuters News Service - Central and South America, January 29, 1990.

[166] La Nacion, Buenos Aires, Sept. 8, 1996.

[167] "Cavallo lashes out against corruption," Latin American Weekly Report, October 31, 1996.

[168] "Argentine candidate says own party men bugged him,," Reuters World Report, June 2, 1998.

[169] "Argentine security services accused over phone tap," Reuters World Report, June 2, 1998.

[170] Código Civil, Art. 1071bis, incorporated by Law No. 21.173. See www.codigos.com.ar

[171] Law 25.065 of December 7, 1998 (Official Bulletin of January 14, 1999).

[172] Credit Card Act, Article 53 ("Bar to inform. Credit Card entities, companies and banks and other finacial entities shall not transfer information about credit card debts to credit report agencies when the data subject has not paid its debts or is having financial problems, without prejudice of personal data that must be transferred to the Central Bank under current regulations. Those who transfer this information to third parties shall be liable for the damages produced by the release of the personal data.")

---

specific right of access to personal data of a financial character. The Central Bank of Argentina, whose jurisdiction includes the overview of the monetary policy in the Argentine financial market has authority to regulate banks. Under that authority it created a public debtor's database,[173] requiring financial entities and banks to collect and classify debtors within a range of risk and to send the information to the database. Under Article 8.1 of the regulation[174] the data subject (a client of a bank) has a right of access to his information and to know the reason why she was included in the database.[175]

In 1996, the national government began a new crackdown on tax evaders. Measures included reviewing citizens' credit cards, insurance, and tax records. One bill allowed citizens whose credit card records had been obtained to sue for invasion of privacy.[176] The same year, the Argentina Passport and Federal Police Identification System, developed by Raytheon E-Systems, was inaugurated at the Buenos Aires airport. The system combines personal data, color photos and fingerprints.[177]

In November 1998, the City of Buenos Aires approved a law on access to information. The law gives all persons the right to ask for and to receive information held by the local authorities and creates a right of judicial review. Individuals have the right under habeas data to updating, rectification, confidentiality or suppression of information.[178] But critics say that government agencies jealously keep public records and that it is very difficult to obtain information.[179]

In 1984, Argentina adopted the American Convention on Human Rights into domestic law. Since 1994, the Convention was "constitutionalized" and is used by the Argentine Supreme Court to determine domestic cases.[180]

---

[173] See Financial System Debtors Database "Central de Deudores del Sistema Financiero," regulated by the Central Bank Circular A 2729 (consolidated version by Circular 2930).

[174] Article 8.1, Central Bank Circular A 2729 (consolidated version by Circular 2930).

[175] The information is published also on the Internet <http://www.bcra.gov.ar> and on CD-ROMs. The last CD-ROM contained a list with 1,950,000 individuals including data on their financial status.

[176] New York Times, June 10, 1996.

[177] Business Wire, September 12, 1996.

[178] See Pablo Andrés Palazzi, El derecho de acceso a la información pública en la ley N° 104 de la Ciudad Autónoma de Buenos Aires. REDI, Número 11 - Junio de 1999 <http://publicaciones.derecho.org/redi/index.cgi?/N%FAmero_11_-_Junio_de_1999>.

[179] See La Nación, "Es de difícil cumplimiento la ley de acceso a la información," 11 de Julio de 2000.

[180] See Janet Koven Levit, "The Constitutionalization of Human Rights in Argentina: Problem or Promise?" 37 Columbia Journal of Transnational Law 281. See also Néstor Pedro Sagues, Judicial Censorship of the Press in Argentina, 4 Sw. J. Of L. & Trade Am 45 (1997) (explaining the importance of understanding the make-up of

---

Commonwealth of Australia

While privacy issues are now featured prominently in the daily news in Australia, the legal safeguards for personal information remain limited. Neither the Australian Federal Constitution nor the Constitutions of the six States contain any express provisions relating to privacy. There is periodic debate about the value of a Bill of Rights, but no current proposals.[181]

The principal federal statute is the Privacy Act of 1988.[182] It creates a set of eleven Information Privacy Principles (IPPs), based on those in the OECD Guidelines, that apply to the activities of most federal government agencies. A separate set of rules about the handling of consumer credit information, added to the law in 1989, applies to all private and public sector organizations. The third area of coverage is the use of the government issued Tax File Number (TFN), where the entire community is subject to Guidelines issued by the Privacy Commissioner, which take effect as subordinate legislation. The origins of the Privacy Act were the protests in the mid-1980s against the Australia Card scheme – a proposal for a universal national identity card and number. The controversial proposal was dropped, but use of the tax file number was enhanced to match income from different sources with the Privacy Act providing some safeguards. The use of the tax file number has been further extended by law to include benefits administration as well as taxation. Some controls over this matching activity were introduced in 1990.[183]

After several policy reversals, the re-elected conservative government introduced legislation to extend privacy protection to the private sector in April 2000. The Privacy Amendment (Private Sector) Bill 2000 applies a set of National Privacy Principles developed by the Privacy Commissioner during 1997 and 1998, originally as a self-regulatory substitute for legislation. The National Principles impose a lower standard of protection in several areas than the EU Directive. For example, organizations are required to obtain consent from customers for secondary use of their personal information for marketing purposes where it is "practicable"; otherwise, they can initiate direct marketing contact, providing they give the individual the choice to opt out of further communications.

---

both the Inter-American Court and the Inter-American Commission on Human Rights because the Argentine Supreme Court relies on their opinions as a guide for interpreting personal rights issues).

[181] The Commonwealth of Australia Constitution Act, <http://www.republic.org.au/const/cconst.html>.

[182] Privacy Act 1988 (Cwth), <http://www.austlii.edu.au/au/legis/cth/consol_act/pa1988108/longtitle.html>.

[183] The Data-matching program (Assistance and Tax) Act 1990. <http://www.austlii.edu.au/au/legis/cth/consol_act/dpata1990349/>.

Controls on the transfer of personal information overseas are also limited, requiring only that organizations take "reasonable steps" to ensure personal information will be protected, or "reasonably believes" that the information will be subject to similar protection as applied in the Australian law. Nevertheless, the Bill includes an innovative principle of anonymity. Principle 8 states that: "Wherever it is lawful and practicable, individuals must have the option of not identifying themselves when entering into transactions with an organisation."

The Government has described the Bill as a "light touch legislative regime" which establishes a minimum standard of privacy protection which can be substituted by approved industry codes, which must meet at least the minimum standards in the National Principles. The Bill attracted controversy and widespread debate, with privacy and consumer groups and some business groups expressing concern at its failure to meet international standards of privacy protection. For example, it appeared that the Bill would have a limited effect on the massive database being built by Acxiom Australia, a joint business of U.S.-based Acxiom and PBL, the media conglomerate owned by Australia's richest man, Kerry Packer. When details of the Acxiom database became public in late 1999, a storm of protect ensued, with concerns heightened by the appointment of Andrew Robb as CEO of Acxiom. Robb was previously the Federal Director of the Liberal Party and was widely credited as playing a major role in the electoral success of the Liberals in the late 1990s with the use of sophisticated campaign techniques.

The Bill provided broad exemptions for employment-related use of employee records; small businesses (under $A3m annual turnover) that do not disclose personal information for a benefit; and media organizations, broadly defined to include organizations which provide information to the public and political parties. The Bill was also criticized for weaknesses in its enforcement regime, including allowing privacy complaints to be handled by an industry-appointed code authority with limited oversight by the Privacy Commissioner.

The House of Representative Legal and Constitutional Affairs Committee conducted an inquiry into the Bill and released its report in June 2000.[184] The Committee, the majority of which consisted of government members, acknowledged many of the criticisms and made 23 recommendations for amendments. The legislation is expected to reach the Senate, where government

---

[184] Parliament of the Commonwealth of Australia, House of Representative Standing Committee on Legal and Constitutional Affairs, Advisory Report on the privacy Amendment (Private Sector) Bill 2000 <http://www.aph.gov.au/house/committee/laca/PrivacyBill/contents.htm>.

members are in a minority and opposition parties have indicated their plan to strengthen the legislation, by late 2000.

Public sector privacy issues continue to raise concerns. As part of reforms to the Australian tax system from July 2000, the Australian Taxation Office required all enterprises to obtain an Australian Business Number. The ATO collected registration details including address and email contact, and planned to make this available to the public through the Australian Business Register and through selling it to database companies. A storm of protest occurred in June 2000 when it was realized that the register would include the home address and other details of almost 2 million individuals, who were sole traders, contractors or even had just a minor income from a hobby or some other activity. The Government agreed to amend the legislation, limit the content of the Australian Business Register and allow individuals to suppress their details. At the same time, the Government was forced into another backdown after receiving legal advice that the Australian Electoral Commission had illegally disclosed information on around 10 million registered Australian voters, after the Prime Minister had asked for this information in order to conduct a targeted direct mailing campaign outlining the benefits of the tax reform package.

The Office of Privacy Commissioner[185] has a wide range of functions, including handling complaints, auditing compliance, promoting community awareness, and advising the government and others on privacy matters. The Commissioner's office, which was initially well funded, suffered major budget cutbacks in 1997, at the same time as the Commissioner's range of responsibilities under several laws and in response to government requests was expanding.

In the period of 1998-99, the Commissioners Office received 8,980 calls, of which 3,142 or 35 percent related to matters falling within the Privacy Commissioner's jurisdiction. Of the remaining calls, 3,212 related to privacy issues outside of the scope of the Privacy Act. Some 718 written inquiries were received, of which 131 were formally investigated as complaints. Ninety-one complaints were closed and 11 audits conducted.[186] The Commissioner released a strategic plan in 2000 outlining his office's role under forthcoming private sector legislation. Guidelines were also released for employee use of email and for government websites. The Commissioner also released a report on the application of the National Privacy Principles to personal health information in

---

[185] Homepage: http://www.privacy.gov.au/

[186] Eleventh Annual Report, Office of the Federal Privacy Commissioner, 1998-99 <http://www.privacy.gov.au/pdf/99annrep.pdf>.

December 1999, proposing modifications to the National Privacy Principles to take account of specific issues relating to the handling of health care information. These suggestions were largely implemented in the Bill released in April 2000.

The Telecommunications (Interception) Act of 1979[187] regulates the interception of telecommunications. A warrant is required under the Act, which also provides for detailed monitoring and reporting, but in 1997 the authority for issuing warrants was extended from federal court judges to designated members of the Administrative Appeals Tribunal, who are on term appointments rather than tenured. Significant loopholes exist within the legislation, such as section 6(2) which some experts argue allows the recording and monitoring of communications in specific circumstances such as when the equipment is provided by a telecommunications carrier. The Interception Act safeguards also need to be read alongside Part 15 of the Telecommunications Act of 1997, which places obligations on telecommunications providers to provide an interception capability and to positively assist law enforcement agencies with interception.

In November 1999, the Australian Security Intelligence Organisation Legislation Amendment Act 1999 was passed by the Commonwealth Parliament. The Act gives ASIO new powers to access e-mails and data inside computers, use tracking devices on vehicles, obtain tax and cash transaction information and intercept mail items carried by couriers. ASIO is authorized to modify private computer files as long as there is reasonable cause to believe that it is relevant to a security matter.[188]

The Parliament approved the Telecommunications (Interception) Legislation Amendment Bill 2000 on June 7, 2000. The legislation will allow for the issuing of "named person" warrants based on a name of person only, not specifying the location of the tap to allow for the interception of multiple services without a new warrant. The bill also expands the use of wiretap information in other proceedings. Intelligence agencies can get a "foreign communications warrant" to "enable ASIO, operating 'within Australia,' to intercept communications 'sent or received outside Australia' for the purposes of collecting foreign intelligence."

---

[187] Telecommunications (Interception) Act 1979,
<http://www.austlii.edu.au/au/legis/cth/consol_act/ta1979350/>.

[188] "Orwellian Nightmare Down Under?" Wired News, December 4, 1999.

Taps increased substantially in the last year reported. In 1998-1999, there were 1,284 warrants issued, up from 675 warrants issued in the year 1997-1998.[189] This excludes an undisclosed number of interception warrants issued to the Australian Security Intelligence Organisation by the Attorney General.

The Crimes Act[190] also contains a range of other privacy related measures, such as offenses relating to unauthorized access to computers, unauthorized interception of mail and telecommunications and the unauthorized disclosure of Commonwealth government information.[191] It also contains provisions relating to "spent" convictions, allowing individuals convicted of minor offenses to lawfully "deny" them in most circumstances after a period of time.

A mix of privacy standards apply to the telecommunications sector. Part 13 of the Telecommunications Act of 1997[192] contains a general prohibition on the disclosure of telecommunications-related personal information. However, this principle contains a detailed list of exceptions.[193] The telecommunications industry is regulated through voluntary codes of practice which are developed by the Australian Communication Industry Forum (ACIF), but, once they are registered by the Australian Communications Authority (ACA), the Authority can direct a company to comply with certain provisions of a code. Early in 2000 the ACA registered the Code of Practice for the Protection of the Personal Information of Customers of Telecommunications Providers[194] and Code of Practice on Calling Number Display.[195]

During 2000, Commonwealth and State governments have announced plans to move towards unique patient identifiers in the health sector, likely to be centered around a health smart card. Health services are primarily delivered by the public sector in Australia, with only around a third of the population having private health insurance. The responsibility for delivery of health services is shared between the Commonwealth Government, which is responsible for much of the funding of the health system, and the States, which operate hospitals and

---

[189] Attorney General's Department, Report on the Telecommunications (Interception) Act for the year ending 30 June 1998.

[190] Crimes Act, 1989 <http://www.austlii.edu.au/au/legis/cth/consol_act/ca191482/s85zl.html>.

[191] See http://www.austlii.edu.au/au/legis/cth/consol_act/ca191482/index.html#s85m.

[192] See http://www.austlii.edu.au/au/legis/cth/consol_act/ta1997214/.

[193] The Data-matching program (Assistance and Tax) Act 1990, <http://www.austlii.edu.au/au/legis/cth/consol_act/dpata1990349/>.

[194] http://www.aca.gov.au/codes/abtem8.htm

[195] http://www.aca.gov.au/codes/abtem9.htm

community health services. The Commonwealth's proposal, HealthConnect, is intended as a voluntary national health information network under which health-related information about an individual would be collected in a standard, electronic format at the point of care.[196] The New South Wales Government established a committee to review health privacy issues, which is intended to report at the end of 2000. The Victorian Government released a draft Health Records Bill in mid-2000.[197]

The Australian States and Territories have varying privacy laws. The New South Wales Privacy and Personal Information Protection Act of 1998 recently came into effect. It is based on a set of OECD-style Information Protection Principles and requires all government departments and agencies to develop a Privacy Management Plan demonstrating their compliance plans. It also allows government agencies to weaken the Information Protection Principles which form the foundation of the legislation.[198] In Victoria, an information privacy bill was introduced in May 2000 and is expected to be enacted later in the year.[199] It covers the public sector with principles similar to the National Privacy Principles. The Australian Capital Territory (ACT) enacted a health privacy law in 1997,[200] and the Queensland government has committed to implement the April 1998 recommendation of a Parliamentary Committee for a public sector privacy law,[201] but with no timetable yet announced. Specific privacy provisions are also found in many State laws dealing with such diverse matters as health, adoption, drug controls and registration of births, deaths and marriages. Most States and Territories also have laws relating to listening devices, although these are generally recognized as being badly in need of updating to cope with new technologies.[202]

The federal Freedom of Information Act of 1982[203] provides for access to government records. The Commonwealth Ombudsman promotes the Act and

---

[196] http://www.health.gov.au/healthonline/connect.htm

[197] http://www.dhs.vic.gov.au/ahs/healthrecords

[198] See http://www.lawlink.nsw.gov.au/pc.nsf/pages/index.

[199] See http://www.dms.dpc.vic.gov.au/.

[200] See http://www.austlii.edu.au/au/legis/act/consol_act/hraaa1997291/

[201] See http://www.parliament.qld.gov.au/comdocs/legalrev/lcarc9.PDF

[202] See the NSW Law Reform Commission's Issues Paper
<http://www.lawlink.nsw.gov.au/lrc.nsf/pages/IP12TOC> and the ACIF Guideline on Participant monitoring at <http://www.acif.org.au/>.

[203] Freedom of Information Act 1982 <http://www.austlii.edu.au/au/legis/cth/consol_act/foia1982222/>, Freedom of Information (Fees and Charges) Regulations 1982, <http://www.austlii.edu.au/au/legis/cth/consol_reg/foiacr432/index.html>, Freedom of Information

---

handles complaints about procedural failures. Merits review (appeal) of adverse FOI decisions is provided by the Administrative Appeals Tribunal, with the possibility of further appeals on points of law to the Federal Court. Budget cuts have severely restricted the capacity of the AGs Department and Ombudsman to support the Act and there is now little central direction, guidance or monitoring. All of the States and the ACT (but not the Northern Territory) also have Freedom of Information laws which include rights for individuals to access and correct personal information about themselves.[204]

Republic of Austria

The Austrian Constitution does not explicitly recognize the right of privacy.[205] Some sections of the data protection law (Datenschutzgesetz – DSG) have constitutional status. These rights may only be restricted under the conditions of Article 8 of the European Convention of Human Rights (ECHR). The entire ECHR has constitutional status and Article 8 is often cited by the constitutional court in privacy matters.

A new data protection bill (Datenschutzgesetz 2000)[206] which incorporates the EU Directive into Austrian law was approved in December 1999 and went into force in January 2000. However, experts criticize the new bill as being inadequate because it retains the cumbersome structure of the original 1978 Act[207] rather than replacing it.[208]

The Act is enforced by the Data Protection Commission. The Commission reports that there are 100,000 Data Controllers registered. It also handles around 85 formal complaints and 1,200 informal requests each year. The Commission has 21 staff members (six legal professionals, two IT experts and 13 support staff).

(Miscellaneous Provisions) regulations 1982.
<http://www.austlii.edu.au/au/legis/cth/consol_reg/foipr612/index.html>.

[204] For an overview of FOI laws in Australia and links to relevant government sites, see the University of Tasmania's FOI Review web pages at http://www.comlaw.utas.edu.au/law/foi/.

[205] Constitution of Austria <http://www.uni-wuerzburg.de/law/au00t___.html>.

[206] See <http://www.ad.or.at/office/recht/dsg2000.htm>.

[207] Datenschutzgesetz – DSG, BGBl 1978/565 changed by 1981/314, 1982/228, 1986/370, 1987/605, 1988/233, 1989/609, 1993/91, 1994/79, 1994/632. <http://www.ad.or.at/office/recht/dsg.htm>.

[208] See Viktor Mayer-Schoenberger and Ernst Brandl, Datenschutzgesetz 2000, (Line Publishing Vienna, 1999).

Wiretapping, electronic eavesdropping and computer searches are regulated by the code of criminal procedure.[209] Telephone wiretapping is permitted if it is needed for investigating a crime punishable by more than one year in prison. Electronic eavesdropping and computer searches are allowed if they are needed to investigate criminal organizations or crimes punishable by more than ten years in prison. The provision concerning electronic eavesdropping and computer searches became effective between October 1, 1997, and July 1, 1998. Due to long and intensive discussion, the provisions are in effect only until December 31, 2001. Criticism of the drafts for this law has led to a number of restrictions, but whether or not these provisions can effectively prevent eavesdropping on innocent persons remains unresolved.

There are also a number of specific laws relating to privacy. The telecommunication law contains special data protection provisions for telecommunication systems, particularly problems like phone directories, unsolicited calls or ISDN calling line identification.[210] The Genetic Engineering Act of 1994 requires prior written consent for information to be used for purposes other than the original purpose. Austrians can have an anonymous "Sparbuch" bank account. The Financial Action Task Force, an anti-money laundering group coordinated by the OECD, has been pressuring Austria to change its laws to require that each account be personally identified.[211] In June 2000, the First Chamber of the Parliament approved legislation to identify anyone who withdraws or deposits from an account by 2002.[212]

The Auskunftspflichtgesetz is a Freedom of Information law that obliges federal authorities to answer questions regarding their areas of responsibility.[213] However, it does not permit citizens to access documents, just to receive answers from the government on the content of information. The nine Austrian Provinces have laws that place similar obligations on their authorities.

Austria is a member of the Council of Europe and has signed and ratified the Convention for the Protection of Individuals with Regard to Automatic

---

[209] § 149a to § 149p Strafprozeßordnung – StPO.

[210] § 87 to § 101, Telekommunikationsgesetz – TKG, BGBl I 1997/100.

[211] Financial Action Task Force on Money Laundering Issues: a Warning about Austrian Anonymous Savings Passbooks, February 11, 1999.

[212] Financial Action Task Force, FATF welcomes proposed Austrian legislation to eliminate anonymous passbooks, 15 June 2000.

[213] BGBl 1987/285 (15 May 1987). <http://www.rz.uni-frankfurt.de/~sobotta/Austria.htm>.

Processing of Personal Data (ETS No. 108).[214] It has signed and ratified the European Convention for the Protection of Human Rights and Fundamental Freedoms.[215] It is a member of the Organization for Economic Cooperation and Development and has adopted the OECD Guidelines on the Protection of Privacy and Transborder Flows of Personal Data.

Kingdom of Belgium

The Belgian Constitution recognizes the right of privacy and private communications.[216] Article 22 states, "Everyone has the right to the respect of his private and family life, except in the cases and conditions determined by law. . . . The laws, decrees, and rulings alluded to in Article 134 guarantee the protection of this right." Article 29 states, "The confidentiality of letters is inviolable. . . . The law determines which nominated representatives can violate the confidentiality of letters entrusted to the postal service." Article 22 was added to the Belgian Constitution in 1994. Prior to the constitutional amendment, the Cour de Cassation ruled that Article 8 of the European Convention applied directly to the law and prohibited government infringement on the private life of individuals.[217]

The processing and use of personal information is governed by the Data Protection Act of 1992. Amending legislation to update this Act and make it consistent with the EU Directive was approved by the Parliament in December 1998.[218] A Royal Decree to implement the Act was approved in July 2000. There was concern among independent experts that the amended Act may not be fully consistent with the Directive, especially in areas relating to government files. The Decree may remedy some of the defects of the Act, including reducing exceptions in favor of the social security institutions. In September 1998, the state security office announced that it was "cleaning" the files on 570,000 individuals that it had been collecting since 1944 to bring the files into

---

[214] Signed 28/01/81, Ratified 30/03/88, Entered into force 01/07/88, <http://conventions.coe.int/>.

[215] Signed 13/12/57, Ratified 03/09/58, Entered into force 03/09/58, <http://conventions.coe.int/>.

[216] Constitution of Belgium,<http://www.fed-parl.be/constitution_uk.html.>.

[217] Cour de Cassation, 26 September 1978.

[218] Act concerning the protection of privacy with regard to the treatment of personal data files, December 8, 1992., as amended by the Act of December 11, 1998 transposing EU Directive 95/46/CE of October 24, 1995. <http://www.law.kuleuven.ac.be/icri/papers/legislation/privacy/tabel/index.html>. An unofficial English translation is available at http://www.law.kuleuven.ac.be/icri/papers/legislation/privacy/engels/.

---

compliance with the 1992 law.[219] In 1995, the Belgian Government admitted spying on the peace and environmental movements.[220]

The Commission de la Protection de la Vie Privée oversees the law.[221] The Commission investigates complaints, issues opinions and maintains the registry of personal files. In 1999, the Commission answered approximately 6,000 complaints and requests for information. According to the Commission, this number is much larger than in previous years as now it is its policy to answer all complaints rather than only those which were "formally" filed. It is currently handling about 1,000 formal investigations.[222] The commission has also issued a number of recommendations relating to workplace privacy, and video surveillance.[223] Under the old law, there were 24,000 processings registered. As of July 2000, there are 21 permanent members on the staff.

Surveillance of communications is regulated under a 1994 law.[224] Prior to its enactment, there was no specific law. The law requires permission of a juge d'instruction before wiretapping can take place. Orders are limited to a period of one month. There were 114 orders issued in 1996.[225] The law was amended in 1997 to remove restrictions on encryption.[226] The Parliament also amended the law in 1998 to require greater assistance from telecommunications carriers.[227]

---

[219] La Sûreté de l'Etat trie 570.000 fiches individuelles, Le Soir, September 19, 1998.

[220] Statewatch Bulletin, Vol. 5 No 6, November-December 1995.

[221] Commission de la protection de la vie privée homepage: http://www.privacy.fgov.be/

[222] E-mail from the Commission de la Protection de la Vie Privée, July 11, 2000.

[223] Avis n° 34/99 d'initiative relatif aux traitements d'images effectués en particulier par le biais de systèmes de vidéo-surveillance <http://www.privacy.fgov.be/av034def.pdf>, Avis n° 3/2000 d'initiative relatif à l'utilisation de systèmes de vidéo-surveillance dans les halls d'immeubles à appartements, <http://www.privacy.fgov.be/av003def.pdf>.

[224] loi de 30 juin 1994 relative à la protection de la vie privée contre les écoutes, la prise de connaissance et l'enregistrement de communications et de télécommunications privées.

[225] Ecoutes: une pratique décevante et. flamande! Le résultat judiciaire des écoutes téléphoniques est médiocre. La Chambre va modifier la donne, Le Soir, December 12, 1997.

[226] Chapitre 17, Loi modifiant la loi du 21 mars 1991 portant réforme de certaines entreprises publiques économiques afin d'adapter le cadre réglementaire aux obligations en matière de libre concurrence et d'harmonisation sur le marché des télécommunications découlant des décisions de l'Union européenne, 19 Decembre 1997.

[227] Loi modifiant la loi du 30 juin 1994 relative à la protection de la vie privée contre les écoutes, la prise de connaissance et l'enregistrement de communications et de télécommunications privées, 10 Juin 1998. See "Le GSM en toute sécurité ? Pas sûr", Le Soir, 20 Feb. 1998.

In spring 2000, the Chamber of Deputies of the Belgian Parliament approved a bill on computer-related crime.[228] The bill would amend the Criminal Procedure Code, adding a paragraph giving the Juge d'Instruction the authority to request the cooperation of experts or network managers to help decrypt telecommunications messages which have been intercepted. The experts, network managers, etc. could not refuse providing cooperation; criminal sanctions would be possible in cases of refusal. The bill would also require that Internet Service Providers retain records for law enforcement purposes. The Bill is currently being debated in the Senate. In December 1999 the Commission de la Protection de la Vie Privée issued an opinion on the bill, in which it raised serious concerns about it's potential impact on the privacy of personal data. It recommended certain amendments to the Bill including the establishment of a "police monitoring system," which would report back to the Commission, and a three year review provision.[229]

There are also laws relating to consumer credit,[230] social security,[231] electoral rolls,[232] the national ID number,[233] professional secrets,[234] and employee rights.[235] There are Freedom of Information laws on the right of access to administrative documents on the national[236] and local and regional levels.[237] Each jurisdiction has a Commission d'accès aux documents administratifs which oversees the act.

Belgium is a member of the Council of Europe and has signed and ratified the Convention for the Protection of Individuals with Regard to Automatic

---

[228] Projet de loi relative à la criminalité informatique,
<http://www.law.kuleuven.ac.be/icri/papers/comcrimefr.html>.

[229] Opinion 33/99 de la Commission de la Protection de la Vie Privée. Available at http://www.privacy.fgov.be/.

[230] La loi du 12 juin 1991 relative au crédit à la consommation. l'arrêté royal du 11 janvier 1993 modifiant l'arrêté royal du 20 novembre 1992 relatif à l'enregistrement par la Banque Nationale de Belgique des défauts de paiement en matière de crédit à la consommation. <http://www.privacy.fgov.be/loicrÈdit.PDF>.

[231] La loi du 15 janvier 1990 relative à l'institution et à l'organisation d'une banque-carrefour de la sécurité sociale. Modified by la loi du 29 avril 1996. <http://www.privacy.fgov.be/loicarrefour.PDF>.

[232] La loi du 30 juillet 1991.

[233] La loi du 8 août 1993: le registre national. <http://www.privacy.fgov.be/loiregistre.PDF>.

[234] Article 458 of the Penal Code.

[235] See Roger Blanpain, Employee Privacy Issues: Belgian Report, 17 Comp. Lab. L. 38, Fall 1995.

[236] 11 avril 1994 relative à la publicité de l'administration Law, la loi du 12 novembre 1997 relative à la publicité de l'administration dans les provinces et les communes.
<http://perso.infonie.fr/ledru.b/citoyen/info/cig01.htm>.

[237] Commission Communautaire Commune de Bruxelles-Capitale, Ordonnance relative à la publicité de l'administration, 26 Juin 1997; Flanders law of 23.10.1991.

Processing of Personal Data (ETS No. 108).[238] It has signed and ratified the European Convention for the Protection of Human Rights and Fundamental Freedoms.[239] It is a member of the Organization for Economic Cooperation and Development and has adopted the OECD Guidelines on the Protection of Privacy and Transborder Flows of Personal Data.

Federative Republic of Brazil

Article 5 of the 1988 Constitution of Brazil provides, in part: "the privacy, private life, honor and image of persons are inviolable, and the right to compensation for property or moral damages resulting from the violation thereof is ensured; . . . the home is the inviolable asylum of the individual, and no one may enter it without the dweller's consent, save in the case of 'in flagrante delicto' or disaster, or to give help, or, during the day, by court order; . . . the secrecy of correspondence and of telegraphic, data and telephone communications is inviolable, except, in the latter case, by court order, in the events and in the manner established by the law for purposes of criminal investigation or criminal procedural discovery; . . . access to information is ensured to everyone and confidentiality of the source is protected whenever necessary for the professional activity."[240]

A bill promoting the privacy of personal data in conformance with the OECD guidelines, to affect both public and private sector databases, was proposed in the Senate in 1996 and has yet to be voted on. The bill provides that, "No personal data nor information shall be disclosed, communicated, or transmitted for purposes different than those that led to structuring such data registry or database, without express authorization of the owner, except in case of a court order, and for purposes of a criminal investigation or legal proceedings . . . It is forbidden to gather, register, archive, process, and transmit personal data referring to: ethnic origin, political or religious beliefs, physical or mental health, sexual life, police or penal records, family issues, except family relationship, civil status, and marriage system . . . Every citizen is entitled to, without any charge; access to his/her personal data, stored in data registries or databases, and correct, supplement, or eliminate such data, and be informed by data registry or

---

[238] Signed 07/05/82, Ratified 28/05/93, Entered into Force 01/09/93, <http://conventions.coe.int/>.

[239] <http://conventions.coe.int/>.

[240] The Constitution of Brazil, 1988. <http://www.uni-wuerzburg.de/law/br00t___.html>.

---

database managers of the existence of data regarding his/her person."[241] It is widely expected that the law will move forward following the approval of legislation in neighboring countries such as Argentina and Chile.

The 1990 Code of Consumer Protection and Defense[242] allows all consumers to "access any information derived from personal and consumer data stored in files, archives, registries, and databases, as well as to access their respective sources. Consumer files and data shall be objective, clear, true, and written in a manner easily understood, and shall not contain derogatory information for a period over five years. Whenever consumers find incorrect data and files concerning their person, they are entitled to require immediate correction, and the archivist shall communicate the due alterations to the incorrect information within five days. Consumer databases and registries, credit protection services, and similar institutions are considered entities of public nature. Once the consumer has settled his/her debts, Credit Protection Services shall not provide any information which may prevent or hinder further access to credit for this consumer." The Informatics Law of 1984[243] protects the confidentiality of stored, processed and disclosed data, and the privacy and security of physical, legal, public, and private entities. Citizens are entitled to access and correct their personal information in private or public databases.

Individuals have a constitutional right of Habeas Data to access information about themselves held by public agencies which has been adopted into law.[244]

In 1996, a law regulating wiretapping was enacted.[245] Official wiretaps are permitted for 15 days, renewable on a judge's order for another 15 days, and can only be resorted to in cases where police suspect serious crimes punishable by imprisonment, such as drug smuggling, corruption, contraband smuggling, murder and kidnapping. The granting of judicial eavesdropping permits by judges was previously an ad hoc process without any legal basis.[246] Illegal wiretapping by police and intelligence agencies is still ongoing. The Agencia Brasileira de Informacoes (Abin) was suspected of wiretapping President

---

[241] Federal Senate Bill No. 61, 1996 (in English)
<http://www.privacyexchange.org/legal/ppl/nat/brazilpending.html>.

[242] Law No. 8078, September 11, 1990.

[243] Law No. 7.232, October 29, 1984.

[244] Lei Nº 9.507, de 12 de Novembro de 1997.

[245] Lei Nº 9.296, de 24 de Julho de 1996.

[246] "Brazil makes police phone-taps legal," Reuters World Service, July 24, 1996.

Cardoso after tapes of his conversations were leaked to the press in May 1999.[247] Several ministers resigned in 1998 after tapes of wiretapped conversation involving the Brazilian Development Bank were disclosed in what was called the "Telegate scandal." In 1992, amid a scandal that toppled President Fernando Collor de Mello, it was discovered that Vice President Itamar Franco's phones at his official residence in Brasilia and in a Rio de Janeiro hotel room had been tapped.[248] In 1996, Abin was put under military control with the task of evaluating the background of people appointed to government posts. According to the new director, "every instrument authorized by the courts will be used to keep the president well informed, including wiretapping of phones, opening of personal mail, and infiltration of Abin agents into social movements such as the Landless Peasant's Movement (Movimento sem Terra)." Abin is the central body of an intelligence system that is spread out through federal, state, municipal and even private organizations. The intelligence system operates under the name of Sisbin (Brazilian Intelligence System).[249] The Agency's guidelines prevent it from performing police operations, and require it to obtain a judicial order to perform wiretaps.[250] A computer crimes act was approved in July 2000.

A candidate for mayor of São Paulo, Celso Pitta, discovered wiretaps on two of his telephone lines in 1996.[251] A man with AIDS charged the city of Morretes, Paraná of discrimination and invasion of privacy after a city government proclamation identifying him and his HIV status was posted in public buildings.[252]

Brazil signed the American Convention on Human Rights on September 25, 1992.

Republic of Bulgaria

The Bulgarian Constitution of 1991 recognizes rights of privacy, secrecy of communications and access to information. Article 32 states, "(1) The privacy of citizens shall be inviolable. Everyone shall be entitled to protection against any

---

[247] "Is Abin behind Telegate?," Latin America Weekly Report, June 8, 1999.

[248] "Brazil vice-president claims his phone was tapped," Reuters North American Wire, September 9, 1992.

[249] "'O Globo', Rio de Janeiro," August 4, 1996, BBC Monitoring Service: Latin America, August 7, 1996.

[250] "President transfers control of new intelligence agency to military," Agencia Estado news agency, Sao Paulo, BBC Summary of World Broadcasts, April 11, 1996.

[251] Reuters News Service, October 2, 1996.

[252] SEJUP (Servico Brasileiro de Justica e Paz), Number 117, February 17, 1994.

illegal interference in his private or family affairs and against encroachments on his honor, dignity and reputation. (2) No one shall be followed, photographed, filmed, recorded or subjected to any other similar activity without his knowledge or despite his express disapproval, except when such actions are permitted by law." Article 33 states, "(1) The home shall be inviolable. No one shall enter or stay inside a home without its occupant's consent, except in the cases expressly stipulated by law. (2) Entry into, or staying inside, a home without the consent of its occupant or without the judicial authorities' permission shall be allowed only for the purposes of preventing an immediately impending crime or a crime in progress, for the capture of a criminal, or in extreme necessity." Article 34 states, "(1) The freedom and confidentiality of correspondence and all other communications shall be inviolable. (2) Exceptions to this provision shall be allowed only with the permission of the judicial authorities for the purpose of discovering or preventing a grave crime." Article 41 states, "(1) Everyone shall be entitled to seek, obtain and disseminate information. This right shall not be exercised to the detriment of the rights and reputation of others, or to the detriment of national security, public order, public health and morality. (2) Citizens shall be entitled to obtain information from state bodies and agencies on any matter of legitimate interest to them which is not a state or other secret prescribed by law and does not affect the rights of others."[253]

There are currently efforts to enact comprehensive data protection legislation in Bulgaria. In 1996, the government began developing data protection legislation in preparation for integration into the EU Internal Market under the Treaty for Association of Bulgaria to the EU. Data protection is also a key element of the information legislation which is a priority in the National Assembly's legislative activities.

The draft Personal Data Protection Act closely follows the EU Data Protection Directive. It sets rules on the fair and responsible handling of personal information by the public and private sector. Entities collecting personal information must do the following: inform people why their personal information is being collected and what it is to be used for; allow people reasonable access to information about themselves and the right to correct it if it is wrong; ensure that the information is securely held and cannot be tampered with, stolen or improperly used; and limit the use of personal information, for purposes other than the original purpose, without the consent of the person affected, or in certain

---

[253] Constitution of the Republic of Bulgaria of 13 July 1991, <http://www.uni-wuerzburg.de/law/bu00t___.html>.

other circumstances. The draft law creates a the State Commission for the Protection of Personal Data to oversee the act.

The European Commission stated in 1997 that "considerable efforts are still needed to adopt and implement measures to meet Community requirements on data protection."[254]

Electronic surveillance used in criminal investigations is regulated by the criminal code and requires a court order.[255] The Telecommunications Law also requires that agencies must ensure the secrecy of communications.[256] The 1997 Special Surveillance Means Act regulates the use of surveillance techniques by the Interior Ministry for investigating crime but also for loosely defined national security reasons. A court order is generally required but in cases of emergency, an order from the Interior Minister is sufficient.[257]

The U.S. State Department in its 1999 human rights report said, "One nongovernmental organization (NGO) complained that the Minister of Interior's discretionary authority to authorize telephone wiretaps without judicial review is excessive, although it is unknown to what extent this authority is employed. It is also alleged that warrants to investigate suspects' private financial records sometimes are abused to give police broad and openended authority to engage in far-ranging investigations of a suspect's family and associates. There are regular, albeit not conclusive or systematic, reports of mail, especially foreign mail, being delayed and/or opened."[258] In August 2000, listening devices were found in the apartment of the Prosecutor General Nikola Filchev and several politicians. Filchev blamed the bugs on the Interior Ministry's Criminal Intelligence Service (CIS) and a Parliamentary session was held after 53 Democratic Left Parliamentarians demanded a hearing.[259] The head of the National Security Service, Col. Yuli Georgiev, resigned in February 1997 after allegations of wiretapping politicians.[260] Bulgaria's military prosecutor filed a suit in December 1996 against an unidentified state official for illegally bugging telephones at the

---

[254] <http://europa.eu.int/comm/dg1a/agenda2000/en/opinions/bulgaria/b1.htm>.

[255] Art. 170-171 (1) (As amended - SG, Nos. 28/1982, 10/1993).

[256] Telecommunications Law, Art. 5.

[257] Bulgarian Helsinki Committee, Human Rights in Bulgaria in 1997.

[258] 1999 Country Reports on Human Rights Practices: Bulgaria, U.S. Department of State, February 25, 2000.

[259] "Buggate Scandalizes Bulgaria." Transitions online, 31 July - 6 August 2000.

[260] "Security chief resigns: reportedly was to be dismissed," BBC Summary of World Broadcasts, February 7, 1997.

offices of the main opposition, Union of Democratic Forces (UDF), including those of president-elect Petar Stoyanov.[261]

In December 1998, the Bulgarian Committee for Post and Telecommunications issued an executive decree to license Internet Service Providers. The decree gave governmental employees the authorization to enter ISPs' offices at any time and obtain any documentation, including user names and passwords, as well as other private information.[262] The decision was extensively crticized by Internet users, service providers and others, including German Chancellor Shroeder who said that licensing was not appropriate. The Bulgarian Internet Society (ISOC) chapter filed a case at the Supreme Administrative Court to stop the decree in January 1999.[263] The Court ordered a temporary restraint of the decree on June 17, 1999. In November 1999, the Bulgarian Prime Minister ordered the Minister of Telecommunications to negotiate an out of court agreement with ISOC. A few weeks later, the decree was changed, and the ISPs were removed from the licensing requirements and placed in the "free regime" category.

There are additional provisions relating to privacy in laws such as the Statistics Law, Tax Administration Law, Insurance Law,[264] and Social Assistance Law.[265] The Radio and Television Act sets limits[266] on broadcasting of personal information. In conjunction with the preparation of the Law on Protection of Citizens' Personal Data, analyses of Bulgarian legal acts related to personal data of individuals are planned. Proposals of reforms and supplements in the relevant acts also can be made, if necessary.

The Law for Access to Information to provide access to government records was enacted in June 2000 and went into force in July.[267] The law allows for access to records except in cases of state security or personal privacy. Minor fines are anticipated against officials who unlawfully withhold documents.[268] The Bulgarian National Bank announced in July 1999 that it would be the first state institution to open up its archive of documents from the Communist era, starting

---

[261] Reuters World Service, December 19, 1996.

[262] Committee for Post and Telecommunications, "List of telecommunication services, Dec. 18, 1998. published at the State Gazette on Dec. 29. 1998. <http://www.cpt.acad.bg/BG/>.

[263] See http://www.isoc.bg/kpd/legal3-eng.html

[264] Insurance Law, Art.7 par. 1.

[265] Social Assistance Law, Art. 32 par. 2.

[266] Radio and Television Act, Articles 10, 15.

[267] Access to Public Information Act (draft), <http://www.aip-bg.org/documents/access.htm>.

[268] National Assembly Adopts Access to Public Information Bill, FBIS, 22 June 2000.

in September.[269] The 1997 Access to Documents of the Former State Security Service Act regulates the access, proceedings of disclosure and use of information kept in the documents of the former State Security Service.

Bulgaria is a member of the Council of Europe and has signed but not ratified the Convention for the Protection of Individuals with Regard to Automatic Processing of Personal Data (ETS No. 108).[270] It has signed and ratified the European Convention for the Protection of Human Rights and Fundamental Freedoms.[271]

Canada

There is no explicit right to privacy in Canada's Constitution and Charter of Rights and Freedoms.[272] However, in interpreting Section 8 of the Charter, which grants the right to be secure against unreasonable search or seizure, Canada's courts have recognized an individual's right to a reasonable expectation of privacy.[273]

Senator Sheila Finestone proposed a "Charter of Privacy Rights" in March 2000.[274] The Charter would create a broad constitutional right of privacy for all Canadians in all spheres and prevail over acts of Parliament. According to Senator Finestone:

> Under the bill, every individual would be given the right to privacy. This right would include, but not be limited to, personal privacy, which includes physical and psychological privacy; privacy of space, which includes freedom from surveillance; privacy of communication, which includes freedom from monitoring and interception; privacy of information, which includes freedom from collection, use and disclosure of their personal information by others. Any interference with an individual's privacy would be an infringement of the individuals right to privacy unless the interference is reasonably justified and unless it is impossible or inappropriate to do so, the individual's informed consent has been obtained.

---

[269] RFE/RL NEWSLINE Vol. 3, No. 142, Part II, 23 July 1999

[270] Signed 02/06/98, <http://conventions.coe.int/>.

[271] Signed 107/05/92, Ratified 007/09/92, Entered into force 07/09/92, <http://conventions.coe.int/>.

[272] Canadian Charter of Rights and Freedoms. <http://canada.justice.gc.ca/Loireg/charte/const_en.html>.

[273] Hunter v. Southam, 2 Supreme Court Reports 2 (1984) 159-60.

[274] The Hon. Sheila Finestone, P.C., Charting Our Future Together: Consultation On A Draft Charter Of Privacy Rights, March 9, 2000. <http://www.ltinc.net/fipa/finestone1.htm>.

A four-part test is required to determine if interferences are reasonably justified. The only permissible interferences would be:

1) where lawful;
2) where necessary to achieve a compelling societal interest that warrant's limiting an individual's privacy;
3) where no other lesser measure will accomplish this objective; and
4) where both the importance of the objective and the beneficial effects of the interference outweigh the privacy loss.

The Federal Parliament approved Bill C-6, the Personal Information Protection and Electronic Documents Act in April 2000.[275] The Act adopts the CSA International Privacy Code (a national standard: CAN/CSA-Q830-96) into law for enterprises that process personal information "in the course of a commercial activity," and for federally regulated employers with respect to their employees. It does not apply to information collected for personal, journalistic, artistic, literary, or non-commercial purposes. The law will go into effect for companies that are under federal regulation, such as banks, telecommunications, transportation and businesses that trade data interprovincially and internationally in January 2001, except with respect to medical records, which are exempted from the new law until 2002 (most medical records, however, fall under provincial jurisdiction). In three years, the Act will cover provincially regulated sectors unless the province enacts "substantially similar" laws, such as Quebéc's law.

The scope of the act is still limited. As noted by the federal Privacy Commissioner Bruce Phillips, "it is by no means the whole answer. Still missing is an adequate legal regime covering such things as video surveillance, physical privacy, biomedical privacy, drug and DNA testing, to mention a few." The European Commission said in July 2000 that it would begin a review of the Canadian law to determine that it provides adequate protection to allow for transborder data flows.[276]

---

[275] Bill C-6, Personal Information Protection and Electronic Documents Act
<http://www.parl.gc.ca/36/2/parlbus/chambus/house/bills/government/C-6/C-6_4/C-6_cover-E.html>.

[276] European Commission, Data protection: Commission adopts decisions recognising adequacy of regimes in US, Switzerland and Hungary, July 27, 2000.
<http://europa.eu.int/comm/internal_market/en/media/dataprot/news/safeharbor.htm>.

The federal Privacy Act[277] provides individuals with a right of access to personal information held by the federal public sector. In addition, the Privacy Act contains provisions regulating the confidentiality, collection, correction, disclosure, retention and use of personal information. Individuals may request records directly from the institution that has the custody of the information. The Act establishes a code of fair information practices that apply to government handling of personal records. However, its provisions can be ignored when another federal Act allows for the processing of personal information.

Individuals can appeal to a federal court for review if access to their records is denied by an agency, but are not authorized to challenge the collection, use or disclosure of information. In the Fall of 1998, the Commissioner asked a court to review the matching of the Customs declarations of returning travelers against the Employment Insurance database. The Federal Privacy Commissioner asked the court to decide whether the Customs Act overrides the government's obligation in the Privacy Act to use personal information only for the purpose for which it is collected unless the individual consents. In February 1999, the court ruled that the matching could not be conducted without ministerial approval and the program was suspended. This was overturned by the Court of Appeals and the Privacy Commissioner has appealed the case to the Supreme Court.

The Privacy Commissioner finished an extensive review of the Act in 1999 and has recommended over 100 changes to the law to improve and update it including giving it primary authority over all information collecting by the federal government, extending its coverage beyond "recorded" information, increasing notices of disclosures, expanding court reviews, creating rules on data matching, controlling "publicly available" information and expanding the mandate of the Privacy Commissioner.[278]

Both the Personal Information Protection and Electronic Documents Act and the Privacy Act are overseen by the independent Privacy Commissioner of Canada.[279] Under the Privacy Act, the Commissioner has the power to investigate, mediate and make recommendations, but cannot issue binding orders. The office received 1,584 complaints in 1999-2000, down from 3,105 in 1998-1999 and completed 1,399 complaint investigations in 1999-2000.[280] In ten

---

[277] Privacy Act, c. P-21. <http://canada.justice.gc.ca/stable/EN/Laws/Chap/P/P-21.html>.

[278] Privacy Commissioner, 1999-2000 annual report, May 2000.
<http://www.privcom.gc.ca/english/02_04_08_e.htm>.

[279] Privacy Commissioner of Canada, <http://www.privcom.gc.ca>.

[280] See infra, Privacy Commissioner, 1999-2000 annual report.

years, the Office has received 15,526 complaints. The Office also received 11,256 calls and letters in 1999-2000. The commission has received 82,422 inquiries in ten years.

The Commissioner can initiate a Federal Court review in limited circumstances relating to denial of access to records. In May 2000, the Commissioner called for an update of the Federal Privacy Act and expressed concern about the misuse of the Social Insurance Number, health privacy and the release of census records.

The Commissioner's 1999-2000 report revealed the existence of a government database called the Longitudinal Labour Force File, managed by Human Resources Development Canada, which contained over 2,000 pieces of information on each Canadian. The information was gleaned from other government data banks and includes details from tax returns, child tax benefit files, provincial and municipal welfare files, federal jobs, job training and employment programs and services, employment insurance files and the social insurance master file. HRDC announced on May 29, 2000 that it was dismantling the Longitudinal Labour Force File and said it was scrapping the software that allowed sharing with other agencies and returning information following a public outcry.[281]

Privacy legislation covering government bodies exists in almost all provinces and territories.[282] In the province of Québec, the Charter of Rights specifically mentions the right to privacy and the law regulates the collection and use of personal information held by private sector businesses operating in the province of Québec.[283] This law sets rules for the collection, confidentiality, correction, disclosure, retention and use of personal information by these businesses. It also provides individuals with a right of access and correction. Nearly every province has some sort of oversight body, but their powers vary. The Québec Commission d'accès à l'information has broad powers over the public and private sectors. The Information and Privacy Commissioners of British Columbia and Ontario have been very active in promoting privacy through their oversight powers of public bodies and public education efforts. A number of provinces are now looking into adopting privacy legislation based on the Personal Information Protection and Electronic Documents Act.

---

[281] Minister of Human Resources Development Canada, HRDC Dismantles Longitudinal Labour Force File Databank, May 29, 2000. <http://www.hrdc-drhc.gc.ca/common/news/dept/00-39.shtml>.

[282] A list of state laws and commissions is available at <http://infoweb.magi.com/~privcan/other.html>.

[283] <http://www.cai.gouv.qc.ca/commiss.htm>.

Part VI of Canada's Criminal Code makes the unlawful interception of private communications a criminal offense.[284] Police are required to obtain a court order. In 1998, there were 157 orders for warrants under the Criminal Code, a decrease from 187 in 1997, 281 in 1996 and 266 in 1995.[285] Amendments to the Radiocommunication Act[286] also forbid the divulgence of intercepted radio-based telephone communications. The Canadian Security Intelligence Service Act[287] authorizes the interception of communications for national security reasons. A federal court in Ottawa ruled in 1997 that the Canadian Security Intelligence Service was required to obtain a warrant in all cases.[288] In October 1998, Industry Minister John Manley announced a new liberal government policy for encryption that allows for broad development, use and dissemination of encryption products.[289]

Other federal legislation also has provisions related to privacy. The Telecommunications Act[290] has provisions to protect the privacy of individuals, including the regulation of unsolicited communications. Also, the Bank Act,[291] Insurance Companies Act,[292] and Trust and Loan Companies Act[293] permit regulations to be made governing the use of information provided by customers. There are sectoral laws for pensions,[294] video surveillance,[295] immigration,[296] and Social Security.[297] The Young Offenders Act[298] regulates what information can be disclosed about offenders under the age of eighteen while the Corrections and Conditional Release Act[299] speaks to what information can be disclosed to

---

[284] Criminal Code, c. C-46. ss. 184, 184.5, 193, 193.1.

[285] Solicitor General Canada, Annual Report on the Use of Electronic Surveillance, 1998. <http://www.sgc.gc.ca/EPub/Pol/eESurveillanceAR98/eEsurveillanceAR1998%20.htm>.

[286] Radiocommunication Act, R.S.C. 1985, c. R-2, s. 9.

[287] CHAPTER C-23, Canadian Security Intelligence Service Act, <http://canada.justice.gc.ca/STABLE/EN/Laws/Chap/C/C-23.html>.

[288] "CSIS has wiretap green light," The Hamilton Spectator, October 1, 1997.

[289] Industry Canada, Building Trust in the Digital Economy, <http://e-com.ic.gc.ca/english/crypto/631d1.html>.

[290] Telecommunications Act, 1993, c. 38, s. 39, s. 41.

[291] Bank Act, c. 46, ss. 242, 244, 459.

[292] Insurance Companies Act, s. 489, s. 607.

[293] Trust and Loan Companies Act, s. 444.

[294] Canada Pension Plan, R.S.C. 1985, c. C-8, s. 104.07.

[295] Criminal Code, c. C-46, s. 487.01.

[296] Immigration Act, S.C. 1985, c. I-2, s. 110.

[297] Old Age Security Act, c. O-9, s. 33.01.

[298] Young Offenders Act, C. Y-1, s. 38.

[299] Corrections and Conditional Release Act, 1992, c. 20, s. 26, 142.

victims and victims' families. In addition, most provinces have some form of legislation protecting consumer credit information. However, the vast majority of information collected by the private sector is on the provincial level and is not currently protected by any provincial laws. A poll in April 1999 found that 88 percent of people said the government should "not allow banks to use information about their customer's bank accounts and other investments to try to sell customers insurance."[300]

Identity issues are currently under debate in Canada. There is great concern about the use of the Social Insurance Number (SIN) by the private sector and identity theft. A Parliamentary committee recommended in May 1999 that an Act setting out limitations on the use of the SIN be developed and that agencies use of the SIN should be documented.[301] Human Resources Development Canada released it recommendations in November 1999 recommending that the SIN not become a national client identifier because of "severe privacy concerns" and costs but it also recommending against new laws to prevent its use and expanding access to the Social Insurance Register by users of the SIN to prevent fraud.[302] The Committee was critical of these recommendations.[303]

Québec considered creating a mandatory ID card but dropped the idea in 1998. In April 1999, it hired DMR Consulting Group to examine the possibility of creating a central database of all government records on residents.[304] In Toronto, a system to fingerprint all welfare recipients was dropped in March 1999 after Citibank, the contractor, was unable to create a working system.[305] The Ontario government continues to discuss a smart card system for all citizens to access government services. The UN Human Rights Commission was critical of the increasing use of fingerprinting in Canada and recommended in April 1999 "that Canada take steps to ensure the elimination of increasingly intrusive measures which affected the right of privacy of people relying on social assistance,

---

[300] "88% of Canadians Oppose Banks Target-Marketing Insurance: Compas Poll," Canada NewsWire, April 27, 1999.

[301] Report of the Standing Committee on Human Resources Development and the Status of Persons with Disabilities, "Beyond the Numbers: The Future of the Social Insurance Number System in Canada," May 1999 <http://www.parl.gc.ca/InfocomDoc/36/1/HRPD/Studies/Reports/hrpdrp04-e.htm#TOC>.

[302] HRDC, A Commitment to Improvement: The Government of Canada's Social Insurance Number, December 1999.

[303] Hearing of the Standing Committee on Human Resources Development and the Status of Persons with Disabilities, November 18, 1999.

[304] "Quebec hires DMR to study ID database," Computing Canada, April 30, 1999.

[305] "City Welfare Fingerprint Plan Flops," The Toronto Star, May 21, 1999.

---

including identification techniques such as fingerprinting and retinal scanning."[306]

The federal Access to Information Act[307] provides individuals with a right of access to information held by the federal public sector. The Act gives Canadians and other individuals and corporations present in Canada the right to apply for and obtain copies of federal government records. "Records" include letters, memos, reports, photographs, films, microforms, plans, drawings, diagrams, maps, sound and video recordings, and machine-readable or computer files. About 12,000 requests are made annually for government records.[308]

The Act is overseen by the Office of the Information Commissioner of Canada.[309] The Commissioner can investigate and issue recommendations but does not have power to issue binding orders. The Office handed 1,670 complaints in 1998-99. It also released report cards on several agencies and issued seven subpoenas to government officials. The Canadian Federal Court has ruled that government has an obligation to answer all access requests regardless of the perceived motives of the requesters. Similarly, the commissioner must investigate all complaints even if the government seeks to block him from so doing on the grounds that the complaints are made for an improper purpose. Each of the provinces also has a Freedom of Information law.[310] A new coalition formed in March 2000 to promote freedom of information in Canada.[311]

Republic of Chile

Article 19 of Chile's Constitution secures for all persons: "Respect and protection for public and private life, the honor of a person and his family. The inviolability of the home and of all forms of private communication. The home

---

[306] Human Rights Committee concludes sixty-fifth session held at headquarters from 22 March to 9 April, April 12, 1999.

[307] Access to Information Act, C. A-1. <http://canada.justice.gc.ca/STABLE/EN/Laws/Chap/A/A-1.html>.(Annotated).

[308] Office of the Information Commissioner of Canada, Annual Report 1998-9, July 21, 1999. <http://fox.nstn.ca/~smulloy/oic98_9e.pdf>.

[309] Information Commissioner of Canada, <http://magi.com/~accessca/>.

[310] See Alasdair Roberts, Limited Access: Assessing the Health of Canada's Freedom of Information Laws, April 1998. <http://qsilver.queensu.ca/~foi/foi.pdf.

[311] Home Page: http://www.opengovernmentcanada.org/

---

may be invaded and private communications and documents intercepted, opened, or inspected only in cases and manners determined by law."[312]

Recently, Chile become the first Latin American country to enact a data protection law. The Act No. 19628, titled "Law for the protection of Private Life,"[313] came into force on October 28, 1999. The law has 24 articles, covering processing and use of personal data in the public and the private sector and the rights of individuals (to access, correction, and judicial control). The law contains a chapter dedicated to the use of financial, commercial and banking data, and specific rules addressing the use of information by government agencies. The law includes fines and damages for the unlawful denial of access and correction rights. Only databanks in the government must be registered.

There is no data protection authority, and enforcement of the law is done individually by each affected person. There is no case law yet interpreting the law. Another deficiency is that the law does not contain restrictions on transfers to third countries.

Chile's transition to democratic rule in 1990 did not eliminate personal privacy violations by government agencies. The Investigations Police – a plainclothes civilian agency that functions in close collaboration with the International Criminal Police Organization (Interpol) and with the intelligence services of the army, navy, and air force – keeps records of all adult citizens and foreign residents and issues identification cards that must be carried at all times.[314] The personal data compiled during military rule was never destroyed. In January 1998, former dictator Gen. Augusto Pinochet threatened to use "compromising information" from secret military intelligence files against those who were trying to keep him from becoming a Senator for Life, a position which would provide immunity from civil suits and public accountability for crimes which took place during his dictatorship.[315] Under current law, the voter registration list is publicly disclosed and used for direct marketing purposes. In 1999, the UN Human Rights Committee criticized the requirement that hospitals report all women who receive abortions.[316]

---

[312] Constitution of Chile, 1980,
<http://www.georgetown.edu/LatAmerPolitical/Constitutions/Chile/chile97.html>.

[313] Law for the Protection of Private Life (Ley Sobre Proteccion de la Vida Privada), Law No.19628 of August 30, 1999, published in the Official Journal in August 28, 1999.

[314] Chile: A Country Report, 1994: U.S. Library of Congress.

[315] "Chile's Ex-Dictator Tries to Dictate His Future Role," The New York Times, February 1, 1998.

[316] United Nations, Human rights committee concludes consideration of Chile's fourth periodic report, March 25, 1999.

A 1995 law bars the collection of information by undisclosed taping, telephone intercepts, and other surreptitious means, and bars the dissemination of such information, except by judicial order in narcotics-related cases.[317] In August 1996, the head of the Direccion de Inteligencia Policial (Dipolcar), the police intelligence service, was charged with authorizing a surveillance operation against the defense ministry official responsible for Carabineros, the militarized national police force. His resignation in disgrace allowed a greater role for the civilian security police, Investigaciones, in anti-drug operations.[318] In 1992, a surveillance center with 24-hour scanning devices was uncovered in downtown Santiago. It was run by an active army intelligence unit (DINE, incorporating former members of the secret police, the CNI) and, among other incidents, was found to have tapped into presidential candidate Sebastian Pinera's cellular phone[319] and taped the calls of President Patricio Aylwin.[320] The Army admitted to tapping telephones in order to comply with its mission, but reaffirmed that it "does not tap phones in an attempt to interfere with peoples' privacy."[321] The scandal provoked the retirement of General Ricardo Contreras, head of the Army Telecommunications Command.[322]

Chile signed the American Convention on Human Rights on August 20, 1990.

People's Republic of China

There are limited rights to privacy in the Chinese Constitution. Article 37 provides that the "freedom of the person of citizens of the People's Republic of China is inviolable," and Article 40 states: "Freedom and privacy of correspondence of citizens of the People's Republic of China are protected by law. No organization or individual may, on any ground, infringe on citizens' freedom of privacy of correspondence, except in cases where to meet the needs of state security or of criminal investigation, public security or prosecutorial

---

[317] Ley No.19.423.

[318] "Rows grow over security services," Southern Cone Report, September 12, 1996.

[319] "Television Nacional de Chile," BBC Summary of World Broadcasts, September 26, 1992.

[320] "Army's bugging centre uncovered," Latin America Weekly Report, October 8, 1992.

[321] "Navy, Air Force Deny Allegations of Telephone Tapping," BBC Summary of World Broadcasts, September 28, 1992.

[322] "Chile army to take action against servicemen involved in telephone-tapping case," BBC Summary of World Broadcasts, November 27, 1992.

---

organs are permitted to censor correspondence in accordance with procedures prescribed by law."[323]

There is no general data protection law in China and few laws that limit government interference with privacy. China has a long-standing policy on keeping close track of its citizens. According to expert W.J.F. Jenner, "Chinese states by the fourth century BC at latest were often remarkably successful in keeping records of their whole populations so that they could be taxed and conscripted. The state had the surname, personal name, age and home place of every subject and was also able to ensure that nobody could move far from home without proper authorization."[324]

Concerns with the growing use of the Internet has led to technical and legal restrictions. With the assistance of American companies such as Bay Networks, China has developed a "Great Firewall" which limits traffic to the Internet outside China to only three gateways.[325] The firewall also blocks some western news web sites such as the BBC, *New York Times* and the Voice of America. In February 1999, the government announced the creation of the State Information Security Appraisal and Identification Management Committee which, according to the official Xinhua state news agency, "will be responsible for protecting government and commercial confidential files on the Internet, identifying any net user, and defining rights and responsibilities... The move is intended to guard both individual and government users, protect information by monitoring and keep them from being used without proper authorization."[326] In December 1998, a Chinese businessman was handed a two-year jail sentence for subversion for supplying 30,000 e-mail addresses of Chinese computer users to a U.S.-based electronic dissident magazine.[327]

Under Article 7 of the Computer Information Network and Internet Security, Protection and Management Regulations, "the freedom and privacy of network

---

[323] PRC Constitution from ChinaLaw Web - Constitution of the People's Republic of China – 1993 (Adopted at the Fifth Session of the Fifth National People's Congress and Promulgated for Implementation by the Proclamation of the National People's Congress on December 4, 1982, as amended at the First Session of the Seventh National People's Congress on April 12, 1988, and again at the First Session of the Seventh National People's Congress on March 29,1993.) <http://www.qis.net/chinalaw/prccon5.htm>.

[324] W.J.F Jenner "China and Freedom" in Kelly & Reid, Asian Freedoms (Cambridge University Press, 1998).

[325] Gary Chapman, "China Represents Ethical Quagmire in High-Tech Age," Los Angeles Times, January 27, 1997.

[326] "China forms information security oversight committee," Xinhua News Agency, February 12, 1999.

[327] "Beijing convicts Internet dissident; Businessman sold Chinese e-mail addresses," The Washington Times, January 21, 1999.

---

users is protected by law. No unit or individual may, in violation of these regulations, use the Internet to violate the freedom and privacy of network users."[328] Article 8 states that "units and individuals engaged in Internet business must accept the security supervision, inspection, and guidance of the public security organization. This includes providing to the public security organization information, materials and digital documents, and assisting the public security organization to discover and properly handle incidents involving law violations and criminal activities involving computer information networks."[329] Articles 10 and 13 stipulate that Internet account holders must be registered with the public security organization and lending or transferring of accounts is strictly prohibited. Sections 285 to 287 of the Criminal Code prohibit intrusions into computer systems and punish violations of the regulations. In August of 1999, under orders from China's Ministry of Information and Industry, Intel agreed to disable the "Processor Serial Number" function of its Pentium III chips, which makes it possible to identify and track Internet users as they engage in e-commerce.[330]

The secrecy of communications is cited in the constitution and in law, but apparently with little effect. In practice, authorities often monitor telephone conversations, fax transmissions, electronic mail, and Internet communications of foreign visitors, businessmen, diplomats, and journalists, as well as Chinese dissidents, activists, and others.[331] British Prime Minister Tony Blair was reported to be upset by the bugging and wiretapping of his rooms during his state visit to China in October 1998.[332] The U.S. State Department said in a 1999 report: "Chinese authorities often monitor telephone conversations, fax transmissions, electronic mail, and Internet communications of foreign diplomats and journalists, as well as Chinese dissidents, activists, and others." The report also noted that the government has created "special Internet police units to increase control over Internet content and access." Frank Lu, the head of the Hong Kong-based Information Center of Human Rights and Democratic Movement in China, reported in November 1999 that 300 computer graduates

---

[328] Computer Information Network and Internet Security, Protection and Management Regulations (Approved by the State Council on December 11, 1997 and promulgated by the Ministry of Public Security on December 30, 1997) <http://www.usembassy-china.gov/english/sandt/index.html>.

[329] Charles D. Paglee, Chinalaw Web - Computer Information Network and Internet Security, Protection and Management Regulations (last modified April 7, 1998) <http://www.qis.net/chinalaw/prclaw54.htm>.

[330] "China Security Blitz Bugs Intel PCs," Australasian Business Abstracts, July 8, 1999.

[331] U.S. Department of State, Bureau of Democracy, Human Rights, and Labor, China Country Report on Human Rights Practices for 1998, February 26, 1999; Amnesty International, 1999 World Report: China.

[332] "Blair: I Never Want to Visit Beijing Again; Blair Claims He was Bugged by China's Secret Police," The Mirror, October 12, 1998.

had been recruited by Shanghai security officials to carry out cyber-surveillance in 1999 alone.[333] Canadian, American, and British members of the Falun Gong movement claimed to be targets of such surveillance in fall of 1999, reporting assaults on their websites by various means commonly used to block or penetrate sites. [334]

The Chinese government announced and then retracted a broad-sweeping rule that required all entities other than embassies to register any software using encryption or including encryption technology. The original rule was announced on November 10, 1999 by the PRC State Encryption Management Commission and required registration by January 31, 2000.[335] However, after few companies registered by the due date, and under increasing pressure due to successful China's WTO bid, officials reversed the hugely unpopular law, which would have banned foreign encryption software and likely would have delayed or prevented the launch of Microsoft's Office 2000 and Cisco's installation of new mobile phone networks.[336]

Postal enterprises and postal staff are prohibited from providing information to any organization or individual about users' dealings with postal services except as otherwise provided for by law.[337] However, Article 21 of the Postal Law permits postal staff to examine, on the spot, the contents of non-letter postal materials. Mail handed in or posted by users must be in accordance with the stipulations concerning the content allowed to be posted; postal enterprises and their branch offices have the right to request users to take out the contents for examination, when necessary.

The Practicing Physician Law requires that doctors not reveal health information obtained during treatment. Doctors who violate the law face criminal penalties. In May of 1999, the Ministry of Health, with the approval of the State Council, published an administrative order declaring that personal information about HIV/AIDS sufferers be kept secret, and that the legal rights and interests of those

---

[333] Kevin Platt, "China's 'cybercops' clamp down," Christian Science Monitor, November 17, 1999.

[334] Michael Laris, "China sniffing out dissent on the Internet; Government accused of web sabotage," The Washington Post, Aug 5, 1999.

[335] State Council Order Number 273, October 22, 1999.

[336] Matt Forney, "Ban Raised Fears Involving Privacy in Communications," The Wall Street Journal, March 13, 2000.

[337] Chinalaw Computer-Assisted Legal Research Center Peking University – Postal Law of the People's Republic of China (Adopted at 18th Meeting of the Standing Committee of the National People's Congress, promulgated by Order No. 47 of the President of the People's Republic of China on December 2, 1986, and effective as of January 1, 1987) CHINALAW No. 396.

people and their relatives should not be infringed. The Ministry of Health order asked all units and individuals in charge of diagnosis, treatment, and management work not to publish any personal information about HIV/AIDS sufferers, such as the name and the family address.[338]

Since 1984, all Chinese citizens over the age of 16 have been required to carry identification cards issued by the Ministry of Public Security. Identification cards include name, sex, nationality, date of birth, address and term of validity, of which there are three. Between the ages of 16 and 25, it is 10 years, between the ages of 25 and 45, it is 20 years and for those aged 45 and over it is permanent. In carrying out their duties, public security organs have the right to ask citizens to show their ID cards. In handling political, economic and social affairs, which involve rights and interests, government offices, people's organizations and enterprises may also ask citizens to show their ID cards.[339] Failure to register for an identification card, forging or otherwise altering a residence registration, or assuming another person's registration are all prohibited by law and punishable by fine. Failure to notify local authorities concerning visiting guests is also punishable by fine.[340] In 1997, the State Bureau of Technical Supervision began working on a new number system that will be used for Social Security and ID cards.[341] Smart card development is reportedly underway in China, with both domestic and international players competing to develop chips and modules to meet design and regulatory specifications.[342] In December 1998, authorities began a test program requiring five hotels in Guangzhou to fax copies of the data of all customers to the Public Security Bureau to capture "unwanted elements."[343]

---

[338] Xinhua news agency, Beijing, 20 May 1999.

[339] Xinhua news agency, Beijing, in English, 7 May 1984, via BBC Summary of World Broadcasts; Regulations of the People's Republic of China Concerning Resident Identity Cards (Adopted at the 12th Meeting of the Standing Committee of the Sixth National People's Congress, promulgated for implementation by Order No. 29 of the President of the People's Republic of China on September 6, 1985, and effective as of September 6, 1985) CHINALAW No. 304.

[340] Chinalaw Computer-Assisted Legal Research Center Peking University – Regulations of the People's Republic of China on Administrative Penalties for Public Security (Adopted at the 17th Meeting of the Standing Committee of the Sixth National People's Congress, promulgated by Order No. 43 of the President of the People's Republic of China on September 5, 1986, and effective as of January 1, 1987) CHINALAW No. 368

[341] China: Numbering system aids social security, China Daily, November 27, 1997.

[342] "With eye on Security, China nurtures domestic IC cards," Electronic Engineering Times, August 9, 1999.

[343] Guangzhou Hotels Send Personal Data on Guests To Police, Hong Kong Standard, 30 Dec 1998.

Special Administrative Region of Hong Kong

Following the People's Republic of China's resumption of sovereignty over Hong Kong on July 1, 1997, the constitutional protections of privacy are contained in the Basic Law of the Hong Kong Special Administrative Region of the People's Republic of China. Article 29 provides "The homes and other premises of Hong Kong residents shall be inviolable. Arbitrary or unlawful search of, or intrusion into, a resident's home or other premises shall be prohibited." Article 30 provides, "The freedom and privacy of communications of Hong Kong residents shall be protected by law. No department or individual may, on any grounds, infringe upon the freedom and privacy of communications of residents except that the relevant authorities may inspect communications in accordance with legal procedures to meet the needs of public security or of investigation into criminal offenses." Also relevant is Article 17 of the International Covenant on Civil and Political Rights, which was incorporated into Hong Kong's domestic law with the enactment of the Bill of Rights Ordinance.[344] Article 39 of the Basic Law provides that the Covenant as applied to Hong Kong shall remain in force and implemented through the laws of Hong Kong.

In 1995, Hong Kong enacted its Personal Data (Privacy) Ordinance,[345] and most of its provisions took effect in December 1996. The legislation enacts most of the recommendations made by the Hong Kong Law Reform Commission following its six-year comparative study.[346] The statutory provisions adopt features of a variety of existing data protection laws and the draft version of the EU Directive is also reflected in several provisions. It sets six principles to regulate the collection, accuracy, use and security of personal data as well as requiring data users to be open about data processing and conferring on data subjects the right to be provided a copy of their personal data and to effect corrections.

The Ordinance does not differentiate between the public and private sectors, although many of the exemptions will more readily apply to the former. A broad definition of "personal data" is adopted so as to encompass all readily retrievable data recorded in all media that relates to an identifiable individual. It does not

---

[344] Chapter of Laws (Cap) 383: 288: <http://www.justice.gov.hk>.

[345] Chapter of Laws (Cap) 486: <http://www.justice.gov.hk>. See generally Berthold M. & Wacks R., Data Privacy Law in Hong Kong (FT Law & Tax, 1997).

[346] Hong Kong Law Reform Commission, 1994 Report on the Law Relating To The Protection Of Personal Data. Website information on the Hong Kong Law Reform Commission is available at <http://www.info.gov.hk>.

---

attempt to differentiate personal data according to its sensitivity. The Ordinance imposes additional restrictions on certain processing, namely data matching, transborder data transfers, and direct marketing. Data matching requires the prior approval of the Privacy Commissioner. The transfer of data to other jurisdictions is subject to restrictions that mirror those of the EU Directive. Also based on the directive is the requirement that upon first use of personal data for direct marketing purposes, a data user must inform the data subject of the opportunity to opt-out from further approaches. The Commissioner had informal discussions with the EU over the question of adequacy but has not received a formal note on the adequacy of the statute.

The Ordinance establishes the Office of the Privacy Commissioner to promote and enforce compliance with statutory requirements.[347] The Commissioner is given strong enforcement powers based on those contained in the UK Data Protection Act. In addition to investigating complaints, the commissioner may initiate his own investigations of reasonably suspected contraventions. He may also conduct audits of selected data users. A contravention of any provision other than a data protection principle is a criminal offense. A contravention causing the data subject damage (including injured feelings) is a basis for claiming compensation. The Commissioner is empowered to designate classes of data users required to publicly register the main features of their data processing. The Commissioner may issue codes of conduct to provide guidance on compliance with the Ordinance's necessarily general provisions. The provisions of a code are legally subordinate but have evidentiary relevance in determining whether a contravention of the Ordinance has occurred. To date the Commissioner has issued two codes: The code on the use of personal identifiers[348] and of credit information[349] and is currently developing a code of practice for human resources management. In 1999, the offce received 15,243 inquiries and 541 complaints. Ten percent of the complaints related to direct marketing. The office has 33 staff members.[350] It also released "Privacy.SAFE" -- a privacy compliance self-assessment kit, to assist organizations in assessing whether their personal data management practices and procedures meet with the requirements of the Ordinance.

---

[347] Home Page: http://www.pco.org.hk

[348] The Code of Practice on the Identity Card Number and other Personal Identifiers was gazetted on 19 December 1997 and took effect in 1998.

[349] The Code of Practice on Consumer Credit Data was issued on 27 February 1998 and took effect on 27 November 1998. A summary is available at the commissioner's website at <http://www.pco.org.hk>.

[350] Operations Division, Office of the Privacy Commissioner for Personai Data, May 1999.

A Hong Kong court ruled in June 1999 against attempts to subject Xinhua, the Chinese News agency which acted as the Chinese government representative in Hong Hong, to the Privacy Ordinance. In December 1996, pro-democracy legislator Emily Lao demanded access to the secret dossier that Xinhua maintained on her. Xinhua refused to respond and the HK government declined to take action. She filed suit but the court quashed her attempt to subpoena the director.[351]

The interception of communications is presently regulated by the Telecommunications Ordinance[352] and the Post Office Ordinance.[353] These enactments provide sweeping powers of interception upon public interest grounds. The vagueness of the powers and the lack of procedural safeguards are inconsistent with the International Covenant of Civil and Political Rights and the Basic Law. No official figures are released on the number of intercepts, which are believed to be widespread and efforts to make the numbers public have been rebuffed in the name of confidentiality.[354] A detailed set of reform proposals released by the Hong Kong Law Reform Commission[355] in 1996 resulted in two legislative initiatives. In early 1997, the government released a draft bill for public consultation regulating the interception of communications. When that initiative stalled, James To, an independent legislator, introduced a private members bill, the last enactment to be passed by the colonial legislature prior to July 1, 1997. That enactment has yet to be brought into force and to date the government has declined to indicate when any legislation regulating the interception of communications will take effect. In January 1999, Mr. To introduced another bill to force the ordinance to go into effect. According to the HK government in its report to the UN Human Rights Commission, "It was drawn up without consultation with the administration and contained provisions which, if implemented, would seriously affect the ability of the law enforcement agencies to combat crime. For example, one provision allows the law enforcement agencies to renew warrants for interceptions once only, that single renewal being valid for just 90 days. This would seriously incapacitate the law enforcement agencies in tackling certain serious crimes, such as kidnapping and money laundering, that usually entail protracted operations. Therefore, the Government is carefully assessing the implications of the Ordinance before

---

[351] "HK Court Blocks Lawsuit Against China News Agency," Reuters, Jun 8, 1999.

[352] Section 33, Chapter of Laws (Cap) 106.

[353] Section 13 Chapter of Laws (Cap) 98.

[354] "Phone tap figures to remain secret," South China Morning Post, October 1, 1998.

[355] Hong Kong Law Reform Commission, Hong Kong Law Reform Commission's 1996 Report on Privacy: Regulating the Interception of Communications. <http://www.info.gov.hk/hkreform/reports/intercept-e.pdf>.

deciding on the way forward and has not appointed a commencement date for this Ordinance."[356]

The Law Reform Commission's sub-committee on privacy released consultation papers on "Civil Liability For Invasion Of Privacy"[357] and "The Regulation Of Media Intrusion" in 1999.[358] The Hong Kong Legislative Council voted 39-0 against the media intrusion proposal in a non-binding vote in November 1999.[359] The Commission is expected to complete its consultation on the proposal by the end of 2000.

The Code on Access to Information[360] requires civil servants to provide records held by government departments unless there are specific reasons for not doing so. Departments can withhold information if it relates to 16 different categories including defense, external affairs, law enforcement and personal privacy. Formal complaints of denials can be filed with the Ombudsman.

Czech Republic

The 1993 Charter of Fundamental Rights and Freedoms provides for extensive privacy rights. Article 7(1) states, "Inviolability of the person and of privacy is guaranteed. It may be limited only in cases specified by law." Article 10 states, "(1) Everybody is entitled to protection of his or her human dignity, personal integrity, good reputation, and his or her name. (2) Everybody is entitled to protection against unauthorized interference in his or her personal and family life. (3) Everybody is entitled to protection against unauthorized gathering, publication or other misuse of his or her personal data." Article 13 states, "Nobody may violate secrecy of letters and other papers and records whether privately kept or sent by post or in another manner, except in cases and in a manner specified by law. Similar protection is extended to messages communicated by telephone, telegraph or other such facilities."[361]

---

[356] Fifth periodic report : China. 16/06/99. CCPR/C/HKSAR/99/1. (State Party Report), 16 June 1999.

[357] Law Reform Commission's sub-committee on Privacy, Civil Liability For Invasion Of Privacy, <http://www.info.gov.hk/hkreform/reports/privacy-e.pdf>.

[358] Law Reform Commission's sub-committee on Privacy, The Regulation Of Media Intrusion. <http://www.info.gov.hk/hkreform/reports/media-e.pdf>.

[359] Government-proposed press council loses vote in Hong Kong, Freedom Forum, November 24, 1999.

[360] Code on Access to Information, March 1995 <http://www.info.gov.hk/access/code.htm>.

[361] Charter of Fundamental Rights and Freedoms, 1993, <http://www.psp.cz/cgi-bin/eng/docs/laws/charter.html>.

The new Act "On Personal Data Protection" went into effect on June 1, 2000.[362] The new law is based on the EU Data Protection Directive as part of the Czech Republic's efforts for accession into the EU. It implements the basic requirements of the Directive, but the police and intelligence services are exempt from many of the key provisions. The EU had been pressuring the Republic to move more quickly in adopting new legislation for several years.[363] The new act replaces the 1992 Act on Protection of Personal Data in Information Systems.[364]

The new act creates an Office for Personal Data Protection as an independent oversight body.[365] The new office will register databases, conduct audits, and impose fines for violations. The Office also has authority over the certificate authorities for digital signatures.

The previous bill was considered to be quite weak and there were a number of high profile scandals involving abuse of personal information. In 1992, the Interior Ministry sold the addresses of all children under the age of two and all women between 15 and 35 – a total of two million people – to Procter & Gamble. The company used the information for a direct marketing campaign for Pampers diapers and Always brands. One official was charged with violating the law. In 1995, Prague City Police Chief Rudolf Blazek admitted his men had access to information about criminal suspects that is by law available only to the Czech Republic Police.[366] In 1996, a black-market CD-ROM that listed all telephone numbers in the Czech Republic, including President Vaclav Havel's home number, appeared on the market. Also in 1996, Internet service providers handed over data about their users in response to a police investigation of a bomb found inside a ketchup bottle. Police believe the information was obtained from the Internet and were attempting to determine who accessed it.[367] In September 1999, a 21-year-old bank employee was arrested for stealing confidential client information from Ceska sporitelna, the largest bank in the Czech Republic. He offered to sell lists of accounts or "the name, address, the account number, balance and transactions at the account" for any of the 2.5 million members via the Internet.[368]

---

[362] Act no. 101 of 2000 "On Personal Data Protection."

[363] "E.U. warns applicants on slow preparations," Financial Times, November 5, 1998.

[364] Act of April 29, 1992 on Protection of Personal Data in Information Systems (No. 256/92).

[365] Home Page: http://www.uoou.cz/

[366] "Information Protection Laws Must Be Passed Now," The Prague Post, January 11, 1995.

[367] "Ketchup-Bottle Bomb Sparks Internet Privacy Row," The Prague Post, September 25, 1996.

[368] CTK National News Wire, September 14, 1999.

A poll conducted in January 1997 found that seventy-nine percent of Czechs cite undisturbed privacy as a top personal priority,[369] while one released in October 1998 found that 75 percent believe that their personal data is misused and two thirds consider data protection a serious problem.[370]

Wiretapping is regulated under the criminal process law.[371] Police must obtain permission from a judge to conduct a wiretap. The judge can approve an initial order for up to six months. There are special rules for intelligence services. In 1996, the Czech secret service (BIS) was accused of monitoring politicians, civic and environmental groups such as Greenpeace, including the use of illegal wiretaps.[372] In 1993, Justice Minister Jiri Novak's telephone was reportedly tapped. A secret service employee found a bugging device in the ministry's central telephone switchboard in the middle of September 1993.

The Penal Code covers the infringement of the right to privacy in the definitions of criminal acts of infringement of the home,[373] slander[374] and infringement of the confidentiality of mail.[375] There are also sectoral acts concerning statistics, medical personal data, banking law, taxation, social security and police data. Unauthorized use of personal data systems is considered a crime.[376] The Ministry of Interior is currently working on a draft on the Czech police which will contain data protection provisions lacking in the Data Protection Act.

The Parliament approved the Freedom of Information Law in May 1999.[377] The law is based on the U.S. FOIA and provides for citizens' access to all government records held by State bodies, local self-governing authorities and certain other official institutions, such as the Chamber of Lawyers or the Chamber of Doctors, except for classified information, trade secrets or personal data.[378] A 1998 act governs access to environmental information.[379]

---

[369] "Undisturbed Privacy Top Priority -- Poll," CTK National News Wire, January 23, 1997.

[370] "Most People Believe that their Personal Data is Misused– Poll," CTK National News Wire, October 6, 1998.

[371] Article 88 of Criminal Process Law.

[372] CTK National News Wire, November 8, 1996.

[373] Penal Code, section 238.

[374] Penal Code, section 206.

[375] Penal Code, section 239.

[376] Centre de Recherches Informatique et Droit, Legal Aspects of Information Services and Intellectual Property Rights in Central and Eastern Europe, Feb 1995.

[377] Act no. 106/1999 Coll., on free access to information

[378] "Freedom of info clears last hurdle," The Prague Post, May 19, 1999.

In April 1996, the Parliament approved a law that allows any Czech citizen to obtain his or her file created by the Communist-era secret police (StB). Non-Czech citizens are not allowed to access their records. The Interior Ministry holds 60,000 records but it is estimated that many more were destroyed in 1989. In October 1998, there was a controversy over the rumors that the records showed that former Vienna Mayor Helmut Zilk, who was about to receive an award from Czech President Vaclav Havel, was a collaborator with the StB. It was suspected that the Office for the Documentation and Investigation of the Crimes of Communism was the source of the documents.

The Czech Republic is a member of the Council of Europe but has not signed the Convention for the Protection of Individuals with Regard to Automatic Processing of Personal Data (ETS No. 108).[380] In May 2000, the cabinet approved a proposal to sign and ratify the Convention. The Czech Republic has signed and ratified the European Convention for the Protection of Human Rights and Fundamental Freedoms.[381] It is a member of the Organization for Economic Cooperation and Development and has adopted the OECD Guidelines on the Protection of Privacy and Transborder Flows of Personal Data.

Kingdom of Denmark

The Danish Constitution of 1953 contains two provisions relating to privacy and data protection. Section 71 provides for the inviolability of personal liberty. Section 72 states, "The dwelling shall be inviolable. House searching, seizure, and examination of letters and other papers as well as any breach of the secrecy to be observed in postal, telegraph, and telephone matters shall take place only under a judicial order unless particular exception is warranted by Statute."[382] The European Convention on Human Rights was formally incorporated into Danish law in 1992.

The Act on Processing of Personal Data entered into force on July 1, 2000.[383] The act implements the EU Data Protection into Danish law. The new act

---

[379] Act no. 123/1998 Coll., on the right to information about the environment.

[380] See <http://conventions.coe.int/>.

[381] Signed 21/02/91, Ratified 18/03/92, Entered into Force 01/01/93. <http://conventions.coe.int/>.

[382] Constitution of Denmark <http://www.uni-wuerzburg.de/law/da00t___.html>.

[383] The Act on Processing of Personal Data, Act No. 429 of 31 May 2000 (Lov om behandling af personoplysninger). <http://147.29.40.90/_GETDOC_/ACCN/A20000042930-REGL>.

---

replaces the Private Registers Act of 1978, which governed the private sector,[384] and the Public Authorities' Registers Act of 1978, which governed the public sector.[385]

An independent agency, the Data Surveillance Agency (Registertilsynet), enforces the act.[386] The Agency supervises registries established by public authorities and private enterprises in Denmark. It ensures that the conditions for registration, disclosure and storage of data on individuals are complied with. It mainly deals with specific cases on the basis of inquiries from public authorities or private individuals, or cases taken up by the agency on its own initiative. According to the Registertilsynet, 11,500 public data bases, 75 large national databases, and 5,000 private databases were registered between January 1994 and July 2000. Of the 5,000 private databases, 500 were run by private firms such as credit bureaus, data-processing bureaus, headhunters and recruitment agencies.[387] The agency handled 1,171 complaints in 1999 under the Private Registers Act and 269 under the Public Authorities Registers Act. It also conducted 14 inspections.

Wiretapping is regulated by the Penal Code.[388] There were calls for an investigation in 1998 into whether the security service (Politiets Efterretningstjeneste - PET) conducted illegal surveillance of leftist activists between the 1960s and 1980s even though a 1968 law outlawed the practice. A former PET agent admitted in 1998 that the Conservative government in 1983 authorized PET to infiltrate and monitor leftist political parties, peace organizations, trade unions, solidarity committees and right wing groups.[389] Danish Justice Minister, Frank Jansen ordered an investigation in 1998 but insisted that some of the investigation be conducted in secret.[390] He later widened the investigation to examine surveillance occurring since 1945.

There was an increased interest in Echelon in Denmark in the past year. In 1999, it was revealed that there is a listening post at Sandagergard on the island of

---

[384] Private Registers Act of 1978 (Lov nr 293 af 8 juni 1978 om private registre mv), in force 1 January 1979.

[385] Public Authorities' Registers Act of 1978 (Lov nr 294 af 8 juni 1978 om offentlige myndigheders registre), also in force 1 January 1979.

[386] Home Page: <http://www.registertilsynet.dk/eng/index.html>.

[387] Letter from the Registertilsynet to EPIC, August 13, 1999.

[388] Penal Code Section 263.

[389] "Denmark: Surveillance of political activity admitted," Statewatch bulletin, vol 8 no 2, March-April 1998.

[390] "Denmark: PET involved in "illegal" surveillance," Statewatch bulletin, vol 8 no 5, September-October 1998.

Amager, south of Copenhagen. Ekstra Bladet, a major paper, ran a series of 50 articles on Echelon prompting calls in the Parliament for an investigation.[391] In April, U.S. Ambassador Richard Swett responded to reports by a former Canadian spy that the U.S. Embassy in Copenhagen was spying on Danes, saying "The U.S. government does not spy on the government of Denmark. I am outraged by these allegations."[392] The Minister of Defense in December 1999 declined suggestions to ask the U.S. not to spy on Denmark, saying "In my opinion, this would merely involve a false sense of security for Danish companies and citizens if we -- and I'm being totally hypothetical now -- were even able to enter into agreements of this kind, because there would still be a great number of countries and organizations that would be able to monitor Danish communication."[393]

Two police detectives in Hjorring were charged in December 1999 with conducting illegal surveillance to discover the source of an anonymous tip about police corruption. The police reportedly spent more time attempting to identity the source, including taking a DNA sample from the letter's stamp and demanding the phone records of a local attorney, than they did investigating the allegations.[394]

Other pieces of legislation with rules relating to privacy and data protection include the Criminal Code of 1930,[395] Act on Video Surveillance,[396] the Administrative Procedures Act of 1985,[397] the Payment Cards Act of 1994,[398] and the Access to Health Information Act of 1993.[399] All citizens in Denmark are provided with a Central Personal Registration (CPR) number that is used to identify them in public registers.

---

[391] See http://www.eb.dk/netdetect/echelon/; http://www.cryptome.org/echelon-eb2.htm

[392] "Envoy to Denmark: We're Not Spies," Associated Press, April 3, 2000.

[393] "HÆKKERUP: Many Are monitoring us," Ekstra Bladet December 9. 1999.

[394] "TVIVLSOM JAGT PAA ANONYM KILDE," Politiken Weekly, March 1, 2000.

[395] Borgerlig Straffelov.

[396] Act No. 278 respecting the prohibiting against video surveillance by private persons, etc, 9 June 1982 (Lovtidende A, No. 44, 1982, p. 644).

[397] lov nr 571 af 19 desember 1985 om forvaltning.

[398] ovbekendtgørelse nr 811 af 12 september 1994 om betalingskort mv.

[399] lov nr 504 af 30 juni 1993 om aktindsigt i helbredsoplysninger.

The Access to Information Act and the Access to Public Administration Files Act[400] govern access to government records.

Denmark is a member of the Council of Europe and has signed the Convention for the Protection of Individuals with Regard to Automatic Processing of Personal Data (ETS No. 108).[401] It has signed and ratified the European Convention for the Protection of Human Rights and Fundamental Freedoms.[402] It is a member of the Organization for Economic Cooperation and Development and has adopted the OECD Guidelines on the Protection of Privacy and Transborder Flows of Personal Data.

Greenland

The original unamended Danish Public and Private Registers Acts of 1979 continue to apply within Greenland, a self-governing territory. The 1988 amendments that brought Denmark into compliance with the Council of Europe's Convention 108 do not apply to Greenland. Greenland is not part of the European Union and therefore has not adopted the EU Privacy Directive. Greenland's data protection requirements are much less stringent than those of Denmark and the other nations of the EU.

Republic of Estonia

The 1992 Estonia Constitution recognizes the right of privacy, secrecy of communications, and data protection. Article 42 states, "No state or local government authority or their officials may collect or store information on the persuasions of any Estonian citizen against his or her free will." Article 43 states, "Everyone shall be entitled to secrecy of messages transmitted by him or to him by post, telegram, telephone or other generally used means. Exceptions may be made on authorization by a court, in cases and in accordance with procedures determined by law in order to prevent a criminal act or for the purpose of establishing facts in a criminal investigation." Article 44 (3) states, "Estonian citizens shall have the right to become acquainted with information about themselves held by state and local government authorities and in state and local

---

[400] lov nr 572 af 19 desember 1985 om offentlighed i forvaltningen).
<http://www.au.dk/da/regler/1985/lov572/index.html>.
< http://www.vissenbjergkommune.dk/postli/offlov.htm>.

[401] Signed 28/01/81, Ratified 23/10/89, Entered into Force 01/02/90, <http://conventions.coe.int/>.

[402] Signed 21/02/91, Ratified 18/03/92, Entered into Force 01/01/93, <http://conventions.coe.int/>.

---

government archives, in accordance with procedures determined by law. This right may be restricted by law in order to protect the rights and liberties of other persons, and the secrecy of children's ancestry, as well as to prevent a crime, or in the interests of apprehending a criminal or to clarify the truth for a court case."[403]

The Riigikogu – Estonia's Parliament – enacted the Personal Data Protection Act in June 1996.[404] The Act protects the fundamental rights and freedoms of persons with respect to the processing of personal data and in accordance with the right of individuals to obtain freely any information which is disseminated for public use. The Personal Data Protection Act divides personal data into two groups – non-sensitive and sensitive personal data. Sensitive personal data are data which reveal political opinions, religious or philosophical beliefs, ethnic or racial origin, health, sexual life, criminal convictions, legal punishments and involvement in criminal proceedings. Processing of non-sensitive personal data is permitted without the consent of the respective individual if it occurs under the terms that are set out in the Personal Data Protection Act. Processed personal data are protected by organizational and technical measures that must be documented. Chief processors must register the processing of sensitive personal data with the data protection supervision authority.

In April 1997, the Riigikogu passed the Databases Act.[405] The Databases Act is a procedural law for the establishment of national databases. The law sets out the general principles for the maintenance of databases, prescribes requirements and protection measures for data processing, and unifies the terminology to be used in the maintenance of databases. Pursuant to the Databases Act, the statutes of state registers or databases that were created before the law took effect must be brought into line with the Act within two years. The Databases Act also mandates the establishment of a state register of databases that registers state and local government databases, as well as databases containing sensitive personal data which are maintained by persons in private law. The chief processor of the register has the right to make proposals to the government, to the chief processors of various databases, and to the state information systems. He or she would also be responsible for coordinating authority with respect to the expansion, merger or liquidation of databases, interbase cross-usage, or the organization of data

---

[403] Constitution of Estonia, <http://www.uni-wuerzburg.de/law/en00t___.html>.

[404] Law on the protection of personal data (RT I 1996, 48, 944).
<http://www.dp.gov.ee/eng/Personal_Data_Protection_Act.html>.

[405] Databases Act (RT* I 1997, 28, 423) <http://www.dp.gov.ee/eng/Databases_Act.html>.

processing or data acquisition in a manner aimed at avoiding duplication of effort or substantially repetitive databases.

The Data Protection Inspectorate is the supervisory authority for the Personal Data Protection Act and the Databases Act. The Inspectorate, a division of the Ministry of Internal Affairs, monitors compliance, issues licenses, takes complaints, and settles disputes. The agency can conduct investigations and demand documents, impose fines, and impose administrative sanctions.[406] As of October 1999, there were only 8 staff members. The EU called for an increase in the size of the authority, "In order to ensure the proper implementation of the EU rules in this area, the administrative capacity of the inspectorate needs to be increased."[407]

Following a complaint by the Inspectorate, the Estonian Statistics Office announced in June 2000 that it had reached an agreement with the Inspectorate to modify its population and housing database to remove personally identifiable information. The Inspectorate demanded in May 2000 that the Office stop the creation of the database as a violation of the Databases Act. The Inspectorate also asked the police to start a criminal investigation into the Census' head.[408] The Parliament enacted a new law on June 1, 2000 on the Census to ensure that privacy is protected.[409] According to Estonian press reports in November 1996, databases of the financial and police records of thousands of Estonians are easily available on the black market. The records were available on CD-ROM and sold for $4,000 each, and included details of individual's bank loans and police files.[410] The Digital Signatures Act was approved in March 2000.[411]

In August 2000, the Cabinet approved a bill to create a national genetic database to be used for research into disease. The database would hold genetic samples on two-thirds of the population of Estonia.[412]

---

[406] Home Page: <http://www.dp.gov.ee:8020/>.

[407] European Commission, Regular Report from the Commission on Progress towards Accession - Estonia - October 13, 1999 <http://europa.eu.int/comm/enlargement/estonia/rep_10_99/b4.htm>.

[408] "Estonian Statistics Office to Bring Census Database Into Accordance With Law," Baltic News Service, June 6, 2000.

[409] "Estonian parliament adopts law on population register," BBC Worldwide Monitoring, June 1, 2000.

[410] The Baltics Worldwide, Spring 1997.

[411] Digital Signatures Act, (RT I 2000, 26, 150), Passed 8 March 2000, entered into force 15 December 2000. <http://www.riik.ee/riso/digiallkiri/digsignact.rtf>.

[412] "Estonia To Set Up One Of World's First Gene Banks," Associated Press, August 10, 2000. See Estonian Genome Foundation Web site: http://www.genomics.ee/genome/

The 1994 Surveillance Act regulates the interception of communications, covert surveillance, undercover informants and police and intelligence data bases.[413] Surveillance can be approved by a "reasoned decision made by the head of a surveillance agency." "Exceptional surveillance" requires the permission of a judge in the Tallinn Administrative Court for serious crimes. The punishment for illegal surveillance is a fine and three years imprisonment for general surveillance activity, and five years imprisonment for special measures like opening correspondence or telephone bugging.[414] In October 1999, the Estonian Police Department refused to grant the Tallinn city police authority the right to plant eavesdropping devices in apartments, offices and telephones to combat organized crime.[415] The law was amended in May 2000 to allow the tax police to conduct surveillance.[416] Under the Telecommunications Act approved in February 2000, surveillance agencies can obtain information on the sender and receiver of messages by written or oral request.[417] Telecommunications providers are also required to delete data within one year and prevent unauthorized disclose of users' information.

In May 1996, the Estonian Intelligence Service started an inquiry on the involvement of former Vice Prime Minister Edgar Saavisar in a politically motivated wiretapping scandal. It eventually led to a change of government.[418] Swedish papers reported in January 2000 that the Estonian secret services had spied on Swedish diplomats.[419]

The Parliament ordered the government to draft a FOIA bill in 1997. A draft Access to Public Information Act is pending before the Parliament and is expected to be approved by the end of 2000.[420] The bill also includes significant provisions on electronic access. Government departments and other holders of public information will have a duty to post information on the web, and e-mail requests must be treated as official requests for information. Citizens have a right

---

[413] Surveillance Act (RT* I 1994, 16, 290, 22 February 1994).
<http://vlf.juridicum.su.se/master99/library2/teste/Surv.htm>.

[414] Criminal Code article 134.

[415] Baltic News Service, October 8, 1999.

[416] Estonian government approves plans for tax police, BBC Worldwide Monitoring, May 16, 2000.

[417] Telecommunications Act Passed 9 February 2000 (RT I 2000, 18, 116), entered into force 19 March 2000.
<http://www.legaltext.ee/tekstid/X/en/X30063.HTM>.

[418] Deutsche Presse-Agentur, "Estonian intelligence begins probe into former premier Saavisar," May 16, 1996.

[419] Estonian MP rejects reports that Estonian secret services spied on Swedes, BBC Worldwide Monitoring, January 13, 2000.

[420] Draft Public Information Act. < http://www.netexpress.ee/eall/eelnou.html>.

under the Surveillance Act to obtain access to information held about them by surveillance agencies. Agencies must respond within three months if the agency maintains information about them.[421]

Estonia is a member of the Council of Europe and signed the Convention for the Protection of Individuals with Regard to Automatic Processing of Personal Data (ETS No. 108) on January 21, 2000.[422] Estonia has signed and ratified the European Convention for the Protection of Human Rights and Fundamental Freedoms.[423]

Republic of Finland

Section 8 of The Constitution Act of Finland states, "The private life, honor and home of every person shall be secured. More detailed provisions on the protection of personal data shall be prescribed by Act of Parliament. The secrecy of correspondence and of telephone and other confidential communications shall be inviolable. Measures impinging on the sphere of the home which are necessary for the protection of fundamental rights or the detection of crime may be prescribed by Act of Parliament. Necessary restrictions on the secrecy of communications may also be provided by Act of Parliament in the investigation of offenses which endanger the security of society or of the individual or which disturb domestic peace, in legal proceedings and security checks as well as during deprivation of liberty."[424]

The Personal Data Protection Act 1999[425] went into effect on June 1, 1999. The law replaced the 1987 Personal Data File Act[426] to make Finnish law consistent with the EU Data Protection Directive.

The Data Protection Ombudsman (DPO) enforces the Act and receives complaints. The office conducted 450 complaints and 10 investigations in 1998. It also receives 5,000 to 8,000 requests for advice each year.[427] A Data Protection

---

[421] Surveillance Act (RT* I 1994, 16, 290, 22 February 1994) <http://vlf.juridicum.su.se/master99/library2/teste/Surv.htm>.

[422] <http://conventions.coe.int/>.

[423] Ratified 14/05/93, Enacted 16/04/96, Entered into Force 16/04/96, <http://conventions.coe.int/>.

[424] Constitution of Finland <http://www.eduskunta.fi/kirjasto/Lait/constitution.html>.

[425] Personal Data Act (523/99). <http://www.tietosuoja.fi/uploads/hopxtvf.HTM>.

[426] Personal Data Files Act (Law No. 471/87).

[427] Home Page: <http://www.tietosuoja.fi/engl.html>.

Board resolves disputes and hears appeals of decisions rendered by the DPO. It also determines if personal information can be exported.[428]

The Finnish government has enacted special ordinances that apply to particular personal data systems. These include those operated by the police such as criminal information systems,[429] the national health service, passport systems, population registers,[430] farm registers, and the agency responsible for motor vehicle registration.[431]

Electronic surveillance and telephone tapping are governed by the Criminal Law. A judge can give permission to tap the telephone lines of a suspect if the suspect is liable for a jail sentence for crimes that are exhaustively listed in the Coercive Criminal Investigations Means Act. Transactional data of a suspect's telecommunications activity can be obtained if the suspect faces at least four months of jail. Electronic surveillance is possible, with the permission of the judge, if the suspect is accused of a drug related crime or a crime that can be punished with more than four years in jail. There were 12 orders for wiretapping in 1997. Although cases of political telecommunications eavesdropping are rare in Finland, there have been published reports that the Finnish military has either supported Western signals intelligence operations (via its large base at Santahamina on the outskirts of Helsinki), or acquiesced to a Swedish/U.S. eavesdropping collaborative effort from the Swedish embassy in downtown Helsinki.[432] In 1996, the PENET anonymous remailer was forced to shut down after Scientologists demanded that the identity of users posting critical messages be revealed to the Church. The court order was later enjoined by the Court of Appeals.[433]

The Finnish government in December 1999 began issuing new national id cards (FINEID) based on smart card technology.[434] The cards will include digital signatures to communicate online with government agencies and companies. The Finnish Population Register Centre will be the digital signature certificate

---

[428] <http://www.tietosuoja.fi/>.

[429] Criminal Records Act (770/93).

[430] Act on Population Information (1993/507).

[431] Jorma Kuopus, "Data Protection Regulatory System," Data Transmission and Privacy, D. Campbell and J. Fisher, eds., (Netherlands: Martinus Nijhoff Publishers, 1994).

[432] See <http://www.qainfo.se/~lb>.

[433] See <http://www.penet.fi/injuncl.html>.

[434] See Finnish Population Register Centre, <http://www.vaestorekisterikeskus.fi/>.

authority. The cards can be used in smart card readers in PCs and there are plans to put them in the SIM cards in mobile phones and interactive television systems.

In 1998, there were a series of controversial raids on animal rights activists by police. The Finnish League for Human Rights raised concerns in its 1998 report on police raids on NGOs including animal rights organizations and journalists and the seizure of their equipment and documents without a search warrant.[435]

The Publicity (of Public Actions) Act[436] went into effect in 1999 replacing the Publicity of Official Documents Act of 1951.[437] It provides for a general right to access any document created by a government agency, or sent or received by a government agency, including electronic records. Finland is a country that has traditionally adhered to the Nordic tradition of open access to government files. In fact, the world's first Freedom of Information act dates back as far as the Riksdag's (Swedish Parliament) 1766 "Access to Public Records Act." This Act also applied to Finland, then a Swedish-governed territory.[438]

Finland is a member of the Council of Europe and has signed and ratified the Convention for the Protection of Individuals with Regard to Automatic Processing of Personal Data (ETS No. 108).[439] Finland has signed and ratified the European Convention for the Protection of Human Rights and Fundamental Freedoms.[440] Finland is a member of the Organization for Economic Cooperation and Development and has adopted the OECD Guidelines on the Protection of Privacy and Transborder Flows of Personal Data.

Aland Islands

The Parliament of the self-governing Aland Islands (Landsting) passed its own Data Protection Act in 1991 and independently ratified the Council of Europe's Convention 108.[441] Although the Aland act makes reference to the Finnish Data Protection Act, there has always been some resistance by the Aland Swedish-

---

[435] Finnish League for Human Rights, Human Rights in Finland: 1998 Audit, December 1998.

[436] http://www.om.fi/1184.htm.

[437] Act 83/9/2/1951.

[438] Wayne Madsen, Handbook of Personal Data Protection (New York: Stockton Press, 1992).

[439] Signed 10/04/91, Ratified 02/12/91, Entered into force 1/04/92, <http://conventions.coe.int/>.

[440] Signed 05/05/89, Ratified 10/05/90, Entered into force 10/05/90, <http://conventions.coe.int/>.

[441] Kuopus, ibid.

speaking majority to following orders from Helsinki. Constitutionally, the Aland Parliament may nullify Finnish laws on its territory.[442]

French Republic

The right of privacy is not explicitly included in the French Constitution of 1958. The Constitutional Court ruled in 1994 that the right of privacy was implicit in the Constitution.[443]

The Data Protection Act was enacted in 1978 and covers personal information held by government agencies and private entities.[444] Anyone wishing to process personal data must register and obtain permission in many cases relating to processing by public bodies and for medical research. Individuals must be informed of the reasons for collection of information and may object to its processing either before or after it is collected. Individuals have rights to access information being kept about them and to demand the correction and, in some cases, the deletion of this data. Fines and imprisonment can be imposed for violations.

As a member of the EU, France should have amended this Act to make it consistent with the European Data Protection Directive (95/46/EC) by October 1, 1998. In August 1997, Prime Minister Lionel Jospin ordered Guy Braibant, president of a government advisory council, to issue a report setting out a plan for the changes to be made in the law. This report was issued in February 1998.[445] On January 19, 1999, in a press conference held by the Interministerial Committee on the Information Society, the Prime Minister announced that a proposal for a new legislative framework on data protection was being sent to the national Parliament.[446] This framework, he stated, would amend the 1978 Act to incorporate the European directive in law and strengthen the role of the national data protection agency (CNIL). During the press conference, the Prime Minister

---

[442] Madsen, ibid.

[443] Dècision 94-352 du Conseil Constitutionnel du 18 Janvier 1995.

[444] Loi N° 78-17 du Janvier 1978 relative à l'informatique, aux fichiers et aux libertés. Journal officiel du 7 janvier 1978 et rectificatif au JO du 25 janvier 1978, modifiée par la loi n° 88-227 du 11 mars 1988, article 13 relative à la transparence financière de la vie politique (JO du 12 mars 1988), la loi n° 92-1336 du 16 décembre 1992 (JO du 23 décembre 1992) et la loi n° 94-548 du ler juillet 1994 (JO du 2 juillet 1994), <http://www.cnil.fr/textes/text02.htm>.

[445] Guy Braibant, Donnees Personnelles et Societe De 'Information: Rapport au Premier Ministre sur la transposition en droit français de la directive no 95/46, le 3 mars 1998,

[446] See <http://www.internet.gouv.fr/francais/index.html>.

---

also announced the relaxation of controls on encryption in France and the intended introduction of a new law on electronic signatures. In January 2000, the European Commission initiated a case before the European Court of Justice against France and four other countries for failure to implement the data directive on time.[447] Draft legislation to update the law is currently being reviewed by the Commission Nationale de L'informatique et des Libertés.

The Commission Nationale de L'informatique et des Libertés (CNIL) is an independent agency which enforces the Data Protection Act and other related laws.[448] The Commission takes complaints, issues rulings, sets rules, conducts audits and issues reports. It reported in its 1999 annual report that the number of complaints received annually has more than doubled in the last five years.[449] In 1999 it received a total of 3,508 complaints, 3,538 requests for advice and approximately 100,000 phone calls. The report notes that there was a 67 percent increase in the number of requests for access to police records and credits this increase to the public concern over the creation of the Système de Traitement des Infractions Constatées (STIC), an initiative by the Minister of Interior to merge police and other records. The report also addresses personal identification numbers, electronic commerce and online profiling, genetic and DNA databases, workplace monitoring, tracking of wireless devices, recruitment practices and the registration of HIV patients. In October 1999 the Commission issued a report on spamming and privacy rights.[450] In April 2000 it published a survey on the top 100 commercial web-sites and their compliance with data protection laws.[451]

Electronic surveillance is regulated by a 1991 law that requires permission of an investigating judge before a wiretap is installed. The duration of the tap is limited to four months and can be renewed.[452] The law created the Commission National de Contrôl des Interceptions de Sécurité, which sets rules and reviews wiretaps each year. The number of wiretaps has been between 4,500 and 4,700 since 1995. There were 4,687 requests for wiretaps in 1999. In total, 4,577 wiretaps (2,978

---

[447] 'Data protection: Commission takes five Member States to court', Press Release, 11 January 2000. <http://europa.eu.int/comm/internal_market/en/media/dataprot/news/2k-10.htm>.

[448] Home Page: <http://www.cnil.fr>.

[449] Commission nationale de l'informatique (CNIL), 20eme rapport d'activite 1999, July 5, 2000.

[450] "Le publipostage électronique et la protection des données personnelles," 14 octobre 1999. http://www.cnil.fr/actu/tactu.htm

[451] 'Protection des données personnelles et e-commerce en France' 19 avril, 2000. <http://www.cnil.fr/actu/tactu.htm>.

[452] La loi n° 91-636 du 10 juillet 1991 relative au secret des correspondances émises par la voie des télécommunications.

---

new and 1,599 renewals) were authorized by the Commission.[453] The interception of cellular telephones rose from 12 percent of all wiretaps in January 1999 to 27.5 percent in December 1999.

The European Court of Human Rights has ruled against France a number of times for violations of Article 8 of the Convention. The Court's 1990 decision in *Kruslin v. France* resulted in the enactment of the 1991 law.[454] Most recently, the court fined France FF 25,000 for wiretap law violations.[455] There have been many cases of illegal wiretapping, including most notably a long running scandal over an anti-terrorist group in the office of President Mitterand monitoring the calls of journalists and opposition politicians.[456] The CNCIS estimated that there were over 100,000 illegal taps conducted by private companies and individuals in 1996, many on behalf of government agencies. A decree was issued in 1997 to limit the dissemination of tapping equipment.[457]

The tort of privacy was first recognized in France as far back as 1858[458] and was added to the Civil Code in 1970.[459] There are additional specific laws on administrative documents,[460] archives,[461] video surveillance,[462] correspondence,[463] and employment.[464] There are also protections incorporated in the Penal Code.[465]

---

[453] 8e rapport d' activité 1999, Commission national de contrôl des interceptions de sécurité, May 2000.

[454] Kruslin v. France, 176-A, Eur. Ct. H.R. (ser. A) (1990).

[455] la France condamnée par la Cour européenne des droits de l'homme, Le Monde, 27 Août 1998.

[456] see Capitaine Paul Barril, Guerres Secrètes à L'Élysée, (Albin Michel, 1996), Francis Zamponi, Les RG à l'écoute de la France: Police et politique de 1981 à 1997, (La Découverte, 1998).

[457] 5e rapport d' activité 1997, Commission national de contrôl des interceptions de sécurité, May 1998.

[458] The Rachel affaire. Judgment of June 16, 1858, Trib. pr. inst. de la Seine, 1858 D.P. III 62. See Jeanne M. Hauch, Protecting Private Facts in France: The Warren & Brandeis Tort is Alive and Well and Flourishing in Paris, 68 Tul. L. Rev. 1219 (May 1994).

[459] Civil Code, Article 9, Statute No. 70-643 of July 17, 1970.

[460] Loi n° 78-753 du 17 juillet 1978 portant diverses mesures d'amélioration des relations entre l'administration et le public et diverses dispositions d'ordre administratif, social et fiscal. (Journal officiel du 18 juillet 1978, page 2851). <http://www.cnil.fr/textes/text05.htm>.

[461] Loi n° 79-18 du 3 janvier 1979 sur les archives (Journal officiel du 5 janvier 1979, page 43, rectificatif au journal officiel du 6 janvier 1979, page 55). <http://www.cnil.fr/textes/text052.htm>.

[462] Loi d'orientation et de programmation n° 95-73 du 21 janvier 1995 relative à la sécurité (Journal officiel du 24 janvier 1995, page 1249). <http://www.cnil.fr/textes/text054.htm>. Also see Décret n° 96-926 du 17 octobre 1996 relatif à la vidéo-surveillance pris pour l'application de l'article 10 de la loi n° 95-73 du 21 janvier 1995 d'orientation et de programmation relative à la sécurité (Journal officiel du 20 octobre 1996, page 15432). <http://www.cnil.fr/textes/text055.htm> and Circulaire du 22 octobre 1996 relative à l'application de l'article 10 de la loi n° 95-73 du 21 janvier 1995 d'orientation et de programmation relative à la sécurité (décret sur la vidéosurveillance) (Journal officiel du 7 décembre 1996, page 17835). <http://www.cnil.fr/textes/text056.htm>.

[463] Code of Post and Telecommunications, L. 41.

The French Liberty of Communication Act was adopted on June 28th, 2000.[466] The Act requires all persons wishing to post content on the Internet to identify themselves, either to the public, by publishing their name and address on their web-site (in the case of a business) or to their host provider (in the case of a private individual). Earlier provisions, which would have imposed large penalties and jail sentences on anybody violating this requirement and required Internet Service Providers (ISPs) to check the accuracy of the personal details given to them, were dropped in the final version of the legislation.[467] The law requires ISPs to keep logs of all data which could be used to identify a content provider in the case of later legal proceedings. ISPs are subject to the "professional secret" rule regarding this data, meaning that they cannot disclose it to anyone except a judge. The law, as passed, also held ISPs liable for failing to delete content once ordered to do so by a judge or for failing to "take appropriate actions" once informed by a third party that they are hosting illegal or harmful content. The passage of this law provoked widespread criticism from civil liberties groups and privacy advocates who argued that it would restrict rights to anonymity and free speech. In June 2000, IRIS, a French civil liberties group, drew up a petition in opposition to the law.[468]

In a review of this law, brought before it on June 29, 2000 by 60 opposition members of Parliament,[469] the French Constitutional Council struck down this provision as contrary to Art 34 of the Constitution.[470] This article states that any measures which could impact upon civil liberties must be detailed in the law. In this case, the Council ruled that the "appropriate actions" to be taken by ISPs should have been specified in the law.

---

[464] Loi n° 92-1446 du 31 décembre 1992 relative à l'emploi, au développement du travail à temps partiel et à l'assurance chômage. (Journal officiel du 1er janvier 1993, page 19). <http://www.cnil.fr/textes/text053.htm>.

[465] Penal Code, Article 368.

[466] Loi no 553 du 28 juin 2000, modifiant la loi n° 86-1067 du 30 septembre 1986 relative à la liberté de communication. <http://www.assemblee-nationale.fr/2/pdf/ta0553.htm>.

[467] A full history of the developments since the law was first introduced on May, 1999 is available (in French) at http://www.iris.sgdg.org/actions/loi-comm/index.html

[468] Loi sur la liberté de communication, Déclaration des acteurs d'Internet. <http://www.iris.sgdg.org/actions/loi-comm/declaration.html>.

[469] Saisine du Conseil constitutionnel par plus de 60 députés, 29 juin 2000. <http://www.conseil-constitutionnel.fr/decision/2000/2000433/index.htm>.

[470] Conseil Constitutionnel, Décision n° 2000-433 DC du 27 juillet 2000, <http://www.conseil-constitutionnel.fr/decision/2000/2000433/2000433dc.htm>.

Two laws in France provide for a right to access government records.[471] The Commission d'accèss aux documents administratifs is charged with enforcing the acts.[472] According to the CADA, it handled 4,000 inquiries per year between 1996 and 1999. The law was amended in April 2000 to clarify access to legal documents and also identify the civil servant processing the request.[473]

France is a member of the Council of Europe and has signed and ratified the Convention for the Protection of Individuals with Regard to Automatic Processing of Personal Data (ETS No. 108).[474] It has signed and ratified the European Convention for the Protection of Human Rights and Fundamental Freedoms.[475] It is a member of the Organization for Economic Cooperation and Development and has adopted the OECD Guidelines on the Protection of Privacy and Transborder Flows of Personal Data.

Federal Republic of Germany

Article 10 of the Basic Law states: "(1) Privacy of letters, posts, and telecommunications shall be inviolable. (2) Restrictions may only be ordered pursuant to a statute. Where a restriction serves to protect the free democratic basic order or the existence or security of the Federation, the statute may stipulate that the person affected shall not be informed of such restriction and that recourse to the courts shall be replaced by a review of the case by bodies and auxiliary bodies appointed by Parliament." Attempts to amend the Basic Law to include a right to data protection were discussed after reunification when the constitution was revised and were successfully opposed by the then-conservative political majority.

In 1983, the Federal Constitutional Court, in a case against a government census law, acknowledged formally an individual's "right of informational self-determination" which is limited by the "predominant public interest." The central

---

[471] Loi no. 78-753 du 17 juillet 1978 de la liberté d'accès au documents administratifs <http://www.legifrance.gouv.fr/textes/html/fic197807170753.htm>; Loi no 79-587 du juillet 1979 relative à la motivation des actes administratifs et à l'amélioration des relations entre l'administration et le public.

[472] Rapport d'activité - 9ème rapport Commission d'accès aux documents administratifs (CADA) Edition 1999.<http://www.ladocfrancaise.gouv.fr/fic_pdf/cada.pdf>.

[473] Loi n°2000-321 du 12 avril 2000 relative aux droits des citoyens dans leurs relations avec les administrations (J.O. du 13 avril 2000). <http://www.legifrance.gouv.fr/citoyen/jorf_nor.ow?numjo=FPPX9800029L>. Travaux préparatoires, see: <http://www.assembleenationale.fr/2/2dbc_2000.htm#loi2000_321>.

[474] Signed 28/01/81, Ratified 24/03/83, Entered into Force 01/10/85, <http://conventions.coe.int/>.

[475] Signed 04/11/50, Ratified 03/05/74, Entered into Force 03/05/74, <http://conventions.coe.int/>.

---

part of the verdict stated, "Who can not certainly overlook which information related to him or her is known to certain segments of his social environment, and who is not able to assess to a certain degree the knowledge of his potential communication partners, can be essentially hindered in his capability to plan and to decide. The right of informational self-determination stands against a societal order and its underlying legal order in which citizens could not know any longer who what and when in what situations knows about them."[476] This landmark court decision derived the "right of informational self-determination" directly from Article 2 of the German Constitution which declares protective personal rights (Persönlichkeitsrechte).

The world's first data protection law was passed in the German Land of Hessen in 1970. In 1977, a Federal Data Protection Law followed, which was reviewed in 1990.[477] The general purpose of this law is "to protect the individual against violations of his personal right (Persönlichkeitsrecht) by handling person-related data." The law covers collection, processing and use of personal data collected by public federal and state authorities (as long as there is no state-regulation), and of non-public offices, as long as they process and use data for commercial or professional aims. All of the 16 Länder have their own specific data protection regulations that cover the public sector of the Länder administrations.

Germany has been slow to update its law to make it consistent with the EU Directive. The European Commission announced in January 2000 that it was going to take Germany to court for failure to implement the directive. The Government on June 14 approved a draft bill.[478] The bill will be heard by the Parliament in the fall and will likely not go into force until early 2001. Observers are skeptical that the bill will be determined to be sufficient. The government has also expressed an intention to draft a second bill which will more fundamentally change the law to modernize it. The Länders of Berlin, Brandenburg, Schleswig-Holstein and Baden-Württenberg have updated their laws to be consistent with the Directive.

The Federal Data Protection Commission (Bundesbeauftragte für den Datenschutz) is responsible for supervision of the Data Protection Act.[479] There are between 10,000 and 20,000 data controllers registered by the agency and the

---

[476] BverfGE 65,1.

[477] Federal Act on Data Protection, 27 January 1977 (Bundesgesetzblatt, Part I, No 7, 1 February 1977), Amended 1990. <http://www.datenschutz-berlin.de/gesetze/bdsg/bdsgeng.htm>.

[478] <http://www.datenschutz-berlin.de/ueber/aktuell.htm#topofnews>.

[479] Home Page: <http://www.bfd.bund.de/>.

office estimates that that will increase when the new federal legislation is approved.[480] The office also handles around 3,000 complaints each year and carries out on average 45 investigations. There are 60 persons on staff.

There are also commissions in each of the Länders who enforce the Länder data protection acts.[481] Supervision, however, is carried out for the private sector by the Land authority designated by the Land data protection law (usually the Land Data Protection Commissioner). In 1996, the Berlin Data Protection Commissioner reached an agreement with Citibank on the use of RailwayCards as Visa cards. The agreement may be an important precursor for transborder dataflows to the U.S. and other countries without privacy laws.[482]

Wiretapping is regulated by the "G10-Law" and requires a court order for criminal cases.[483] In July 1999, the Constitutional Court issued a decision on a 1994 law which authorizes warrantless automated wiretaps (screening method) of international communications by the intelligence service (BND) for purposes of preventing terrorism and the illegal trade in drugs and weapons.[484] The court ruled that the procedure did violate privacy rights protected by the Basic Law but that screening could continue as long as the intelligence service did not pass on the information to the local police and the Parliament must enact new rules by June 2001. It was reported that the BND has 1,400 operatives listening in on satellite communications.[485] The Constitutional Court ruled in December 1999 that the government could conduct surveillance of political parties if it is believed that they are hostile to the constitution and information can not be obtained by public means.[486]

After a fiercely fought six-year political debate, a two-third majority of the German parliament eventually approved a change to Section 13 of the

---

[480] Fax from Ulrich Dammann, Bundesbeauftragte für den Datenschutz to EPIC, July 27, 2000.

[481] Links to the Ländesbeauftragten für den Datenschutz are available at <http://www.datenschutz-berlin.de/sonstige/behoerde/ldbauf.htm>.

[482] Dr.iur. Alexander Dix, Case Study: North America and the European Directive - The German RailwayCard: A model contractual solution of the "adequate level of protection" issue?, September 1996. <http://www.datenschutz-berlin.de/sonstige/konferen/ottawa/alex3.htm>.

[483] "Gesetz zur Beschraenkung des Brief-, Post- und Fernmeldegeheimnisses - Gesetz zu Artikel 10 des Grundgesetzes (GG10)" (Law on restriction of the right of secrecy of letters, mail and telecommunication - Law applying to article 10 of the constitution). 13. August 1968 (G10 BGBl. I, p. 949) and was changed the last time by the bill of 28.10. 1994 (BGBl. I, p.3186ff) "Verbrechensbekaempfungsgesetz" ('Crime-fighting law').

[484] <http://www.uni-wuerzburg.de/glaw/bv093181.html>.

[485] German Phone Taps are Routine, The Independent, July 10, 1999.

[486] Constitutional Court Upholds Covert Investigation of Political Parties, The Week in Germany December 10, 1999.

Constitution in April 1998, which makes it legal for police authorities to place bugging devices even in private homes (provided there is a court order). The change was the provision for the "Law for the enhancement of the fight against organized crime," which became effective in 1999.

In addition, wherever they deal with the handling of personal information on natural persons either directly or by amendments, nearly all German laws contain references to the respective data protection law or carry special sections on the handling of personal data that reflect the right to privacy. Most recently there have been a number of laws relating to communications privacy. The Telecommunications Carriers Data Protection Ordinance of 1996 protects privacy of telecommunications information.[487] The Information and Communication Services (Multimedia) Act of 1997 sets protections for information used in computer networks.[488] The Act also sets out the legal requirements for digital signatures. The German Federal Supreme Court ruled in March 1999 that Commerzbank AG could not include a clause in their contracts that clients agree to receive telephone "consulting." In April 1998, a law was passed that allows the Bundeskrimalamt to run a nationwide databank of genetic profiles related to criminal investigations and convicted offenders. One month later, the Bundesgrenzschutz, originally a para-military border police force, and now responsible among other tasks for railways and stations, received permission to check persons' identities and baggage without any concrete suspicion. [489]

There is no general Freedom of Information act in Germany. The Land of Brandenberg adopted a Freedom of Information law in 1998 to allow citizen access to government records.[490] The act is enforced by the Information and Data Protection Commissioner. More recently, Berlin[491] and Schleswig Holstein[492] have also adopted FOI laws.

---

[487] Telecommunications Carriers Data Protection Ordinance (TDSV) As of: 12 July 1996 (Federal Law Gazette I p 982), Federal Ministry of Posts and Telecommunications. <http://www.datenschutz-berlin.de/gesetze/medien/tdsve.htm>.

[488] Federal Act Establishing the General Conditions for Information and Communication Services - Information and Communication Services Act - (Informations- und Kommunikationsdienste-Gesetz - IuKDG) 13 June 1997 <http://www.datenschutz-berlin.de/gesetze/medien/iukdge.htm>. Also see Resolution of the Conference of Data Protection Commissioners of the Federation and the Länder of 29 April 1996 on key points for the regulation in matters of data protection of online services. <http://www.datenschutz-berlin.de/sonstige/konferen/sonstige/old-res2.htm>.

[489] "New Powers For The Border Police: Checks Anywhere At Any Time," Fortress Europe, FECL 56 (December 1998).

[490] Akteneinsichts- und Informationszugangsgesetz (AIG), 1998.

[491] <http://www.datenschutz-berlin.de/recht/bln/ifg/ifg.htm>.

[492] <http://www.rewi.hu-berlin.de/Datenschutz/DSB/SH/material/recht/infofrei/infofrei.htm>.

Since 1990, a law allows for access to the files of the Stasi, the former East Germany's security service, by individuals and researchers. The law created a Federal Commission for the Records of the State Security Services of the Former GDR (the Gauck Authority) which has a staff of 3,000 piecing together shredded documents and making files available.[493] There have been 1.6 million requests from individuals for access to the files and 2.7 million requests for background checks since the archives became available.[494] Many of the files were destroyed in 1989, but sometime in 1990, the U.S. Central Intelligence Agency was able to obtain the names, aliases and payment histories of 4,000 spies who worked in various countries for Stasi or informers from the Soviet Union. The U.S. Government refused to give the files to the German government until December 1999, claiming that it would harm the people in the files.[495] In May 2000, files about former Chancellor Helmut Kohl's telephone calls were found to be missing from the archives when they were going to be used to investigate corruption. The Stasi had conducted extensive wiretapping of Kohl for years.[496]

Germany is a member of the Council of Europe and has signed and ratified the Convention for the Protection of Individuals with Regard to Automatic Processing of Personal Data (ETS No. 108).[497] It has signed and ratified the European Convention for the Protection of Human Rights and Fundamental Freedoms.[498] It is a member of the Organization for Economic Cooperation and Development and has adopted the OECD Guidelines on the Protection of Privacy and Transborder Flows of Personal Data.

Hellenic Republic (Greece)

The Constitution of Greece recognizes the rights of privacy and secrecy of communications. Article 9 states, "(1) Each man's home is inviolable. A person's personal and family life is inviolable. No house searches shall be made except when and as the law directs, and always in the presence of representatives of the judicial authorities. (2) Offenders against the foregoing provision shall be punished for forced entry into a private house and abuse of power, and shall be

---

[493] Web Site: <http://www.snafu.de/~bstu/ >.

[494] "Gauck reports steady flow of inquiries about stasi records," The Week in Germany, July 16, 1999 .

[495] "U.S.-Held Files Seen Uncovering E. German Spies." Reuters, February 4, 1999.

[496] "Stasi files on Kohl's tapped calls vanish," The Times, May 17, 2000.

[497] <http://conventions.coe.int/>.

[498] <http://conventions.coe.int/>.

---

obliged to indemnify in full the injured party as the law provides." Article 19 states, "The privacy of correspondence and any other form of communication is absolutely inviolable. The law shall determine the guarantees under which the judicial authority is released from the obligation to observe the above-mentioned right, for reasons of national security or for the investigation of particularly serious crimes."[499]

The Law on the Protection of Individuals with regard to the Processing of Personal Data was approved in 1997.[500] Greece was the last member of the European Union to adopt a data protection law and its law was written to directly apply the EU Directive into Greek law. The law was also necessary for Greece to join the Schengen Agreement. There were major protests during the ratification of the Schengen Agreement for border controls and information sharing. According to news reports, police used tear gas to disperse a group of about 1,000 protesters, including Orthodox priests, when they tried to push their way into Parliament as the pact was being debated.[501]

The Protection of Personal Data Authority is an independent public authority set up under the law. Its mission is to supervise the implementation of the law and the other rulings pertaining to the protection of individuals against the processing of personal data.[502] It also exercises other powers delegated to it from time to time. The Agency ruled on May 14, 2000 that religious affiliations must be removed from state identity cards. The agency also ordered that fingerprints, profession and spouses' names also be removed. The decision was opposed by Archbishop Christodoulos, the leader of the powerful Greek Orthodox Church who said, "These changes are being put forward by neo-intellectuals who want to attack us like rabid dogs and tear at our flesh."[503] Prime Minister Costas Simitis announced on May 24 that new Greek identity cards would not include religion, not even on a voluntary basis. Greece is the only member of the European Union that requires citizens to list their religious beliefs on police identity cards. The European Parliament passed a resolution in 1993 calling on the Greek government not to place religion on its national ID cards.[504]

---

[499] Constitution of Greece, Adopted: 11 June 1975, <http://www.uni-wuerzburg.de/law/gr00t___.html>.

[500] Law no. 2472 on the Protection of Individuals with regard to the Processing of Personal Data.

[501] The Reuters European Community Report, June 10, 1997.

[502] Home Page: <http://www.dpa.gr/>.

[503] The Guardian, May 22, 2000.

[504] The Reuters European Community Report, April 23, 1993.

The law requires that police wishing to conduct telephone taps must obtain court permission.[505] However, there are continuing reports of government surveillance of human rights groups, Orthodox religious groups, and activist members of minority groups by government agents who are conducting illegal wiretapping and interception of mail.[506] In June 1994, a parliamentary investigation committee recommended the indictment of former Prime Minister Mitsotakis and 30 persons from his administration on charges of wiretapping political opponents from 1989 to 1991. In January 1995, the Parliament voted to drop all charges against Mitsotakis, and the Supreme Court ordered the dismissal of other charges in April 1995. The late Greek Prime Minister Andrea Papandreou was also investigated for illegally wiretapping his political opponents.[507]

The law of 1599/1986 regulates the use of the Single Register Code Number (EKAM).[508] The number is the official national ID number for the population register, ID card, voting register, passport number, tax number, drivers license number, and other registers. Until the 1997 data protection law was enacted, this protected the privacy of information in those registers.

Article 5 of the Greek Code of Administrative Procedure (Law No. 2690/1999)[509] is a new Freedom of Information act that provides citizens the right to access administrative documents created by government agencies. It replaces Law 1599/1986.

Greece is a member of the Council of Europe and has signed and ratified the Convention for the Protection of Individuals with Regard to Automatic Processing of Personal Data (ETS No. 108).[510] Greece has signed and ratified the European Convention for the Protection of Human Rights and Fundamental Freedoms.[511] Greece is a member of the Organization for Economic Cooperation and Development and has adopted the OECD Guidelines on the Protection of Privacy and Transborder Flows of Personal Data.

---

[505] Law no 2225/94.

[506] U.S. Department of State, Greece Country Report on Human Rights Practices for 1997, January 30, 1998. See also Greece Report, Human Rights Watch World Report, 1998.

[507] Reuters World Service, November 20, 1996.

[508] Law no 1599/1986 on the relationship of a new type of identification card and other provisions.

[509] See http://www.rz.uni-frankfurt.de/~sobotta/greecenew.htm

[510] Signed 17/02/83, Enacted 11/08/95, Entered into Force 01/12/95, <http://conventions.coe.int/>.

[511] Signed 28/11/50, Enacted 28/11/74, Entered into Force 28/11/74, <http://conventions.coe.int/>.

Republic of Hungary

Article 59 of the Constitution of the Republic of Hungary reads, "Everyone in the Republic of Hungary shall have the right to good reputation, the inviolability of the privacy of his home and correspondence, and the protection of his personal data."[512] In 1991, the Supreme Court ruled that a law creating a multi-use personal identification number violated the constitutional right of privacy.[513]

Act No. LXIII of 1992 on the Protection of Personal Data and Disclosure of Data of Public Interest covers the collection and use of personal information in both the public sector and private sector. It is a combined Data Protection and Freedom of Information Act. Its basic principle is informational self-determination.[514] Hungary is an applicant for EU membership and it is anticipated that only minor changes are required to make the Act compliant with the EU Directive. In June 1999, the Parliament amended the Act to treat "data controllers" and "data processors" differently to make it more consistent with the EU Directive.[515]

The Article 29 Working Group of the European Commission recommended in September 1999 that "the Commission and the Committee established by Article 31 of Directive 95/46/EC note that Hungary ensures an adequate level of protection within the meaning of Article 25(6) of this directive."[516] In July 2000, the European Commission formally adopted this position, thereby approving all future transfers of personal data to Hungary.[517] The Parliament is currently working on more extensive revisions to the act to ensure compliance with the EU Directive, but the changes are not expected to be approved this year.

The Parliamentary Commissioner for Data Protection and Freedom of Information oversees the 1992 Act.[518] Besides acting as an ombudsman for both

---

[512] Constitution of the Republic of Hungary,
<http://centraleurope.com/ceo/country/hungary/constit/hucons01.html>.

[513] Constitutional Court Decision No. 15-AB of 13 April 1991.
<http://www.privacyinternational.org/countries/hungary/hungarian_id_decision_1991.html>.

[514] ACT LXIII OF 1992 on the Protection of Personal Data and the Publicity of Data of Public Interest,
<http://www.osa.ceu.hu/yeast/AccessAndProtection/04.htm>.

[515] Act No. LXXII of 1999.

[516] Opinion 6/99 Concerning the level of personal data in Hungary, Adopted on 7 September 1999,
<http://europa.eu.int/comm/internal_market/en/media/dataprot/wpdocs/wp24en.htm>.

[517] "Commission adopts decisions recognising adequacy of regimes in US, Switzerland and Hungary," July 27, 2000. <http://europa.eu.int/comm/internal_market/en/media/dataprot/news/safeharbor.htm>.

[518] Web Site: <http://www.obh.hu/>.

---

data protection and freedom of information, the Commissioner's tasks include maintaining the Data Protection Register, and providing opinions on DP and FOI-related draft legislation, as well as each category of official secrets. Under the Secrecy Act of 1995, the Commissioner is entitled to change the classification of state and official secrets as well. The Commissioner (along with the two other Parliamentary Commissioners – one for human rights in general, the other for the ethnic minorities) was elected for the first time on June 30, 1995, for a six year term.

The Commission has been very active reviewing cases involving personal information.[519] When reviewing unlawful national security controls in 1995, unlawful information gathering practices were found in 797 cases and files had to be destroyed. In 1995, the names and addresses of the winners of the largest lottery jackpot were broadcast on television against the will of the individuals. In a case involving unlawful gathering of personal data of patients at voluntary drug treatment institutions in 1997, the police had to return the lists to the hospital. In June 2000, the Commission ruled that a large company can not give personal information to debt collectors without the person's consent.[520] In March, the Commissioner expressed concern about U.S. FBI agents based in Hungary having access to personal information while being given diplomatic immunity.[521] The Commission has registered 19,376 databases and conducts about 900 examinations each year. [522] There are 27 people on the staff.

Surveillance by police requires a court order and is limited to investigations of crimes punishable by more than five years imprisonment.[523] Surveillance by national security services requires the permission of a specially appointed judge or the Minister of Justice, who can authorize surveillance for up to 90 days.[524] There have been a number of scandals involving secret service spying on political opponents, environmental activists and ethnic minorities. The Parliamentary National Security Committee is still investigating the illegal surveillance of members of the then-opposition political party Fidesz by the

---

[519] See Hungarian Civil Liberties Union, Data Protection and Freedom of Information, 1997.

[520] Matav told it cannot give customer information to debt collectors, MTI Hungarian News Agency, June 23, 2000.

[521] Ombudsman worry about use of personal data by Hungary-based FBI staff, BBC Monitoring Europe – Political, March 23, 2000.

[522] Letters from László Majtényi, Parliamentary Commissioner for Data Protection and Freedom of Information, August 4, 1999, July 11, 2000.

[523] Act XXXIV of 1994 on Police.

[524] Act LXXV of 1995 on the National Security Services.

intelligence services.[525] Prime Minister Viktor Orbán said in 1998 the surveillance was conducted by former members of the secret service then employed by private companies.[526] In April 1998, the government issued a decree ordering phone companies that offer cellular service to modify their systems to ensure that they could be intercepted. The cost was estimated to be HUF10 billion.[527]

Many laws contain rules for handling personal data including addresses,[528] universal identifiers,[529] medical information,[530] police information,[531] public records,[532] employment,[533] telecommunications,[534] and national security services.[535] The Direct Marketing Act provides for opt-out, but only for name and address information.[536] There is no sectoral legislation covering the Internet. The Criminal Code also has provisions on privacy.[537]

Hungary is a member of the Council of Europe and has signed and ratified the Convention for the Protection of Individuals with Regard to Automatic Processing of Personal Data (ETS No. 108).[538] It has signed and ratified the European Convention for the Protection of Human Rights and Fundamental Freedoms.[539] It is a member of the Organization for Economic Cooperation and Development and has adopted the OECD Guidelines on the Protection of Privacy and Transborder Flows of Personal Data.

---

[525] Hungary: government, far-right clash with opposition over surveillance case, BBC Monitoring Europe - Political, March 2, 2000.

[526] "Fidesz 'bugging' probe underway, The Budapest Sun," September 3, 1998.

[527] "Technical costs of phone tapping estimated at HUF 10bn," MTI Econews, April 17, 1998.

[528] Act No. LXVI of 1992 on the register of personal data and addresses of citizens.

[529] Act No. XX of 1996 on the identification methods replacing the universal personal identification number, and on the use of identification codes.

[530] Act XLVII of 1997 on the use and protection of medical and related data.

[531] Act No. XXXIV of 1994 on the Police (Chapter VIII: "Data handling by the Police").

[532] Act No. LXVI of 1995 on public records, public archives, and the protection of private archives (restricting rules on the publicity of documents containing personal data).

[533] Act No. IV of 1991 on furthering employment and provisions for the unemployed.

[534] Act No. LXXII of 1992 on telecommunications.

[535] Act No. CXXV of 1995 on the National Security Services etc.

[536] Act No. CXIX of 1995 on the use of name and address information serving the purposes of research and direct marketing.

[537] Criminal Code, Sections 177-178.
<http://www.privacy.org/pi/countries/hungary/hungary_criminal_code.html>.

[538] Signed 13/05/93, Enacted 08/10/97, Entered into Force 01/02/98, <http://conventions.coe.int/>.

[539] Signed 06/11/90, Enacted 05/11/92, Entered into Force 05/11/92, <http://conventions.coe.int/>.

Republic of Iceland

Section 72 of the Constitution states, "The dwelling shall be inviolable. House searching, seizure, and examination of letters and other papers as well as any breach of the secrecy to be observed in postal, telegraph, and telephone matters shall take place only under a judicial order unless particular exception is warranted by Statute."[540]

The Act on Protection of Individuals with regard to the Processing of Personal Data is a new law on the processing of personal information for government agencies and corporation enacted to ensure compliance with the EU Directive.[541] The act covers both automated and manual processing of personal information. It also covers video surveillance and limits the use of National Identification Numbers. The Statistical Bureau of Iceland shall maintain a registry of individuals not willing to allow the use of their names in product marketing. It replaces the 1979 Act on the Registration and Handling on Personal Data.[542]

The Act is enforced by the Icelandic Data Protection Commission (Datatilsynet). The Commission maintains the registry of activities and can investigate and issue rulings. It can also impose fines for non-compliance and can seek criminal sanctions. The Authority can also prohibit or mandate the use of the National Identification Numbers and is in charge of overseeing the Schengen Information System. In 1998, the Commission registered 509 activities.

In December 1998, the Parliament approved a bill to create a nationwide centralized health database to be used for genetic research.[543] The Government gave an exclusive 12-year license for the database to American bio-tech company deCODE Genetics, which will create a nationwide genetic database of the entire Icelandic population based on 30 years of patients' records. The company is spending $200 million over the next five years for research. Patients were originally required to opt out of the database by June 1999. After that date, their

---

[540] Constitution of the Kingdom of Iceland, Adopted: 5 June 1953. <http://www.uni-wuerzburg.de/law/da00t___.html>.

[541] Act on Protection of Individuals with regard to the Processing of Personal Data No. 77/2000. <http://brunnur.stjr.is/interpro/tolvunefnd/tolvunefnd.nsf/pages/1E685B166D04084D002569050056BF6F>.

[542] Act on the Registration and Handling on Personal Data, No. 121, 28 December 1989. The law was originally introduced in 1979 and renewed in 1984 and 1989 after the law automatically expired after five years because of the 'sunset' provisions attached to laws by Iceland's Parliament.

[543] Act on a Health Sector Database no. 139/1998, 17 December 1998. <http://brunnur.stjr.is/interpro/htr/htr.nsf/pages/gagngr-log-ensk>.

---

information could not be removed. DeCode plans to register on the U.S. NASDAQ stock market in the summer of 2000.

This proposal has been very controversial both in Iceland and with medical and privacy experts around the world. As of May 2000, over 18,000 people have opted out of the database. The Icelandic Medical Association is opposing the effort and many doctors are refusing to hand over their patients' records without consent. The World Medical Association in April 1999 supported the Icelandic Medical Association's opposition to the database.[544] Security experts have examined the database and have found that its encryption does not protect the identities of individuals.[545] At their annual meeting in Santiago de Compostela, Spain in September 1998, the other European Data Protection Commissioners recommended that the Icelandic authorities reconsider the project in light of the fundamental principles laid down in the European Convention on Human Rights, the Council of Europe Convention and Recommendation (97)5 on medical data, and the EC Directive.

Responding to the protests, the Government enacted the Act on Biobanks on May 13, 2000.[546] The act sets rules for the "collection, keeping, handling and utilization of biological samples from human beings" to ensure confidentiality and prohibit discrimination. The Act requires informed consent from the person for the collection of samples. However, under the Act "if samples have been collected for the purpose of clinical tests or treatment, the consent of the patient may be assumed for the storage of the biological sample in a biobank" if the doctor gives general information to the patient. The Data Protection Authority is to set the procedures on the linking of the sample with the patient's identification.

Under the Law on Criminal Procedure, wiretapping, tape recording or photographing without consent requires a court order and must be limited to a short period of time. After the recording is complete, the target must be informed and the recordings must be destroyed after they are no longer needed.[547] There were 42 wiretaps authorized between 1992 and February 1996.[548] Complaints against the orders can be submitted to the Supreme Court. Chapter XXV of the

---

[544] World Medical Association Opposes Icelandic Gene Database, EBMJ, 24 April 1999.

[545] Dr. Ross Anderson, Icelandic Database is Insecure, EBMJ, 18 May 1999.

[546] Act on Biobanks no. 110/2000, May 13, 2000.
<http://brunnur.stjr.is/interpro/tolvunefnd/tolvunefnd.nsf/pages/95EAE39BAC9DFA25002569050057034C>.

[547] Articles 86-87, Law on Criminal Procedure

[548] <http://www.icenews.is/daily/1996/09feb96.html>.

Penal Code also penalizes violations of privacy such as violating the secrecy of letters and revealing secrets to the public.

The Freedom of Information Act of 1996 (Upplysingalög) governs the release of records.[549] Under the Act, individuals (including non-residents) and legal entities have a legal right to documents without having to show a reason for the document. There are exceptions for national security, commercial and personal information. Copyrighted material can be provided to requestors but it is then their responsibility if they republish the materials in a manner inconsistent with the copyright. Denials can be appealed to the Information Committee.

Iceland is a member of the Council of Europe and has signed and ratified the Convention for the Protection of Individuals with Regard to Automatic Processing of Personal Data (ETS No. 108).[550] It has signed and ratified the European Convention for the Protection of Human Rights and Fundamental Freedoms.[551] It is a member of the Organization for Economic Cooperation and Development and has adopted the OECD Guidelines on the Protection of Privacy and Transborder Flows of Personal Data. Iceland is not an EU member state but has been granted associate status.

Republic of India

The Constitution of 1950 does not expressly recognize the right to privacy.[552] However, the Supreme Court first recognized in 1964 that there is a right of privacy implicit in the Constitution under Article 21 of the Constitution, which states, "No person shall be deprived of his life or personal liberty except according to procedure established by law."[553]

There is no general data protection law in India. The National Task Force on IT and Software Development, established by the Prime Minster's Office in May 1998, submitted an "IT Action Plan" to Prime Minister Vajpayee in July 1998 calling for the creation of a "National Policy on Information Security, Privacy and Data Protection Act for handling of computerized data." It examined the UK

---

[549] Act no. 50/1996, <http://www.rz.uni-frankfurt.de/~sobotta/Enskthyd.doc>.

[550] Signed 27/09/82, Enacted 25/03/91, Entered into Force 01/07/91, <http://conventions.coe.int/>.

[551] Signed 04/11/50, Enacted 29/06/53, Entered into Force 03/09/53, <http://conventions.coe.int/>.

[552] Constitution of India, November 1949. <http://www.commercenetindia.com/constitution/>.

[553] Kharak Singh vs State of UP, 1 SCR 332 (1964); See Mr. R.C. Jain, National Human Rights Commission, India, Indian Supreme Court on Right to Privacy, July 1997.

Data Protection Act as a model and recommended a number of cyber laws including ones on privacy and encryption.[554] The Act was expected to be drafted by the end of 1998 but has not been introduced.[555]

In May of 2000, the government passed the Information Technology Act, a set of laws intended to provide a comprehensive regulatory environment for electronic commerce. [556] Chapter III of the bill gives electronic records and digital signatures legal recognition, and Chapter X creates a Cyber Appellate Tribunal to oversee adjudication of cybercrimes such as damage to computer systems (Section 43) and breach of confidentiality (Section 72). After strong criticism, sections requiring cybercafes to record detailed information about users were dropped. The legislation gives broad discretion to government law enforcers through a number of provisions – Section 69 allows for interception of any computer resource and requires that users disclose encryption keys or face a jail sentence up to seven years. Section 80 allows deputy superintendents of police to conduct searches and seize suspects without a warrant; Section 44 imposes stiff penalties on anyone who fails to provide requested information to authorities; and Section 67 imposes strict penalties for involvement in the publishing of materials deemed obscene in electronic form.

Wiretapping is regulated under the Indian Telegraph Act of 1885. An order for a tap can be issued only by the Union home secretary or his counterparts in the states. A copy of the order must be sent to a review committee established by the high court. Tapped phone calls are not accepted as primary evidence in India's courts. There have been numerous phone tap scandals in India, resulting in a 1996 decision by the Supreme Court which required the government to promulgate rules regulating taps. The Court ruled that wiretaps are a "serious invasion of an individual's privacy."[557] However, illegal wiretapping by government agencies appears to be continuing. According to prominent Non-Government Organizations, the mail of many NGOs in Delhi and in strife-torn areas continues to be subjected to interception and censorship.[558] There was considerable discussion in 1998 about a rumored new government proposal on

---

[554] National Task Force on IT & SD, Basic Background Report, 9th June 1998. <http://it-taskforce.nic.in/it-taskforce/bg.htm>.

[555] "India: Taskforce suggests slew of measures," The Hindu, July 7, 1998.

[556] Information Technology Act 2000, No. 21 of 2000. <http://www.mit.gov.in/it-bill.htm>.

[557] Peoples Union for Civil Liberties (PUCL) vs. The Union of India & Another, 18 December 1996, on Writ Petition (C) No. 256 of 1991, <http://www.wired.com/news/story/1128.html>.

[558] South Asia Human Rights Documentation Centre, Alternate Report and Commentary to the United Nations Human Rights Committee on India's Third Periodic Report under Article 40 of the International Covenant on Civil and Political Rights, July 1997. <http://www.hri.ca/partners/sahrdc/alternate/fulltext.shtml>.

Internet surveillance. The plan would have required Internet service providers to connect their routers to state security agencies such as the Intelligence Bureau and the Research and Analysis Wing so their traffic could be monitored.[559]

ISPs are barred from violating the privacy rights of their subscribers by virtue of the license to operate they are granted by the Department of Telecommunications.[560]

There is also a right of privacy guaranteed by Indian laws. Unlawful attacks on the honor and reputation of a person can invite an action in tort and/or criminal law.[561] The Public Financial Institutions Act of 1993 codifies India's tradition of maintaining confidentiality in bank transactions.

The Supreme Court ruled in 1982 that access to government information was an essential part of the fundamental right to freedom of speech and expression[562] A draft Freedom of Information Act was introduced into the Parliament in July 2000.[563] The bill would provide a general right to access information and create a National Council for Freedom of Information and State Councils. It contains seven broad categories of exemptions. The draft was heavily criticized by campaigners who said that the bill provided only limited access to government records.[564] The National Centre for Advocacy Studies said, "Many of the aspects towards information availability have been left completely in the hands of bureaucrats, which defeats the very purpose of the bill." In 1997, the state of Tamil Nadu adopted the Act for Right to Information and the states of Gujarat and Rajasthan have administratively provided access to records. The state of Madhya Pradesh enacted a Right to Information Bill in March 1998

---

[559] "New Law to let Govt Intercept Net Mail," Internet Edition of Indian Express, December 14, 1998.

[560] Orijit Das, "Networking Web Caching: Detouring the Access," Computers Today, June 15, 2000.

[561] United Nations, Human Rights Committee, Consideration of Reports Submitted by States Parties Under Article 40 of the Covenant, Third periodic reports of States parties due in 1992 Addendum -India /1, 17 June 1996.

[562] S.P. Gupta vs. Union of India (AIR 1982 SC 149); See Government of India, Report of the Working Group on Right to Information and Promotion of Open and Transparent Government, May 1997.

[563] Freedom on Information Bill, 2000. <http://www.humanrightsinitiative.org/RTI/foibill1.htm>.

[564] "Open-government bill flawed, say activists," South China Morning Post, January 11, 2000. "NGOs oppose information bill," The Times of India, March 7, 2000.

Ireland

Although there is not an express reference to a right to privacy in the Irish Constitution, the Supreme Court has ruled an individual may invoke the personal rights provision in Article 40.3.1 to establish an implied right to privacy. This article provides that "The State guarantees in its laws to respect, and, as far as practicable, by its laws to defend and vindicate the personal rights of the citizens." It was first used to establish an implied constitutional right in the case of *McGee v. Attorney General*,[565] which recognized. the right to marital privacy. This case has been followed by others such as *Norris v. Attorney General*[566] and *Kennedy and Arnold v. Ireland.*[567] In the latter case the Supreme Court ruled that the illegal wiretapping of two journalists was a violation of the constitution, stating:

> *The right to privacy is one of the fundamental personal rights of the citizen which flow from the Christian and democratic nature of the State... The nature of the right to privacy is such that it must ensure the dignity and freedom of the individual in a democratic society. This can not be insured if his private communications, whether written or telephonic, are deliberately and unjustifiably interfered with.*[568]

Ireland has also signed and ratified the European Convention for the Protection of Human Rights and Fundamental Freedoms.[569] Unlike every other European signatory country, Ireland has not incorporated this Convention into national law. However, there have been announcements by the Government that the Convention will soon be written into Irish law as part of the Anglo-Irish peace talks. This will, for the first time, allow the provisions of the Convention (including the right to privacy) and the case law of the European Court of Human Rights to be relied on in Irish courts.

In 1988, the Data Protection Act was passed in order to implement the 1981 Council of Europe Convention for the Protection of Individuals with Regard to Automatic Processing of Personal Data. The Act regulates the collection,

---

[565] 1974 IR 284.

[566] 1984 I.R. 36.

[567] 1987 I.R. 587.

[568] Constitution of Ireland, <http://www.maths.tcd.ie/pub/Constitution/index.html>.

[569] Signed 04/11/50, Enacted 25/02/53, Entered into Force 03/09/53, <http://conventions.coe.int/>.

---

processing, keeping, use and disclosure of personal information processed by both the private and public sectors, but it only covers information which is automatically processed. Individuals have a right to access and correct inaccurate information. Information can only be used for specified and lawful purposes and cannot be improperly used or disclosed. Additional protections can be ordered for sensitive data. Criminal penalties can be imposed for violations. There are broad exemptions for national security, tax, and criminal purposes. Misuse of data is also criminalized by the Criminal Damage Act 1991.

As a member of the EU, Ireland is obliged to amend this Act and extend its scope in order to implement the European Data Protection Directive. Under the terms of the Directive, Ireland should have completed this by October 1, 1998. A consultation paper was released by the Department of Justice in November 1997.[570] However, as of July 2000, draft legislation has not been published. According to the Department of Justice, Equality and Law Reform a draft Data Protection Bill is now in the final stages of its preparation and should be introduced in the fall of 2000.[571] In January 2000, the European Commission initiated a case before the European Court of Justice against Ireland and four other countries for failure to implement the Data Directive on time.[572]

The 1988 Act established the office of the Data Protection Commissioner to oversee enforcement of its principles. The Commissioner can investigate complaints, prosecute offenders, sponsor codes of practice, and supervise the registration process. The Commission generally deals with about 80 to 100 formal complaints each year, together with approximately 1,500 telephone-based queries from the public. In his Annual Reports, the Commissioner has consistently expressed the need for additional resources and staff in order to continue to "provide any reasonable level of service to the public, whether they be data controllers or individual data subjects."[573]

According to a recent survey, conducted by Rits IT Consultants, of the top 500 Irish companies, only 29 per cent undertake an audit on a regular basis to ensure compliance with the Data Protection Act.[574] In addition, an informal Irish Times

---

[570] Department of Justice, Consultation Paper on Transposition into Irish Law, November 1997.
<http://www.irlgov.ie:80/justice/publications/Law/consult.PDF>.

[571] See Dail Debates 20 April 2000. <http://www.irlgov.ie:80/debates-00/20april/sect5.htm>.

[572] European Commission, 'Data protection: Commission takes five Member States to court', 11 January 2000.
<http://europa.eu.int/comm/internal_market/en/media/dataprot/news/2k-10.htm>.

[573] Irish Data Protection Commissioner, Annual Report, 1998, p16

[574] Rits, 'Information Security Survey 2000', April 17 2000. <http://www.rits.ie/survey.htm>.

---

survey of the top Irish websites, including Government institutions and leading private companies, found that these sites routinely breach the terms of the Data Protection Act and the principles laid down in the EU Data Protection Directive. Of the 100 sites studied, it was found that almost none post even the most basic privacy policy explaining to the public what is done with personal information gathered on the site.[575]

In an effort to combat fraud and abuse of public services, the Government passed the Social Welfare Act of 1998 creating a "Public Service Card" which is to carry a unique personal public service number. What was once the "Revenue and Social Insurance" (RSI) number, and used for social welfare and tax purposes only, will now be used as a unique personal identifier in all communications between an individual and specified State Agencies. The Act allows for the exchange of personal data between these bodies in certain circumstances, and its provisions are expressly exempt from the Data Protection Act. The only privacy safeguard laid down by the Act is a provision making it an offence for anyone other than a State agency to attempt to obtain an individual's PPSN. The Data Protection Commissioner criticized this scheme while it was being debated, stating that "the proposed sharing of personal data, obtained and kept by legally separate entities, for such diverse purposes is fundamentally incompatible with … the basic tenets of data protection law."[576] His views were ignored, and the scheme, known as the REACH program, is expected to be fully implemented by 2002.[577]

Proposals by the Minister of Justice to introduce new law enforcement powers have gained recent support in Ireland. A bill to restrict the right to silence, lengthen detention terms and to facilitate the police obtaining search warrants and DNA samples won the approval of the Government in February 2000.[578] The Irish Council for Civil Liberties has criticized all such proposals, claiming them to be contrary to the European Convention on Human Rights.[579] A draft Bill has not yet been introduced in the Dail.

---

[575] "Monitoring your Electronic Footprints Irish Websites are Blatantly Ignoring EU Legislation on Data Protection," Irish Times, October 22, 1999.

[576] Irish Data Protection Commissioner, Annual Report, 1996, p35. See also 'Remarks by the Data Protection Commissioner on the bill to the Dail Select Committee on Social, Community and Family Affairs', 4 March 1998.

[577] "ID card planned for each citizen by 2002," the Irish Times, March 23, 2000.

[578] "Bill Would Extend Curb on Suspect's Right to Silence," the Irish Times, February 18, 2000.

[579] Press Release of the ICCL, September 22, 1998. See also the Irish Times, February 18, 2000.

Wiretapping and electronic surveillance is regulated under the Interception of Postal Packets and Telecommunications Messages (Regulation) Act. The Act followed a 1987 decision of the Supreme Court ruling that wiretaps of journalists violated the constitution (see above). In April 1998, the Gardai investigated allegations that several journalists who had uncovered a scandal at the National Irish Bank had their cellular phone conversations intercepted.[580] In its June 1998 Report on "Privacy, Surveillance and the Interception of Communications," the Law Reform Commission recommended legislation to make illegal the invasion of a person's privacy through secret filming, taping and eavesdropping and the publication of information received from such surveillance. News stories this year carried reports of Ireland joining the controversial surveillance system known as ECHELON.[581] The issue of employee monitoring is also causing growing concern in Ireland and the Manufacturing, Science and Finance Union (MSF) recently called for national and EU legislation to limit the use of electronic surveillance in the workplace.[582]

There were protests in the Irish Parliament in June 1999 after reports that the British government tapped all telephone calls, email, telexes and faxes between Ireland and Britain from a 13-story tower in Capenhurst, Cheshire, from 1989 until 1999. The Irish government asked its ambassador in the UK to demand more information on the activity. [583] In January 2000, the Irish Minister for Foreign Affairs held meetings with the British Foreign Secretary to investigate these allegations.[584] Three English and Irish civil liberties groups, namely the Irish Council for Civil Liberties, Liberty, and British Irish Rights Watch, have brought a case against the UK Government before the European Court of Human Rights alleging breaches of Articles 8 and 13 of the European Convention on Human Rights.[585] The UK Government has neither confirmed nor denied the allegations.

Other incidental causes of action open to those who suffer privacy intrusions in Ireland include claims under the laws of Trespass, Nuisance, Defamation, Negligence and Confidence.

---

[580] "Gardai to Investigate Surveillance Allegations," The Irish Times, April 18, 1998.

[581] The Phoenix, May 5, 200, Vol 18 No.9, p20.

[582] "Law to Limit Monitoring of Workers Urged," the Irish Times, March 7, 2000.

[583] The Independent, July 17, 1999.

[584] "Andrews to Press on Reports of Interceptions," The Irish Times, January 24, 2000.

[585] "UK Military Phone Taps Breached Civil Rights," Irish Times, June 1, 2000. See also, "Government Tapping of Phone Calls between UK and Ireland Challenged," The Guardian, May 31, 2000.

The Freedom of Information Act was approved in 1997 and went into effect in April 1998.[586] The act creates a presumption that the public can access documents created by government agencies and requires that government agencies make internal information on their rules and activities available. The Office of the Information Commissioner enforces the act. According to the Information Commissioner's 1999 Annual Report, over 11,000 FOI requests in total were made to public bodies in 1999. The Commissioner accepted 443 cases for review, of which 141 were completed.[587]

Ireland is a member of the Organization for Economic Cooperation and Development and has adopted the OECD Guidelines on the Protection of Privacy and Transborder Flows of Personal Data. It is also a member of the Council of Europe and as mentioned above it introduced the 1988 Data Protection Act to give effect to Convention for the Protection of Individuals with Regard to Automatic Processing of Personal Data (ETS No. 108). [588]

State of Israel

Section 7 of The Basic Law: Human Dignity and Freedom (1992) states, "(a) All persons have the right to privacy and to intimacy. (b) There shall be no entry into the private premises of a person who has not consented thereto. (c) No search shall be conducted on the private premises or body of a person, nor in the body or belongings of a person. (d) There shall be no violation of the secrecy of the spoken utterances, writings or records of a person."[589] According to Supreme Court Justice Mishael Cheshin, this elevated the right of privacy to the level of a basic right.[590]

The Protection of Privacy Law regulates the processing of personal information in computer data banks.[591] The law set out 11 types of activities that violated the law and could subject violators to criminal or civil penalties. Holders of data banks of over 10,000 names must register. Information in the database is limited

---

[586] Freedom of Information Act, 1997. <http://www.irlgov.ie/finance/free1.htm>.

[587] Irish Information Commissioner, Annual Report, 1999. <http://www.irlgov.ie/oic/report99/pub.htm>.

[588] Signed 18/12/86. Enacted 25/05/90. Entered into Force 01/08/90, <http://conventions.coe.int/>.

[589] The Basic Law: Human Dignity and Freedom (5752 - 1992). Passed by the Knesset on the 21st Adar, 5754 (9th March, 1994). <http://www.israel-mfa.gov.il/gov/laws/dignity.html>.

[590] Israeli Business Law An Essential Guide @ 30.01.

[591] The Protection of Privacy Law 5741-1981, 1011 Laws of the State of Israel 128. Amended by the Protection of Privacy Law (Amendment) 5745-1985.

---

to purposes for which it was intended and must provide access to the subject. There are broad exceptions for police and security services. It also sets up basic privacy laws relating to surveillance, publication of photographs and other traditional privacy features. The law was amended in 1996 to broaden the databases covered such as those used for direct marketing purposes, and also increased penalties.[592]

The Act is enforced by the Registrar of Databases within the Ministry of Justice. The Registrar maintains the register of databases and can deny registration if he believes that a database is used for illegal activities. The registrar can also investigate and enforce the Act.[593] As of mid-1998, 5,200 databases were registered.[594] A public council for the protection of privacy has also been set up to advise the Justice Minister on legislative matters related to the Protection of Privacy Law and its subsidiary regulations and orders. The council sets guidelines for the protection of computerized databases, and guides the Registrar of Databases in his work. Under the 1996 amendments, the Registrar is to be given more independence.

Interception of communications is governed by the Secret Monitoring Law of 1979, which was amended in 1995 to tighten procedures and to cover new technologies such as cellular phones and email. It also increased penalties for illegal taps and allowed interception of privileged communications such as those with a lawyer or doctor.[595] The police must receive permission from the President of the District Court in order to intercept any form of wire or electronic communications or plant microphones for a period up to three months, which can be renewed. According to the Israeli government, the number of wiretap orders, "has averaged roughly 1,000 to 1,100 annually over the last several years. Roughly half of these wiretap permits are given in connection with drug-related offences."[596] Intelligence agencies may wiretap people suspected of endangering national security, after receiving written permission from the Prime Minister or Defense Minister. The agencies must present an annual report to the Knesset. The Chief Military Censor may also intercept international conversations to or from

---

[592] Law of April 11, 1996.

[593] See <http://israel.org/gov/justice.html>.

[594] United Nations Human Rights Committee, Initial report of States parties due in 1993 : Israel. 09/04/98. CCPR/C/81/Add.13. (State Party Report), 9 April 1998.

[595] The Secret Monitoring Law, 5739-1979, Laws of the State of Israel, vol. 33, pp. 141-146.

[596] United Nations Human Rights Committee, Initial report of States parties due in 1993 : Israel. 09/04/98. CCPR/C/81/Add.13. (State Party Report), 9 April 1998.

Israel for purposes of censorship.[597] The State's Attorney's Office in May 2000 submitted a request to the Tel Aviv district court to force ISPs to hand over electronic mail.[598]

A 1991 report by the State Comptroller found that the police were abusing the procedures and that led to the 1995 amendments. In 1996 a Defense Forces employee was tried for misusing the phone records of a journalist.[599] Several people, including Ma'ariv publisher Opher Nimrodi, were convicted in 1998 of ordering wiretaps on business people and media personalities, including Science Minister Silvan Shalom in 1994.[600] In November 1998, wiretaps were discovered on the phone of Labor and Social Affairs Minister Eli Yishai. It was suspected that he was wiretapped by a rival political faction inside the Shas party.

Unauthorized access to computers is punished by the 1995 Computer Law.[601] The Postal and Telegraph Censor, which operates as a civil department within the Ministry of Defense, has the power to open any postal letter or package to prevent harm to state security or public order.[602]

The 1996 Patient Rights Law imposes a duty of confidentiality on all medical personnel.[603] A Genetic Privacy Bill was approved for a first reading by the Knesset's subcommittee on science in March 1998 and is expected to be approved shortly. The bill will limit disclosure of private DNA information.[604] In August 1999, the Cabinet called on the Ministry of Justice to develop legislation creating a national DNA database for police investigations.[605] The Health Ministry issued regulations on the use of video surveillance in hospitals in September 1998 after it was disclosed that cameras had been moved to watch patients undressing.[606]

---

[597] "Shas disputes linking wiretap to Yishai-Deri rivalry," The Jerusalem Post, November 27, 1998.

[598] "State Attorney's Office: We'll Request Permission to Tap ISP's E-mail," Israel's Business Arena, May 7, 2000.

[599] "IDF officer involved in phone record scandal accuses others of involvement," The Jerusalem Post, July 11, 1996.

[600] "Media wiretapper found guilty," The Jerusalem Post, September 4, 1998.

[601] The Computer Law (5755-1995), 1534 Laws of the State of Israel 366, See Miguel Deutch, Computer Legislation: Israel's New Codified Approach, 14 J. Marshall J. Computer & Info. L. 461 (Spring 1996).

[602] Regulation 89 of the Mandatory Defence (Emergency) Regulations, 1945.

[603] Patient's Rights Law, 5756-1996.

[604] "Ha'aretz, Knesset panel debates 'genetic privacy' bill," March 15, 1998.

[605] "Filing our most secret codes," The Jerusalem Post, September 8, 1999.

[606] "Embarrassed by Ichilov disclosure: Ministry issues regulations for hospital cameras," The Jerusalem Post, September 10, 1998.

Criminal records are governed by the Criminal Register and Rehabilitation Law that allows 30 government agencies to access the records.[607]

Finance Minister Yaakov Ne'eman issued an authorization in March 1998 giving the director of the Bureau for Counterterrorism full access to the databases of all Israeli taxation authorities, including the Income Tax Authorities and Customs. It gives the Bureau access to the financial records of any citizen in Israel, including the status of their bank account "for urgent cases of preventing terrorist acts."[608]

The Supreme Court ruled in the *Shalit* case that there was a fundamental right for citizens to obtain information from the government.[609] The Freedom of Information Law was approved unanimously by the Knesset in May 1998. It provides for broad access to records held by government offices, local councils and government-owned corporations. Requests for information must be processed within 30 days. A court can review decisions to withheld information. A Jerusalem Post survey in June 1999 found that many agencies had not began to prepare for the law.[610] According to the ACLI, there have now been several court decisions on the new law, which is being used "effectively."

Italian Republic

The 1948 Constitution has several limited provisions relating to privacy. Article 14 states, "(1) Personal domicile is inviolable. (2) Inspection and search may not be carried out save in cases and in the manner laid down by law in conformity with guarantees prescribed for safeguarding personal freedom. (3) Special laws regulate verifications and inspections for reasons of public health and safety, or for economic and fiscal purposes." Article 15 states, "(1) The liberty and secrecy of correspondence and of every form of communication are inviolable. (2) Limitations upon them may only be enforced by decision, for which motives must be given, of the judicial authorities with the guarantees laid down by law."[611]

---

[607] Criminal Register and Rehabilitation Law, 5741-1981.

[608] "Anti-terror chief to see all tax files," Ha'aritz, May 29, 1998.

[609] H.C. 1601-4/90 Shalit et al. v. Peres el at., 44(3) P.D. 353. See Debbie L. Rabina, Access to government information in Israel: stages in the continuing development of a national information policy. <http://www.ifla.org/IV/ifla66/papers/018-160e.htm>.

[610] "Ministries not ready for info law," The Jerusalem Post, June 25, 1999.

[611] Constitution of the Republic of Italy, Adopted 22 Dec 1947. <http://www.uni-wuerzburg.de/law/it00t___.html>.

The Italian Data Protection Act was enacted in 1996 after twenty years of debate.[612] The Act is intended to fully implement the EU Data Protection Directive. It covers both electronic and manual files, for both government agencies and the private sector. There have also been decrees approved relating to processing of personal information for journalistic purposes,[613] for scientific or research purposes,[614] health,[615] and processing by public bodies.[616]

The Act is enforced by the Supervisory Authority ("Garante") for Personal Data Protection.[617] The Garante maintains a register of databases, conducts audits and enforces the laws. It can also audit databanks not under its jurisdiction, such as those relating to intelligence activities. The Decree on the internal organization of the Authority was published in the Official Journal on February 1, 1999. The decree establishes the procedures for keeping the Register of Data Processes, access to the register by citizens, investigations, registrations and inspections.[618] The Garante ruled in October 1998 that phone companies need not mask the phone numbers on bills and that phone companies should allow for anonymous phone cards to protect privacy.[619] The Guarante has also held investigations into the Echelon surveillance system.

A Milan court ruled in September 1999 that the Data Protection Act only is concerned with the controls on the processing of personal information and is not

---

[612] Legge `31 dicembre 1996 n. 675, Tutela delle persone e di altri soggetti rispetto al trattamento dei dati personali. Amended by Legislative Decree No. 123 of 09.05.97 and 255 of 28.07.97.
<http://elj.strath.ac.uk/jilt/dp/material/l675-eng.htm (Unofficial translation). Legge 31 Dicembre 1996, N. 676, Delega al Governo in materia di tutela delle persone e di altri soggetti rispetto al trattamento dei dati personali. <http://www.privacy.it/legge96676.html>. See <http://www.privacy.it/normativ.html>. for list of decrees.

[613] Decreto legislativo 13 maggio 1998, n. 171. Disposizioni in materia di tutela della vita privata nel settore delle telecomunicazioni, in attuazione della direttiva 97/66/CE del Parlamento europeo e del Consiglio, ed in tema di attività giornalistica. <http://www.privacy.it/dl1998171.html>.

[614] Decreto legislativo del 30/7/1999 n. 281 "Disposizioni in materia di trattamento dei dati personali per finalità storiche, statistiche e di ricerca scientifica," <http://www.privacy.it/dl1999281.html>.

[615] Decreto legislativo del 30/7/1999 n. 282 "Disposizioni per garantire la riservatezza dei dati personali in ambito sanitario" <http://www.privacy.it/dl1999282.html>.

[616] Decreto legislativo 11/5/1999, n.135 Disposizioni integrative della legge 31/12/1996, n. 675, sul trattamento di dati sensibili da parte dei soggetti pubblici. <http://www.privacy.it/dl1999135.html>.

[617] Home Page: http://www.dataprotection.org/

[618] Decreto del presidente della repubblica, 31 marzo 1998, n.501 Regolamento recante norme per l'organizzazione ed il funzionamento dell'Ufficio del Garante per la protezione dei dati personali, a norma dell'articolo 33, comma 3, della legge 31 dicembre 1996, n. 675. (GU n. 25 del 1-2-1999)
<http://193.207.119.193/MV/gazzette_ufficiali/25/2.htm>.

[619] <http://www.privacy.it/garantes981006.html>.

---

a general privacy act. The court reversed the Garante ruling against a newpaper for publishing incorrect details about a countess.[620]

Wiretapping is regulated by articles 266-271 of the penal procedure code and may only be authorized in the case of legal proceedings.[621] Government interceptions of telephone and all other forms of communications, must be approved by a court order. They are granted for crimes punishable by life imprisonment or imprisonment for more than five years; for crimes against the administration punishable by no less than five year imprisonment; for crimes involving the trafficking of drugs, arms, explosives, and contraband; and for insults, threats, abusive activity and harassment carried out over the telephone. The law on computer crime includes penalties on interception of electronic communications.[622] Interception orders are granted for 15 days at a time and can be extended for the same length of time by a judge. The judge also monitors procedures for storing recordings and transcripts. Any recordings or transcripts which are not used must be destroyed. The conversations of religious ministers, lawyers, doctors or others subject to professional confidentiality rules can not be intercepted. There are more lenient procedures for anti-Mafia cases. Some 44,000 orders were approved in 1996, up from 15,000 in 1992.[623] In March 1998, the Parliament issued a legislative decree adopting the provisions of the E.U. Telecommunications Privacy Directive.[624]

There are also sectoral laws relating to workplace surveillance,[625] statistical information, and electronic files and digital signatures.[626] The Workers Charter prohibits employers from investigating the political, religious or trade union opinions of their workers, and in general on any matter which is irrelevant for the purposes of assessing their professional skills and aptitudes.[627] The 1993

---

[620] See http://www.andreamonti.net/jus/demi990927.htm

[621] Intercettazioni di conversoni o comunicazioni, Art 266-271 du code di procedura penale issus de la loi du 22 Septembre 1988.

[622] Legge 23 dicembre 1993 n 547.

[623] French Commission National de Control des Interceptions de securite, Annual Report 1996.

[624] Decreto legislativo 13 maggio 1998, n. 171. Disposizioni in materia di tutela della vita privata nel settore delle telecomunicazioni, in attuazione della direttiva 97/66/CE del Parlamento europeo e del Consiglio, ed in tema di attività giornalistica <http://www.privacy.it/dl98171.html>.

[625] Legge 29 marzo 1983, n. 93 - Legge quadro sul pubblico, ITNTDI, p. 296, § 1114.

[626] Presidential Decree No. 513 of 10 November 1997, "Regulations establishing criteria and means for implementing Section 15(2) of Law No. 59 of 15 March 1997 concerning the creation, storage and transmission of documents by means of computer-based or telematic systems", <http://www.aipa.it/english/law2/pdecree51397.asp>.

[627] Section 8 of Law No. 300 of 20 May 1970.

---

computer crime law prohibits unlawfully using a computer system and intercepting computer communications.[628]

Italy is a member of the Council of Europe and has signed and ratified the Convention for the Protection of Individuals with Regard to Automatic Processing of Personal Data (ETS No. 108).[629] It has signed and ratified the European Convention for the Protection of Human Rights and Fundamental Freedoms.[630] It is a member of the Organization for Economic Cooperation and Development and has adopted the OECD Guidelines on the Protection of Privacy and Transborder Flows of Personal Data.

Japan

Article 21 of the 1946 Constitution states, "Freedom of assembly and association as well as speech, press and all other forms of expression are guaranteed. 2) No censorship shall be maintained, nor shall the secrecy of any means of communication be violated." Article 35 states, "The right of all persons to be secure in their homes, papers and effects against entries, searches and seizures shall not be impaired except upon warrant issued for adequate cause and particularly describing the place to be searched and things to be seized . . . 2) Each search or seizure shall be made upon separate warrant issued by a competent judicial officer."[631]

The 1988 Act for the Protection of Computer Processed Personal Data Held by Administrative Organs governs the use of personal information in computerized files held by government agencies.[632] It is based on the OECD guidelines and imposes duties of security, access, and correction. Agencies must limit their collection to relevant information and publish a public notice listing their files systems. Information collected for one purpose cannot be used for a purpose "other than the file holding purpose."

---

[628] Law No. 547 of 23 December 1993

[629] Signed 02/02/83, Ratified 29/03/97, Entered into force 01/07/97. <http://conventions.coe.int/>.

[630] Signed 04/11/50, Ratified 26/10/55, Entered into force 26/10/55. <http://conventions.coe.int/>.

[631] Constitution of Japan, November 3, 1946. <http://www.ntt.co.jp/japan/constitution/english-Constitution.html>.

[632] The Act for the Protection of Computer Processed Personal Data held by Administrative Organs, Act No. 95, 16 December 1988 (Kampoo, 16 December 1988).

The Act is overseen by the Government Information Systems Planning Division of the Management and Coordination Agency. The agency reports that there have been 1,700 notices filed. The agency does not have any powers to investigate complaints.

The Prefecture of Kanagawa also has legislation that protects privacy in both the public and private sectors.[633]

The Japanese government has followed a policy of self-regulation for the private sector, especially relating to electronic commerce. In June 1998, former Prime Minister Ryutaro Hashimoto announced that he had signed an agreement with U.S. President Clinton for self-regulation for privacy measures on the Internet except for certain sensitive data. "If data in a certain industry is highly confidential, legal methods can be considered for that industry."[634] On March 4, 1997, the Ministry of International Trade and Industry (MITI) issued Guidelines Concerning the Protection of Computer Processed Personal Data in the Private Sector.[635]

Several committees have been set up to develop legislation for the private sector. In July 1999, government set up the Working Party on Personal Data Protection" under the Advanced Information and Telecommunications Society Promotion Headquarters. In January 2000, the government convened the Expert Committee for Drafting Law of Personal Data Protection under the Advanced Information and Telecommunications Society Promotion Headquarters to develop a comprehensive basic law to protect personal information on the basis of the Interim Report of the Working Party. The panel released an interim report in June 2000 urging the adoption of legal protections for the processing of personal information by businesses and the creation of a government office to handle complaints and investigations. It also recommended changes to laws on information held by government agencies. The panel is scheduled to release its final report in September 2000 and the government will introduce a bill into Parliament in 2001.[636]

---

[633] Kanagawa Prefecture Ordinance on the Protection of Personal Data, Ordinance No. 6, dated 30 March 1990.

[634] U.S. Japan Joint Statement on Electronic Commerce, May 15, 1998. <http://www.ecommerce.gov/usjapan.htm>.

[635] MITI, Guidelines Concerning the Protection of Computer Processed Personal Data in the Private Sector, March 4, 1997. <http://www.jipdec.or.jp/security/privacy/guideline-e.html >. For a detailed analysis of the guidelinest, see MITI Handbook Concerning Protection of Personal Data, February 1998. <http://www.jipdec.or.jp/security/privacy/handbook-e.html>.

[636] Advisory Panel to Japanese Government Drafts Law to Protect Personal Information, BNA Daily Report for Executives, June 8, 2000.

The Ministry of Finance and Ministry of International Trade and Industry announced plans to introduce legislation to protect individuals credit data in 2000 after a task force issues proposals.[637] Japan's Ministry of Posts and Telecommunications (MPT) announced plans in June 1998 to study privacy in telecommunications services, establishing a study group to look into the matter.[638] An October 1999 survey by the MPT found that 92 percent of respondents believed that their personal information had been disclosed without their consent. Eighty-three percent believed that organizations and individuals who hold personal information should be regulated.[639]

In February 1998, MITI established a Supervisory Authority for the Protection of Personal Data to monitor a new system for the granting of "privacy marks" to businesses committing to the handling of the personal data in accordance with the MITI guidelines, and to promote awareness of privacy protection for consumers. The "privacy mark" system is administered by the Japan Information Processing Development Center (JIPDEC) – a joint public/private agency.[640] Companies that do not comply with the industry guidelines will be excluded from relevant industry bodies and not granted the privacy protection mark. It is assumed that they will then be penalized by market forces. However, in addition, the new Supervisory Authority will investigate violations and make suggestions as necessary to the relevant administrative authorities.[641] An analysis of the marks done for the European Union by four academic privacy experts found that there were serious shortcomings in the system.[642] In the first two years of the JIDPEC program, companies seeking certification were dominated by businesses that handle personal information like marriage bureaus; in total, the JIPDEC awarded about 140 licenses.[643] In May 2000, the JIPDEC agreed with BBBOnline, a division of the U.S.-based Better Business Bureau, to mutually recognize each other's privacy protection marks.

---

[637] "Japan Ministries To Compile Credit Data Protection Bill," Nikkei, July 4, 1999.

[638] Newsbytes, June 1, 1998.

[639] Ministry of Post and Telecommunications, More than 90% of Telecommunications Service Users Are Interested in Privacy Protection, 14 October 1999.
<http://www.mpt.go.jp/pressrelease/english/telecomm/news991115_5.html>.

[640] Home Page: http://www.jipdec.or.jp/security/privacy/index-e.html

[641] Nigel Waters, 'Reviewing the adequacy of privacy protection in the Asia Pacific Region, IIR Conference Information Privacy - Data Protection, 15 June 1998, Sydney; see also Ministry of International Trade and Industry (MITI) 'Japan's views on the protection of personal data' (April 1998).

[642] Raab, Bennett, Gellman & Waters, European Commission Tender No XV/97/18/D, Application of a Methodology Designed to Assess the Adequacy of the Level of Protection of Individuals with Regard to Processing Personal Data: Test of the Method on Several Categories of Transfer, September 1998.

[643] "Japan, U.S. bodies ink deal on data-privacy certification," The Yomiui Shimbun, May 19, 2000.

Wiretapping is considered a violation of the Constitution's right of privacy and has only been authorized only a few times. A controversial bill to authorize wiretapping for cases involving narcotics, gun offenses, gang-related murders and large-scale smuggling of foreigners was approved by the Diet in August 1999 following strong pressure by the United States government.[644] Under the new law, which went into effect in August 2000, the use of wiretaps is restricted to prosecutors and police officers at the rank of superintendent and above, and requires police officers to obtain warrants from district court judges in order to use wiretaps. The warrants are good for 10 days and can only be extended for a total of 30 days. Further, the presence of a third, independent party, for instance an employee of Nippon Telegraph and Telephone company, is required during monitoring. Finally, police and prosecutors must in principle notify individuals who have been monitored within 30 days after the investigation. Strict penalties are possible for those who abuse the wiretap policy.[645]

The wiretap law was opposed by the Federation of Bar Associations, journalists and trade unions.[646] Nobuto Hosaka, a Social Democratic Party lawmaker filed a suit in July 1999 alleging that the police had intercepted his phone calls after a transcript of a conversation he had with a TV reporter about the wiretap bill was delivered anonymously to two newspapers by someone claiming to have tapped the phone from the police facilities.[647] Over 180,000 people have signed a petition for the repeal of the wiretapping law. The signature-collecting Committee for the Repeal of the Wiretapping Law submitted the petition to the Diet on May 24, 2000.[648] In August, NTT asked that its employees not be required to be present when taps are installed, saying it would likely have a detrimental effect on company performance.[649]

Wiretapping is also prohibited under article 104 of the Telecommunications Business Law and article 14 of the Wire Telecommunications Law.[650]

---

[644] Reuters, June 1, 1999. Also see <http://www.jca.ax.apc.org/~toshi/cen/wiretap.intr.html>.

[645] "Diet passes wiretap, ID bills," Asia Intelligence Wire, August 13, 1999.

[646] "Diet eyes allowing police to bug phones," Mainichi Daily News June 16, 1998.

[647] "Lawmaker files complaint over alleged illegal wiretap," The Daily Yomiuri, July 8, 1999.

[648] See NaST, <http://www.jca.apc.org/privacy/>.

[649] "DoCoMo urges NPA not to seek tapping aid," Yomiuri Shimbun, August 16, 2000.

[650] Telecommunications Business Law, LAW No. 86 of 25 December 1984) As amended last by Law No. 97 of 20 June 1997 <http://www.mpt.go.jp/policyreports/english/laws/Tb_index.html>.

In June 1997, the Tokyo High Court upheld a lower court's finding that the Kanagawa Prefectural Police had illegally wiretapped the telephone at the home of a senior member of the Japanese Communist Party. The court awarded damages of four million yen.[651] A number of NTT employees have also been caught recently selling information about customers.[652] In March 2000, a district court sentenced a former assistant police inspector at the Nara Prefectural Police to two years in prison after finding him guilty of passing information on cellular phone users to a gang informant.[653] A number of companies that provide for pre-paid cellular phone service announced in May 2000 that they would start requiring users to provide identification before they could use the services to prevent crime. [654]

In the same anti-crime package of bills under which the wiretapping law was passed, the Diet also provisionally approved the Basic Resident Registers Law, granting Tokyo the authority to issue a 10-digit number to every Japanese citizen and resident alien, and requiring all citizens and resident aliens to provide basic information – name, date of birth, sex, and address – to the local police. Due to privacy concerns, the bill will be put into effect within three years of its passage on the condition that new privacy-protection legislation is enacted. [655]

The Ministry of Transportation announced in June 1999 a plan to issue "Smart Plates" license plates with embedded IC chips by 2001. The chips will contain driver and vehicle information and be used for road tolls and traffic control.[656] The National Police Agency has operated a comprehensive video surveillance system called the "N-system" with 400 locations on expressways and major highways throughout the country, which has been automatically recording the license plate number of every passing car for the last 11 years. Whenever a "wanted" car is detected, the system immediately issues a notice to police.[657] Eleven motorists filed a lawsuit challenging the system in 1997.

In March 2000, it was discovered that a research company had secretly conducted genetic tests on 1,000 blood samples obtained from people who had

---

[651] Police wiretapping, Mainichi Daily News, June 29, 1997.

[652] NTT Staffers Leaking Customer Information, Newsbytes, July 2, 1999.

[653] "Cop gets suspended jail term for violating people's privacy," Kyodo News International, Inc., March 13, 2000.

[654] Prepaid cell phone companies to require, Kyodo News Service, May 12, 2000

[655] "Diet passes wiretap, ID bills," Asia Intelligence Wire, August 13, 1999.

[656] "License Plates to Bear IC Chips with Driver, Auto Info," Comline, June 09, 1999.

[657] Christian Science Monitor, April 8, 1997.

donated blood to the Japanese Red Cross Society. The Health and Welfare Ministry launched an investigation in November 1999 into reports that a dealer was selling private information on people receiving medical treatment, including their clinical histories. Several months later, Tohoku University in Sendai and the National Cardiovascular Center in the Osaka Prefecture city of Suita also disclosed that they had studied the genes of blood donors without obtaining their consent. A poll conducted by the Mainichi newspaper suggests that this is standard practice, finding that 70 percent of medicine faculties in 64 universities around Japan are conducting gene tests.[658] Health and Welfare Minister Yuya Niwa said that the ministry is investigating the case and will consider setting up laws regulating such leakage of patients' medical data.

The Law Concerning Access to Information Held by Administrative Organs was approved by the Diet in May 1999 after 20 years of debate.[659] The law allows any individual or company to request government information in electronic or printed form. A nine-person committee in the Office of the Prime Minster will receive complaints about information which the government refuses to make public and will examine whether the decisions made by the ministries and agencies were appropriate. Government officials will still have broad discretion to refuse requests but requestors will be able to appeal decisions to withhold documents to one of eight different district courts. The law goes into effect in 2001. A survey by Kyodo News in May 1999 found that 31 city and prefectural governments are in the process of adopting legislation consistent with the new law. Sixteen of them are including a principle of "right to know."[660]

Japan is a member of the Organization for Economic Cooperation and Development and a signatory to the OECD Guidelines on Privacy and Transborder Dataflows.

Republic of Korea (South Korea)

The Constitution provides for protection of privacy and secrecy of communications. Article 16 states, "All citizens are free from intrusion into their place of residence. In case of search or seizure in a residence, a warrant issued by

---

658 Manabu Yoshikawa and Yasuyoshi Tanaka Mainichi Shimbun, "Ethicists OK gene-sample research," Mainichi Daily News, May 8, 2000.

659 The Law Concerning Access to Information Held by Administrative Organs.
<http://www.somucho.go.jp/gyoukan/kanri/translation.htm>.

660 Kyodo News, May 22, 1999.

a judge upon request of a prosecutor has to be presented." Article 17 states, "The privacy of no citizen may be infringed." Article 18 states, "The privacy of correspondence of no citizen shall be infringed."[661]

The Act on the Protection of Personal Information Managed by Public Agencies of 1994 sets rules for the management of computer-based personal information held by government agencies and is based on the OECD privacy guidelines.[662] Under the Act, government agencies must limit data collected, ensure their accuracy, keep a public register of files, ensure the security of the information, and limit its use to the purposes for which it was collected. The Act is enforced by the Minister of Government Administration.

Interest in promotion of electronic commerce has been a major impetus for recent developments. In May 1998 the Ministry of Commerce, Industry and Energy (MoCIE) proposed a set of guidelines for electronic commerce legislation, including protecting privacy in the digital trade environment.[663] The Basic Act on Electronic Commerce was approved in January 1999. Chapter III of the Act requires that "electronic traders shall not use, nor provide to any third party, the personal information collected through electronic commerce beyond the alleged purpose for collection thereof without prior consent of the person of such information or except as specifically provided in any other law." Individuals also have rights of access, correction and deletion and data holders have a duty of security.[664]

The Ministry of Information and Communication (MIC) set up a Cyber Privacy Center in April 2000.[665] The Ministry issued guidelines in May 2000 on privacy. The guidelines requires consent before collecting "sensitive information" such as political orientation, birthplace, and sexual orientation, and ISPs wishing to collect information about users under 14 must obtain parental consent. ISPs must display their privacy policies and establish security policies. The Ministry said it was planning to develop legislation in late 2000 that would incorporate the guidelines.[666] A study by the Korea Information Security Agency in November 1999 found that most sites were collecting information but were lacking adequate

---

[661] Constitution of the Republic of Korea, Adopted: 17 July 1948. <http://www.ccourt.go.kr/english/et.html>.

[662] Act of 7 January 1994.

[663] Nikkei BP AsiaBizTech - 29-Jun-98.

[664] Basic Law on Electronic Commerce, 1999. <http://www.mbc.com/ecommerce/legis/south_korea.html >.

[665] Homepage: http://www.cyberprivacy.or.kr/

[666] "Seoul issues guideline on privacy of information," Korea Herald, May 1, 2000.

privacy policies.[667] The existing national ID card number is widely used on the Internet by e-commerce sites and free web sites.[668]

The cabinet approved a bill in March 1999 creating a National Human Rights Commission which would, among its powers, investigate illegal wiretapping. The proposal was criticized by Amnesty International and local groups who held a week-long hunger strike to protest the bill. Amnesty said that the bill "seems designed to set up a commission which lacks independence and has weak investigative powers over a limited range of violations."[669] The bill has still not been approved by the Parliament because of the controversy.

Wiretapping is regulated by the Law on Protection of Communications Secrecy Act.[670] It requires a court order to place a tap. Intelligence agencies are required to obtain permission from the Chief Judge of the High Court or approval from the President for national security cases. Article 54 of the Telecommunication Business Act prohibits persons who are (or have been) engaged in telecommunication services from releasing private correspondence.[671] There were 2,103 cases of wiretapping in the first half of 1999, down from the 6,638 taps in 1998, of which 1,073 were "emergency taps" conducted without prior court permission; 6,002 taps in 1997; and 2,067 in 1996.[672] The police also issued 93,000 requests for information to telecommunications providers in the first half of 1999, up from 63,000 in the same period in 1998.[673]

Rep. Kim Hyong-o of the opposition Grand National Party (GNP) stated that he believed that over 10,000 taps were actually placed in 1998.[674] Under previous administrations, there were widespread surveillance and wiretapping abuses by intelligence and police officials. In October 1998, President Kim Dae-jung ordered a full-scale probe into illegal wiretapping. The government proposed amendments to the Telecommunications Law in November 1999 which would

---

[667] "Local Internet sites found lax about privacy," Korea Herald, February 22, 2000.

[668] "National ID number privacy," Korea Herald, July 12, 2000.

[669] Amnesty International, "South Korea - Govt proposal will set up a weak National Human Rights Commission," April 12, 1999.

[670] Protection of Communications Secrets Act, Act No. 4650, Dec 27, 1993.
<http://webdb.mic.go.kr/e_home/mic/secrets.html>.

[671] Telecommunications Business Act, Act No. 4394, Aug. 10, 1991.
<http://webdb.mic.go.kr/e_home/mic/business2.html>.

[672] "Wiretappings Number 6,638 Last Yr.," Korea Times, February 10, 1999.

[673] "Police get stern warning on illegal wiretapping," Korea Herald, September 27, 1999.

[674] "Kim Hyong-o Says More Than 10,000 May Be Exposed to Gov't Taps," Korea Times, February 13, 1999.

allow victims of illegal wiretapping to sue in court, limit the number of crimes for which wiretapping is allowed, and provide for notice to targets of wiretapping. The government set up a wiretapping complaint center under the Ministry of Information and Communication in October 1999.[675] The United Nations Human Rights Commission heard testimony on Korean wiretapping at its meeting in October 1999.[676]

Credit reports are protected by the Act Relating to Use and Protection of Credit Information of 1995.[677] Postal privacy is protected by the Postal Services Act.[678]

In 1997, the government proposed an "Electronic National Identification Card Project." The plan was based on a smart card system and according to a local human rights group would "include universal ID card, driver's license, medical insurance card, national pension card, proof of residence, and a scanned fingerprint, among other things."[679] The government was scheduled to issue cards to all citizens by 1999.[680] In November 1997, a law on the ID card project passed the National Assembly. In December 1997, Kim Dae Jung, a former dissident, won the Presidential election. He had publicly opposed the ID card project in his campaign and the project was publicly withdrawn. However, activists believe that government agencies are continuing to quietly develop the proposals. In 1999, the government began replacing existing cards with a plastic card.

The Act on Disclosure of Information by Public Agencies is a freedom of information act that allows Koreans to demand access to government records. It was enacted in 1996 and went into effect in 1998. The Supreme Court ruled in 1989 that there is a constitutional right to information "as an aspect of the right of

---

[675] "Gov't to operate eavesdropping complaint center," Korea Herald, October 30, 1999.

[676] United Nations Human Rights Committee, Summary record of the 1792nd meeting : Republic of Korea. 22/11/99. CCPR/C/SR.1792, 22 November 1999.

[677] Act Relating to Use and Protection of Credit Information, Law No. 4866, Jan. 5, 1995. Enforcement Decree for the Act Relating to Use and Protection of Credit Information.

[678] Amended by Law No. 2372, Dec.16, 1972; Law No.3602, Dec. 31,1982.
<http://www.mic.go.kr/rmic/webdriver?MIval=eng-0000-0&content_page=z320-0002-1&m_code=z320-0012-1>.

[679] <http://kpd.sing-kr.org/idcard/main-e.html>.

[680] Joohoan Kim, Ph.D., Digitized Personal Information and the Crisis of Privacy: The Problems of Electronic National Identification Card Project and Land Registry Project in South Korea, <http://kpd.sing-kr.org/idcard/joohoan2.htm!>.

freedom of expression, and specific implementing legislation to define the contours of the right was not a prerequisite to its enforcement."[681]

South Korea is a member of the Organization for Economic Cooperation and Development and has adopted the OECD Guidelines on the Protection of Privacy and Transborder Flows of Personal Data.

Republic of Latvia

Article 17 of the Constitutional Law on Rights and Obligations of a Citizen and a Person states, "(1) The State guarantees the confidentiality of correspondence, telephone conversations, telegraph and other communications. (2) These rights may be restricted by a judge's order for the investigation of serious crimes."[682]

The Law on Personal Data Protection was adopted by the Parliament on March 23, 2000. The law is based on the EU Data Directive and the Council of Europe Convention No. 108.[683] The bill will also create a Data Protection Inspectorate. The approval follows several years of EU pressure to adopt the law.

The Law on Freedom of Information was adopted by the Saiema in October 1998 and signed into law by the State President in November 1998.[684] It guarantees public access to all information in "any technically feasible form" not specifically restricted by law. Individuals may use it to obtain their own records. Information can only be limited if: there is a law authorizing withholding; the information is for internal use of an institution; it constitutes trade secrets; or concerns the private life of an individual.

In January 1999, the National Human Rights Office (NHRO) threatened to sue the National Compulsory Health Insurance Central Fund (NCHICF) over the mandatory use of personal identification codes by doctors, alleging a violation of the right to privacy in the European Convention on Human Rights.[685]

---

[681] Right to Information (1 KCCR 176, 88 HunMa 22, Sep. 4, 1989). <http://www.ccourt.go.kr/english/case4.html>.

[682]Constitutional Law: The Rights and Obligations of a Citizen and a Person, 1991. <http://www.uni-wuerzburg.de/law/lg03000_.html>.

[683] ESIS, Regulatory Developments: Latvia Master Report, April 2000. <http://www.eu-esis.org/esis2reg/LVreg1.htm>.

[684] Law on Freedom of Information, Adopted 29 October 1998, Signed 6 November 1998.

[685] Baltic News Service, January 5, 1999.

Under the Penal Code, it is unlawful to interfere with correspondence.[686] Wiretapping or interception of postal communications requires the permission of a court.[687] On November 16, 1995, it was reported that telephones in the Latvian Defense Ministry were tapped. The Latvian Defense Ministry responded by stating Latvia's "military counterintelligence service reserves the right to ensure the security of communications at the Ministry of Defense and structures of the national armed forces."[688] In April 1994, a bugging device was found on the switchboard of the "Dienas Bizness" newspaper.[689]

Latvia is a member of the Council of Europe and signed the Convention for the Protection of Individuals with Regard to Automatic Processing of Personal Data (ETS No. 108) on February 11, 2000.[690] It has signed and ratified the European Convention for the Protection of Human Rights and Fundamental Freedoms.[691]

Republic of Lithuania

Article 22 of the Constitution states, "The private life of an individual shall be inviolable. Personal correspondence, telephone conversations, telegraph messages, and other intercommunications shall be inviolable. Information concerning the private life of an individual may be collected only upon a justified court order and in accordance with the law. The law and the court shall protect individuals from arbitrary or unlawful interference in their private or family life, and from encroachment upon their honor and dignity."[692]

Lithuania enacted its Law on Legal Protection of Personal Data in 1996[693] and amended it in March 1998 to extend it to computerized information held by private controllers.[694] The Law regulates the processing of all types of personal

---

[686] Criminal Code of Latvia, art. 132.

[687] Criminal Procedure Code of Latvia, arts. 168, 176, 176.1.

[688] "Defense Ministry issues a statement in response to reports of bugging," Latvian Radio, Riga, November 16, 1995, BBC Summary of World Broadcasts, November 20, 1995.

[689]BBC Summary of World Broadcasts, April 16, 1994.

[690] See <http://conventions.coe.int/>.

[691] Signed 10/2/95, Ratified 26/7/96, Entered into force 26/7/96, <http://conventions.coe.int/>.

[692] Constitution of the Republic of Lithuania.
<http://www.litlex.lt/Litlex/Eng/Frames/Laws/Documents/CONSTITU.HTM>.

[693] The Law on Legal Protection of Personal Data (No 63-1479, 1996).
<http://www.lrs.lt/cgi-bin/preps2?Condition1=38025&Condition2=>.

[694] Law No.VII-662, March 12, 1998.

---

data, not just in state information systems. It defines the time and the general means of protecting personal data and sets rights of access and correction. It also sets rules on the collecting, processing, transferring and using of data. The Administrative Code defines various monetary penalties in cases of the infringement of the processing and use of data.[695] There is also a Law on State Registers[696] which governs the use and legitimacy of state data registers that contain personal information. The law also mandates that data registers may only be erased or destroyed in cooperation with the State Data Protection Inspectorate.

The Seimas is currently reviewing extensive amendments to the law.[697] The amendments would ensure the law's compliance with the EU Directives on Data Protection and Telecommunications. It will cover not just the processing of personal information by computers, but also by other means. It also adopts the Council of Europe recommendations on direct marketing, health care, science research, telecommunications and statistics. The bill is expected to be approved in the summer of 2000.

The State Data Protection Inspectorate was established in 1996 to enforce the provisions of the Law on Legal Protection of Personal Data and the Law on State Registers.[698] It registers data controllers, supervises processing, handles appeals for denial of access to records, and approves transborder data flows. The Inspectorate has eight staff members and has registered 622 data controllers.[699] It has conducted 21 physical inspections and over 400 in writing. It has also drafted 13 legal acts. Under the 1998 Law, it is subordinated to the Minister of Public Administration Reforms and Local Authorities from July 1998. Under the draft act, the office would be reorganized into an independent organization.

Wiretapping requires a warrant issued by the Prosecutor General.[700] On October 27, 1995, the Lithuanian State Security Department Chief, Jurgis Jurgialis, denied opposition charges that his department bugged telephones for political reasons. He said, "we resort to such actions only on the basis of the law and after

---

[695] See Ona Jakstaite, "Regulating Data Security in Lithuania," Baltic IT Review.

[696] The Law on the Public Registers (13 August 1996, No. I-1490). <http://www.is.lt/dsinsp/anglo/docs/Ist_reg.htm>.

[697] New Revision Law on Legal Protection of Personal Data of the Republic of Lithuania <http://www.is.lt/dsinsp/anglo/index.html>.

[698] Resolution No. 1185 "On establishing the State Data Protection Inspectorate, 10 October 1996 (No 100-2293). Home page: <http://www.is.lt/dsinsp/anglo/index.html>.

[699] Email from Ona Jakstatite, State Data Protection Inspectorate, 21 June 2000.

[700] Law on Operative Activities, 1991.

receiving the prosecutor's authorization in each particular case." Jurgialis denied that his department was involved in widespread bugging but conceded such activities were conducted throughout Lithuania "by quite different structures, including foreign intelligence services."[701] In May 1998, *Lietuvos rytas*, the country's largest daily, revealed that a top-secret surveillance unit was monitoring the media, the prosecutor general, cabinet ministers, the Prime Minister, and the President. The unit was shut down after the revelations.[702] The International Helsinki Committee raised concerns about the prosecution of Audrius Butkevicius, a member of the Lithuanian parliament, on corruption charges in 1997 based on wiretaps conducted without a court order.[703]

There are specific privacy protections in laws relating to telecommunications,[704] radio communications,[705] statistics,[706] the population register,[707] and health information.[708] The Penal Code of the Republic of Lithuania provides for criminal responsibility for violations of the inviolability of a residence, infringement on secrecy of correspondence and telegram contents, on privacy of telephone conversations, persecution for criticism, secrecy of adoption, slander, desecration of graves and impact on computer information. Civil laws provide for compensation for moral damage because of dissemination of unlawful or false information demeaning the honor and dignity of a person in the mass media.[709]

The 1996 Law on the Provision of Information to the Public provides for a limited right of access to official documents and to documents held by political parties, political and public organizations, trade union and other entities.[710] A more comprehensive "Law on the Right to Receive Information from the State

---

[701] Vladas Burbulis, "Lithuania Security Chief Refutes Any Telephone Bugging," ITAR- TASS, October 27, 1995.

[702] "Keeping an Eye on Politicians," Transitions, August 1998.

[703] International Helsinki Federation for Human Rights, Annual Report 1999 <http://www.ihf-hr.org/reports/ar99/ar99lit.htm>.

[704] The Law on Telecommunications, 30 November 1995, No. I-1109.

[705] Law on Radio Communication, 7 November 1995, No.I-1086.
<http://www.litlex.lt/Litlex/Eng/Frames/Laws/Documents/366.HTM>.

[706] The Law on Statistics, 12 October 1993, No.I-270.

[707] Law on the Population Register, January 23, 1992, No. I-2237.

[708] Law on the Health System, 19 July 1994, No.I-552.

[709] United Nations Human Rights Committee, Consideration of Reports Submitted by States Parties Under Article 40 of the Covenant, Initial reports of States parties due in 1993, Addendum, Lithuania, 1996.
<http://www.hri.ca/fortherecord1997/documentation/tbodies/ccpr-c-81-add10.htm>.

[710] The Law on the Provision of Information to the Public, 2 July 1996 No.I-1418 (As amended by 23 January 1997). <http://www.lrtv.lt/en_lrtvm.htm>.

---

and Municipal Institutions" drafted by the Lithuanian Centre for Human Rights is currently being reviewed by the Parliament.[711]

Lithuania is in the process of preparing for membership in the EU and has a National Program for the Adoption of EU Regulations. It is a member of the Council of Europe but has not yet signed and ratified the Convention for the Protection of Individuals with Regard to Automatic Processing of Personal Data (ETS No. 108).[712] It has signed and ratified the European Convention for the Protection of Human Rights and Fundamental Freedoms.[713]

Grand Duchy of Luxembourg

Article 28 of the Constitution states, "(1) The secrecy of correspondence is inviolable. The law determines the agents responsible for the violation of the secrecy of correspondence entrusted to the postal services. (2) The law determines the guarantee to be afforded to the secrecy of telegrams." [714]

Luxembourg's Act Concerning the Use of Nominal Data in Computer Processing was adopted in 1979.[715] The law pertains to individually identifiable data in both public and private computer files. It also requires licensing of systems used for the processing of personal data. The law considers all personal data to be sensitive, although special provisions may be applied to medical and criminal information. For personal data processing by the private sector, an application must first be made to the Minister for Justice who thereafter issues an authorization for such processing to take place.

As a member of the EU, Luxembourg should have amended this law by October 1, 1998, in order to implement the European Data Protection Directive (95/46/EC). An amending bill was introduced in the Parliament in 1997, but withdrawn in 1998 and not reintroduced due to Parliamentary elections.[716] In January 2000, the European Commission initiated a case before the European Court of Justice against Luxembourg and four other countries for failure to

---

[711] Memorandum on the Submission of ARTICLE 19 Critique - Lithuanian Draft Law on "The Right to Receive Information" <http://www.article19.org/pubs/mlalitin.htm>.

[712] <http://conventions.coe.int/>.

[713] Signed 14/05/93, Ratified 20/06/95, Entered into force 20/06/95, <http://conventions.coe.int/>.

[714] Constitution of the Grand Duchy of Luxembourg. <http://www.uni-wuerzburg.de/law/lu00t___.html>.

[715] Act on the Use of Nomative Data in Computer Processing, 31 March 1979.

[716] Act on the protection of individuals with regard to the processing of their personal data, no. 4357.

---

implement the Directive on time.[717] A finalized bill has now been drafted but has yet to be approved by the Government and submitted to Parliament.[718] A project on electronic commerce that will implement the EU Telecommunications Privacy Directive is also currently pending.[719]

The Commission à la Protection des Données Nominatives, under the Ministry of Justice, oversees the law. If an application for personal data processing is granted, and there is an objection raised or if the application is refused or the original authorization is withdrawn for some reason, an appeal can be made to the Disputes Committee of the Council of State. A national register of all systems containing personal information is maintained by the Minister for Justice. Public sector personal data systems can only be established upon the issuance of a special law or regulation. Such proposed laws or regulations are reviewed by the Advisory Board. In 1992, the law was amended to include special protection requirements for police and medical data.

Telephone tapping is regulated by articles 88-1 and 88-2 of the Criminal Code.[720] Judicial wiretaps are authorized if it can be shown: that a serious crime or infringement, punishable by two or more years imprisonment, is involved; that there is sufficient evidence to suspect that the subject of the interception order committed or participated in the crime or received or transmitted information to/from or concerning the accused; and that ordinary investigative techniques would be inadequate under the circumstances. Orders are granted for 1 month periods and may be extended repeatedly as long as the cumulative period does not exceed one year. Administrative wiretaps may also be authorized for national security reasons by a special tribunal appointed by the head of government. These interceptions are granted for three months at a time must stop once the requested information is received. The communications of persons bound by professional secrecy rules cannot be intercepted and any recordings of such must be destroyed immediately. Information, gathered during judicial and administrative interceptions but not subsequently used must be destroyed. In the case of judicial warrants persons who formed the subject of the warrant will sometimes be informed of the action taken. This law was highly criticized by

---

[717] European Commission, "Data protection: Commission takes five Member States to court," 11 January 2000. <http://europa.eu.int/comm/internal_market/en/media/dataprot/news/2k-10.htm>.

[718] European Commission, Status of implementation of Directive 95/46, <http://europa.eu.int/comm/internal_market/en/media/dataprot/law/impl.htm>.

[719] Projet de loi relatif au commerce électronique, document parlementaire N° 4641 du 15/03/2000 <http://www.etat.lu/ECO/coel.htm>.

[720] Art 88-1 - 88-4 of the Criminal Code, Law of 26 November 1982, modified by the law of 7 July 1989.

---

human rights activists and the socialist workers party when it was first introduced. In fact the law was challenged on numerous occasions before the European Court of Human Rights. That Court, however, ruled that the law violated neither article 8 (concerning the right to private and family life) nor article 13 (concerning the right to due process) of the European Convention on Human Rights.[721]

The Numerical Identification of Natural and Legal Persons Act of 1979[722] provides for the introduction of an identity number, consisting of 11 digits (including digits to represent date of birth and sex) for every person resident in the country. The law contains specifications for use of this number. These specifications are loosely drafted, however, and leave it open for the number to be widely circulated. The data protection authority is said to be monitoring the adoption of this number closely.[723] There are also sectoral laws on privacy relating to telecommunications,[724] and banking secrecy. Luxembourg's status as a financial haven ensures that unwarranted surveillance of individuals is forbidden. This may change as Luxembourg comes under increasing pressure to amend its financial confidentiality laws to permit greater access to personal financial records by European and American investigators.

There is no general freedom of information law in Luxembourg. Under the 1960 decree on state archives, the archives are to be open to the public, but citizens must make a written request explaining why they want access and ministers have broad discretion to deny requests.[725] The government announced in August 1999 that it was planning to develop a new press bill including a right to access records.[726]

---

[721] Commission Nationale de Control des Interceptions de Security, (Frnace) 8e Rapport d'Activite 1999, p66-67.

[722] Loi du 30 mars 1979 organisant l'identification numérique des personnes physiques et morales <http://www.etat.lu/ECP/30-3-79.doc . Règlement grand-ducal du 7 juin 1979 déterminant les actes, documents et fichiers autorisés à utiliser le numéro d'identité des personnes physiques et morales. <http://www.etat.lu/ECP/7-6-79.doc>. Règlement grand-ducal modifié du 21 décembre 1987 fixant les modalités d'application de la loi du 30 mars 1979, <http://www.etat.lu/ECP/21-12-87.doc>.

[723] The Council of Europe, 'The introduction and use of personal identification numbers: the data protection issues', 1991, <http://www.coe.fr/DataProtection/Etudes_Rapports/epins.htm>.

[724] Loi du 21 mars 1997 sur les télécommunications. <http://www.etat.lu/ILT/co/legal/loi-t.htm> , Règlement grand-ducal du 22 décembre 1997 fixant les conditions du cahier des charges pour l'établissement et l'exploitation de réseaux fixes de télécommunications. <http://www.etat.lu/ILT/co/legal/lic-b.htm>.

[725] Arrêté grand-ducal fixant l'organisation et les conditions de fonctionnement des Archives de l'Etat.

[726] Le programme gouvernemental: Accord de coalition PCS/PDL, August 1999. <http://www.gouvernement.lu/gouv/fr/gouv/progg/coalfr.html#1>.

Luxembourg is a member of the Council of Europe and has signed and ratified the Convention for the Protection of Individuals with Regard to Automatic Processing of Personal Data (ETS No. 108).[727] It has signed and ratified the European Convention for the Protection of Human Rights and Fundamental Freedoms.[728] It is a member of the Organization for Economic Cooperation and Development and has adopted the OECD Guidelines on the Protection of Privacy and Transborder Flows of Personal Data.

Malaysia

The Constitution of Malaysia does not specifically recognize the right to privacy.[729]

The Ministry of Energy, Communications and Multimedia is drafting a Personal Data Protection Act that will create legal protections for personal data as part of the "National Electronic Commerce Master Plan." Secretary-general Datuk Nuraizah Abdul Hamid said the purpose of the Bill was to ensure secrecy and integrity in the collection, processing and utilization of data transmitted through the electronic network.[730] The Ministry is looking at the OECD Guidelines, EU Data Directive and the UK, Hong Kong and New Zealand legislation as models for the act. The bill has been delayed for several years as the Ministry has watched international developments such as the U.S./EU Safe Harbor negotiations.

The government appears to be moving towards embracing a mix of self-regulation and government intervention. At a conference in April 2000, Deputy Prime Minister Datuk Seri Abdullah Ahmad Badawi stressed the role of the private sector in creating a safe and private environment in which electronic commerce could flourish. In likening on-line privacy protection to the steps banks had to take to make ATMs safe, the Deputy Prime Minister characterized privacy safeguards as a cost of doing business rather than a public good.[731]

In 1998, the Parliament approved the Communications and Multimedia Act, which has several sections on telecommunications privacy. Section 234 prohibits

---

[727] Signed 28/01/81. Ratified 10/02/88. Entered into force 01/06/88. <http://conventions.coe.int/>.

[728] Signed 04/11/50. Ratified 03/09/53. Entered into force 03/09/53. <http://conventions.coe.int/>.

[729] Constitution of Malaysia, <http://star.hsrc.ac.za/constitutions/constmalcont.html>.

[730] "Draft of Bill on Personal Data Protection ready by year-end," New Straits Times. October 2, 1998.

[731] Sarban Singh, "Match our commitment, DPM tells private firms," The New Straits Time, April 19, 2000.

---

unlawful interception of communications. Section 249 sets rules for searches of computers and includes access to encryption keys. Section 252 authorizes police to intercept communications without a warrant if a public prosecutor considers that a communication is likely to contain information that is relevant to an investigation.[732] There are regular reports of illegal wiretapping, including on the former deputy premier Anwar Ibrahim. Police detained four people under the Internal Security Act on suspicion of spreading rumors of disturbances in Kuala Lumpur in August 1998. Inspector-General of Police Tan Sri Abdul Rahim Noorsaid told the media then that the suspects were detained after police tracked their activities on the Internet with the assistance of Internet service provider Mimos Berhad.[733] The provider said later that it did not screen private e-mail.[734]

Several other laws relating to technology were approved in 1997, including The Digital Signature Act of 1997[735] and the Computer Crime Act of 1997.[736] Section 8 of the Computer Crime Act allows police to inspect and seize computing equipment of suspects without a warrant or any notice. The suspect is also required to turn over all encryption keys for any encrypted data on his equipment. The act also outlaws eavesdropping, tampering with or falsifying data, sabotage through computer viruses or worms, among a host of cybercrimes.[737] The Energy, Communications and Multimedia Ministry announced in July 2000 that it is developing a National Policy Framework on Information Security to provide guidelines on computer security.[738] Malaysia's Banking and Financial Institutions Act 1989, Pt XIII, also has provisions on privacy.

The pilot program for a Government Multi-Purpose Card will be launched in September 2000 for two million residents in the Multimedia Super Corridor.[739] The card will be used as a national identity card and drivers license, and will contain immigration and passport information, medical records, and eventually be usable as a debit card. It will contain both a photo and a thumbprint. It is planned to expand nationally starting in 2002. Besides the MPC, there are also

---

[732] Communications and Multimedia Act 1998 <http://www.cmc.gov.my/legisframe.htm>.

[733] "Rumours over Internet: Four to be charged soon," New Straits Times, September 24, 1998.

[734] "E-mail not screened, says service provider," The Straits Times, August 17, 1998.

[735] Digital Signature Bill 1997, <http://www.cca.gov.my/1997.htm>. Digital Signature Regulations 1998 <http://www.cca.gov.my/1998.htm>.

[736] Computer Crimes Bill 1997, < http://www.mycert.mimos.my/crime.html >.

[737] Shamsul Yunos, "Legal need to protect privacy on the Net," The Malay Mail, June 9, 2000.

[738] "National guideline on information security," New Straits Times, July 3, 2000.

[739] "Klang Valley residents will be first to use Multi-Purpose Card," New Straits Times, June 1, 1999.

initiatives for a Payment Multi-Purpose Card (PMPC) and a chip-based national passport. The government signed a contract in June 1999 with several companies including Unisys and Iris Technologies to develop these smart cards. All Malaysian over the age of 12 are issued national ID cards. It was announced in 1998 that if citizens do not carry their cards, they risk being detained by immigration police.[740] In January 1999, it was announced that Muslim couples married in the Malaysian capital will be issued cards with computer chips so Islamic police can instantly verify their vows and the police will be equipped with portable card readers. In December 1998, the government began requiring that cybercafes obtain name, address, and identity card information from patrons, but lifted the requirement in March 1999.[741]

United Mexican States

Article 16 of the 1917 Mexican Constitution provides in part: "One's person, family, home, papers or possessions may not be molested, except by virtue of a written order by a proper authority, based on and motivated by legal proceedings. The administrative authority may make home visits only to certify compliance with sanitary and police rules; the presentation of books and papers indispensable to verify compliance with the fiscal laws may be required in compliance with the respective laws and the formalities proscribed for their inspection. Correspondence, under the protective circle of the mail, will be free from all inspection, and its violation will be punishable by law."[742]

On June 7, the Mexican E-Commerce Act took effect.[743] The law amends the Civil Code, the Commercial Code, the Rules of Civil Procedure and the Consumer Protection Act. It covers consumer protection, privacy and digital signatures and electronic documents. It includes a new article in the Federal Consumer Protection Act giving authority to the government "to provide for the effective protection of consumer in electronic transactions or concluded by any other means, and the adequate use of the data provided by the consumer" (Art. 1.VIII); and also to coordinate the use of Code of Ethics by providers including the principles of this law. The law also creates a new chapter in the Consumer

---

[740] "Malaysians told: Carry ICs or risk detention," New Straits Times, May 14, 1998.

[741] "Cabinet: Cybercafes not subjected to restrictions," New Straits Times, March 18, 1999.

[742] Constitucion Politica de los Estados Unidos Mexicanos, <http://info.juridicas.unam.mx/cnsinfo/fed00.htm>.

[743] E-Commerce Act, <http://vlex.com/mx/redm/N@UMERO_7_JUNIO-JULIO_2000_NUMERO_DE_ANIVERSARIO/4>.

Law titled: "Rights of Consumers in electronic transactions and transactions by any other means." The new article 76 now provides, "This article will be applied to the relation between providers and consumers in transactions effectuated by electronics means. The following principles must be observed: I. Providers shall use information provided by consumers in a confidential manner, and shall not be able to transfer it to third parties, unless there is express consent from the consumer or a requirement from a public authority ... II. Providers must use technical measures to provide security and confidentiality to the information submitted by the consumer, and notify the consumer, before the transaction, of the characteristics of the system ... VI. Providers must respect consumer decisions not to receive commercial solicitations ..."

Article 214 of the Penal Code protects against the disclosure of personal information held by government agencies.[744] The General Population Act regulates the National Registry of Population and Personal Identification. The Registry's purpose is to register all persons making up the country's population using data enabling their identity to be certified reliably. The aim is ultimately to issue the citizen's identity card, which will be the official document of identification, fully endorsing the data contained in it concerning the holder.[745]

Chapter 6 of Mexico's Postal Code, in effect since 1888, recognizes the inviolability of correspondence and guarantees the privacy of correspondence.[746] The 1939 General Communication Law provides penalties for interrupting communications and divulging secrets.[747] The Federal Penal Code establishes penalties for the crime of revealing personal secrets by any means, including personal mail.[748] In 1981, the Penal Code was amended to include the interception of telephone calls by a third person.[749] The Law Against Organized Crime, passed in November 1996, allows for electronic surveillance with a judicial order.[750] The law prohibits electronic surveillance in cases of electoral, civil, commercial, labor, or administrative matters and expands protection against

---

[744] Código Penal Federal, Art. 214.

[745] See United Nations Commission on Human Rights, Question of the follow-up to the guidelines for the regulation of computerized personal data files: report of the Secretary-General prepared pursuant to Commission decision 1995/114 <http://www.hri.ca/fortherecord1997/documentation/commission/e-cn4-1997-67.htm>.

[746] El Código Postal de los Estados Unidos Mexicanos (1884).

[747] Ley de Vías Generales de Comunicación de 30 de diciembre de 1939, Arts 571. 576, 578.

[748] Código Penal Federal, Art 210.

[749] Id., Art. 167, part 9.

[750] Ley Federal Contra la Delincuencia Organizada, 7 de noviembre de 1996, <http://info1.juridicas.unam.mx/legfed/247/1.htm>.

unauthorized surveillance to cover all private means of communications, not merely telephone calls.[751]

The Law has been widely criticized by Mexican human rights organizations as violating Article 16 of the Constitution.[752] They noted that telephone espionage had historically been used by the ruling PRI party "to keep the opposition in check."[753] In 1997, the telephones of the Jalisco State Supreme Court were found to have been wiretapped.[754] In March 1998, a large cache of government electronic eavesdropping equipment which had been used since 1991 to spy on members of opposition political parties, human rights groups and journalists was discovered in Campeche.[755] Thousands of pages of transcripts of telephone conversations were uncovered along with receipts for $1.2 million in Israeli surveillance equipment. More than a dozen other cases of government espionage in four other states were exposed, ranging from hidden microphones and cameras found in government offices in Mexico City, to tapes of a state governor's telephone calls. Every government agency identified with the electronic surveillance operations – the federal attorney general and interior ministry, the military, the national security agency and a plethora of state institutions – denied knowing anything about them.[756] The new President-elect, Vicente Fox, has promised to eliminate the security police division that is responsible for much of the illegal government wiretapping in Mexico.

The U.S.-Mexican border has been an area of increased surveillance. Mexican authorities now routinely perform "security sweeps" of homes in areas bordering the United States.[757] On the U.S. side, biometric facial feature recognition systems have been implemented by the Immigration and Naturalization Service at the Otay Mesa border crossing (San Diego-Tijuana) for frequent U.S. commuters to Mexican maquiladora factories. The biometric data is stored with driver's license numbers, vehicle registration numbers and passport status information in an INS database. When a commuter in the program approaches the U.S. border, a transponder under his vehicle sends a signal to the checkpoint

---

[751] "Zedillo to sign sweeping organized crime package," The Los Angeles Times, October 30, 1996.

[752] "Exigen siete ONG la renuncia del titular de Seguridad Publica," La Jornada, October 7, 1997.

[753] "Con la reforma anticrimen, el espionaje entraría a la Constitución," La Jornada, 28 de abril de 1996.

[754] AP, January 18, 1997.

[755] "Spy Network Stuns Mexicans, Raid Opens Door to Exposure of Government Snooping," The Washington Post, April 13, 1998.

[756] "Anger as Big Brother spy tactics exposed," The Guardian (London), April 14, 1998.

[757] "En marcha, amplia operacion anticrimen en la frontera con E.U.," La Jornada, November 5, 1996.

booth, activating the database and displaying the driver's image. Other commuters use a voice-activated device in addition to the facial scan.[758]

Mexico is a member of the Organization for Economic Cooperation and Development, but does not appear to have adopted the OECD Guidelines on the Protection of Privacy and Transborder Flows of Personal Data. Mexico has also signed the American Convention on Human Rights.

Kingdom of the Netherlands

The Constitution grants citizens an explicit right to privacy.[759] Article 10 states, "(1) Everyone shall have the right to respect for his privacy, without prejudice to restrictions laid down by or pursuant to Act of Parliament. (2) Rules to protect privacy shall be laid down by Act of Parliament in connection with the recording and dissemination of personal data. (3) Rules concerning the rights of persons to be informed of data recorded concerning them and of the use that is made thereof, and to have such data corrected shall be laid down by Act of Parliament." Article 13 states, "(1) The privacy of correspondence shall not be violated except, in the cases laid down by Act of Parliament, by order of the courts. (2) The privacy of the telephone and telegraph shall not be violated except, in the cases laid down by Act of Parliament, by or with the authorization of those designated for the purpose by Act of Parliament."

In May 2000, the government-appointed commission for "Constitutional rights in the digital age" presented proposals for changes to the Dutch constitution.[760] The commission was set up after confusion about the legal status of e-mail under the constitutionally protected privacy of letters. The commission's task was to investigate if existing constitutional rights should be made more technology-independent and if new rights should be introduced. According to this proposal, Article 10 will be expanded to the right of persons to be informed about the origin of data recorded about them and the right to correct that data. Article 13 is made technology-independent and gives the right to confidential communications. Breaches of this right can only be made by a judge or a minister.

---

[758] "Human bar codes," The San Diego Union-Tribune, May 13, 1998.

[759]. Constitution of the Kingdom of the Netherlands 1989, <http://www.uni-wuerzburg.de/law/nl00000_.html>.

[760] 'Klant in het web', June 2000, <http://www.registratiekamer.nl/bis/top_1_5_35_13.html>. (Dutch only)

The Personal Data Protection Act of 2000 was approved by the Parliament in June 2000.[761] This bill is a revised and expanded version of the 1988 Data Registration Act that will bring Dutch law in line with the European Data Protection Directive and will regulate the disclosure of personal data to countries outside of the European Union. The Act replaces the Data Registration Act of 1988.[762] The new law will go into effect in January 2001.

The Registration Chamber (Registratiekamer) serves as the Data Protection Authority and exercises supervision of the operation of personal data files in accordance with the Data Registration Act.[763] The Chamber advises the government, deals with complaints submitted by data subjects, institutes investigations and makes recommendations to controllers of personal data files. The Chamber receives around 6,000 inquiries and 300 complaints each year. It also mediated 160 cases in 1999. There are presently over 60,000 databases registered with the Chamber. It has also released several reports on privacy enhancing technologies jointly produced with the Office of the Information and Privacy Commissioner of Ontario, Canada. In June 2000, the Registration Chamber published a report on the privacy policies of Dutch ISPs. The Chamber concluded that policies and procedures of providers are often unclear, contradictory or unlawful.[764]

Two decrees were issued under the Data Registration Act. The Decree on Sensitive Data[765] sets out the limited circumstances when personal data on an individual's religious beliefs, race, political persuasion, sexuality, medical, psychological and criminal history may be included in a personal data file. The Decree on Regulated Exemption[766] exempts certain organizations from the registration requirements of the Data Registration Act.

Interception of communications is regulated by the criminal code and requires a court order.[767] A new Telecommunications Act was approved in December 1998

---

[761] Personal Data Protection Act, Staatsblad 2000 302, 6 July 2000. (unofficial translation), <http://www2.unimaas.nl/~privacy/wbp_en_rev.htm>.

[762] Wet van 28 december 1988, houdende regels ter bescherming van de persoonlijke levenssfeer in verband met persoonsregistraties (Wet persoonsregistraties). Gepubliceerd in het Staatsblad 1988, 655. <http://www.unimaas.nl/~privacy/wpr.htm>.

[763] Homepage: <http://www.registratiekamer.nl.>.

[764] 'Klant in het web', June 2000, <http://www.registratiekamer.nl/bis/top_1_5_35_13.html>.

[765] Decree on Sensitive Data, March 5, 1993, <http://www2.unimaas.nl/~privacy/bgg-e.htm>.

[766] Decree on Regulated Exemption, July 6, 1993, <http://www.unimaas.nl/~privacy/bgv.htm>.

[767] Article 125g of the Code of Criminal Procedure.

which requires that Internet Service Providers have the capability by August 2000 to intercept all traffic with a court order and maintain users logs for three months.[768] The bill was enacted after XS4ALL, a Dutch ISP, refused to conduct a broad wiretap of electronic communications of one of its subscribers. The Dutch Forensics Institute has developed a so-called "black-box" that is used to intercept Internet traffic at an ISP. The black box is under control of the ISP and is turned on after receiving a court order. The box is believed to look at authentication traffic of the person to wiretap and divert the person's traffic to law enforcement if that person is online.[769] In May 2000, Dutch Internet providers canceled a deal with the Justice Department to provide names and addresses of Internet users under criminal investigation without a court order if the case involves a serious crime. Dutch privacy law gives the holder of a data registry the right to give out personal data to third parties in "pressing cases." The agreement between the providers and the Justice Department had to be halted nevertheless after a court ruled that the Justice Department was requesting information without a clear urgency.[770]

The new Telecommunications Act also implements the EU Telecommunications Privacy Directive. The Special Investigation Powers Act of 2000 regulates the use of bugging devices and directional microphones by law enforcement.

The Intelligence services do not need a court order for interception, but obtain their authorization from the responsible minister. A proposed new law on intelligence services (Wet op de Inlichtingenen Veiligheidsdiensten) gives a broad range of new powers to the services. If the law is adopted by Parliament, the BVD will be able to intercept all wireless communications (including mobile phones) without focusing on a particular person. The law gives power to store all intercepted data (including Internet traffic) for one year, and encrypted data can be stored for an unlimited time to facilitate possible decryption in the future. Under the proposal the BVD can also intrude (hack) into computer systems to intercept data or modify software on that system. Finally, the BVD can intercept wireless communications such as satellite traffic for economic espionage using keywords through the satellite interception facility at Zoutkamp.

---

[768] Telecommunications Act <http://www.minvenw.nl/dgtp/data/tweng.doc>. Rules pertaining to Telecommunications (Telecommunications Act), December 1998, <http://www.minvenw.nl/hdtp/hdtp2/wetsite/engels/index.html>.

[769] Homepage: <http://www.holmes.nl/>

[770] "Dutch Internet Providers Cancel Deal With Law Enforcement On Voluntary Assistance In Criminal Investigations," Telepolis, July 12, 2000. <http://www.heise.de/tp/english/inhalt/te/8367/1.html>.

A survey by the Dutch Ministry of Justice in 1996 found that police in the Netherlands intercept more telephone calls than their counterparts in the United States, Germany or Britain.[771] The Parliamentary Investigations Commission into police methods released a 4,700 page report in 1996. The report was critical of legal controls on police surveillance[772] and found that there was a failure among judges, prosecutors and other officials to limit police abuses. Some analysts say that the reason for the high number of taps is that the Netherlands prohibits other forms of investigations such as informers.

The Dutch government has refused to deny, confirm or investigate the existence of the Echelon system. A Parliament hearing on Echelon is scheduled in the autumn of 2000.

There are sectoral laws dealing with the Dutch police,[773] medical exams,[774] medical treatment,[775] social security,[776] entering private homes,[777] and the employment of minorities.[778]

The Government Information (Public Access) Act of 1991[779] is based on the constitutional right of access to information. It creates a presumption that documents created by a public agency should be available to everyone. Information can be withheld if it relates to international relations of the state, the "economic or financial interest of the state," investigation of criminal offenses, inspections by public authorities or personal privacy. However, these exemptions must be balanced against the importance of the disclosure. Requestors can appeal denials to an administrative court which renders the final decision.

The Netherlands is a member of the Council of Europe and has signed and ratified the Convention for the Protection of Individuals with Regard to

---

[771] Ibid.

[772] Tappen in Nederland, WODC, 1996

[773] Dutch Police Registers Act 1990, <http://www.unimaas.nl/~privacy/wpolr.htm>.

[774] Dutch Medical Examinations Act 1997, <http://www.unimaas.nl/~privacy/wmk.htm>.

[775] Dutch Medical Treatment Act 1997, <http://www.unimaas.nl/~privacy/index.htm>.

[776] Dutch Social Security System Act 1997, <http://www.unimaas.nl/~privacy/osv1997.htm>, Compulsory Identification Act.

[777] Dutch Act on the Entering of Buildings and Houses 1994, <http://www.unimaas.nl/~privacy/awbt.htm>.

[778] Dutch Act on the Stimulation of Labor by Minorities 1994, <http://www.unimaas.nl/~privacy/samen.htm>.

[779] Act of 31 October 1991, containing regulations governing public access to government information. This replaced the Act on Public Access to Information of 9 November 1978.

Automatic Processing of Personal Data (ETS No. 108).[780] It has signed and ratified the European Convention for the Protection of Human Rights and Fundamental Freedoms.[781] It is a member of the Organization for Economic Cooperation and Development and has adopted the OECD Guidelines on the Protection of Privacy and Transborder Flows of Personal Data.

New Zealand

Article 21 of the Bill of Rights Act 1990 states, "Everyone has the right to be secure against unreasonable search or seizure, whether of the person, property, or correspondence or otherwise."[782] The Human Rights Act 1994 prohibits discrimination.[783]

New Zealand's Privacy Act was enacted in 1993 and has been amended several times.[784] It regulates the collection, use and dissemination of personal information in both the public and private sectors. It also grants to individuals the right to have access to personal information held about them by any agency. The Privacy Act applies to "personal information," which is any information about an identifiable individual, whether automatically or manually processed. Recent case law has held that the definition also applies to mentally processed information.[785] The news media are exempt from the Privacy Act in relation to their news activities.

The Act creates twelve Information Privacy Principles generally based on the 1980 OECD guidelines and the information privacy principles in Australia's Privacy Act 1988. In addition, the legislation includes a new principle that deals with the assignment and use of unique identifiers. The Information Privacy Principles can be individually or collectively replaced by enforceable codes of practice for particular sectors or classes of information. At present, there is only

---

[780] Signed 07/05/82, Ratified 28/05/93, Entered into Force 01/09/93. <http://conventions.coe.int/>.

[781] <http://conventions.coe.int/>.

[782] Bill of Rights Act, 1990 <http://www.uni-wuerzburg.de/law/nz01t___.html>.

[783] <http://www.hrc.co.nz/welcome.htm>.

[784] The Privacy Act 1993, <http://www.knowledge-basket.co.nz/privacy/legislation/1993028/toc.html>; The Privacy Amendment Act 1993, <http://www.knowledge-basket.co.nz/privacy/legislation/1993059/toc.html>; The Privacy Amendment Act 1994, <http://www.knowledge-basket.co.nz/privacy/legislation/1994070/toc.html>, Privacy Amendment Act 1996, Privacy Amendment Act 1997, Privacy Amendment Act 1998.

[785] See Re Application by Linformation stored in person's memory (1997) 3 HRNZ 716 (Complaints Review Tribunal).

---

one complete sectoral code of practice in force, the Health Information Privacy Code 1994. There are several codes of practice that alter the application of single information privacy principles: the Superannuation Schemes Unique Identifier Code 1995, the EDS Information Privacy Code 1997, and the Justice Sector Unique Identifier Code 1998.[786]

In addition to the information privacy principles, the legislation contains principles relating to information held on public registers; it sets out guidelines and procedures in respect to information matching programs run by government agencies, and it makes special provision for the sharing of law enforcement information among specialized agencies.

The Privacy Commissioner conducted a five-year review in 1998 and recommended over 150 changes to the act, mostly minor. These included limiting use of information on public registers, creating a right to be taken off direct marketing lists, restricting requests by employers for criminal and medical records, limiting exceptions to the act, and providing for more funding for the Office of the Commissioner to enforce the act.[787]

The Office of the Privacy Commissioner is an independent oversight authority that was created prior to the Privacy Act by the 1991 Privacy Commissioner Act.[788] The Privacy Commissioner oversees compliance with the Act, but does not function as a central data registration or notification authority. The Privacy Commissioner's principal powers and functions include promoting the objects of the Act, monitoring proposed legislation and government policies, dealing with complaints at first instance, approving and issuing codes of practice and authorizing special exemptions from the information privacy principles, and reviewing public sector information matching programs. The Commissioner has a 20-person staff.

Complaints by individuals are initially filed with the Privacy Commissioner who attempts to conciliate the matter. The office received 11,141 inquiries and 1,082 complaints in the year ending June 1998 and completed 804 of the complaints. In 121 cases, a final opinion was granted.[789] If conciliation fails, the Proceedings

---

[786] Available at: http://www.privacy.org.nz/comply/comptop.html

[787] Office of the Privacy Commissioner, Necessary and Desirable: Privacy Act 1993 Review, December 1998.

[788] Home Page: <http://www.privacy.org.nz/>.

[789] NZ Privacy Commission, Annual Report for the year ended 30 June 1998.

Commissioner[790] or the complainant (if the Proceedings Commissioner is unwilling) can bring the matter before the Complaints Review Tribunal, which can issue decisions and award declaratory relief, issue restraining or remedial orders, and award special and general damages up to NZ $200,000.

The New Zealand Court of Appeal decided its first case on the Privacy Act of 1993 in 2000.[791] The case concerned a defense barrister who secretly tape recorded a telephone conversation with a women complainant in a domestic assault case. The complaint was made to the Privacy Commissioner alleging a breach of information privacy principles concerning fair collection of personal information. The defendant was ordered to pay $7,500 damages by Complaints Review Tribunal. The respondent appealed to the High Court, which upheld the CRT decision but reduced damages to $2,750. The respondent appealed to the Court of Appeal, which by a 3-2 majority allowed the appeal and quashed the declarations and orders of the Tribunal.

The High Court ruled in July that the implementation of a nationwide drivers license system with a digitized photograph that was required by the 1998 Land Transport Act was legal. The law creates a national database of digitized photographs. The individual challenging the law has said she will appeal to the Court of Appeal.[792]

The New Zealand Crimes Act and Misuse of Drugs Act govern the use of evidence obtained by listening devices.[793] Judicial warrants may be granted for bugging premises or interception of communications. Emergency permits may be granted for the bugging of premises and, following the 1997 repeal of a prohibition, for telephonic interceptions. Those who illegally disclose the contents of private communications illegally intercepted face two years in prison. However, those who illegally disclose the contents of private communications lawfully intercepted are merely liable for a NZ$500 fine. In 1998/99 the New Zealand Police sought and obtained 15 interception warrants under the Misuse of Drugs Act and 11 interceptions warrants under the Crimes Act. A total of 128 warrants (new and renewed) were obtained under the Telecommunications Amendment Act 1997 for obtaining call data analyzers (pen registers and trap

---

[790] The Proceedings Commissioner is a member of the Human Rights Commission, to which the Privacy Commissioner also belongs. The Proceedings Commissioner is empowered to take civil proceedings before the Complaints Review Tribunal on behalf of a complainant if conciliation fails.

[791] The case of Christopher Harder v The Proceedings Commissioner, Court of Appeal, CA240/99, 17 July 2000.

[792] See Standup New Zealand <http://www.standupnz.co.nz/index.html>.

[793] Part XIA, Crimes Act 1961; Misuse of Drugs Act 1978.

---

and trace devices that obtain call information but not the contents of communications). The devices operated for an average duration of 54 days.

The New Zealand Security Intelligence Service (NZSIS) is also permitted to carry out electronic interceptions under the New Zealand Security Intelligence Service Act of 1969. Under the provisions of this act, the Minister in Charge of the NZSIS is required to submit an annual report to the House of Representatives. The Act was amended in 1999 to allow for the service to enter premises to install taps following a Court of Appeal case that prohibited entering of premises without a warrant. The amendment also created a "foreign interception warrant."[794] Another amendment created a Commissioner of Security Warrants to jointly issue warrants with the Prime Minister.[795]   In 1999, the Minister reported six warrants issued to the NZSIS for intercepts and three continued for the previous 15 months.[796] This was up from three the previous reporting period. The average length of time for which these warrants were in force was 150 days. The report further states that "the methods for interception and seizure used were listening devices and the copying of documents."[797]

One agency not governed by the restrictions imposed on law enforcement and the NZSIS is the Government Communications Security Bureau (GCSB), the signals intelligence (SIGINT) agency for New Zealand. Operating as a virtual branch of the U.S. National Security Agency, this agency maintains two intercept stations at Waihopai and Tangimoana. The Waihopai station routinely intercepts trans-Pacific and intra-Pacific communications and passes the collected intelligence to NSA headquarters. David Lange, a former Prime Minister of New Zealand, said he and other ministers were told very little about the operations of GCSB while they were in power. Of particular interest to GCSB and NSA are the communications of the governments of neighboring Pacific island states.[798] GCSB was specifically exempted from the provisions of the Crimes Act in 1997.[799]

---

[794] New Zealand Security Intelligence Service Amendment Act 1999.

[795] New Zealand Security Intelligence Service Amendment (No 2) Act 1999.

[796] Director of Security, Statement on Warrants, 7 March 2000.

[797] Appendix I, Report by the Privacy Commissioner to the Minister of Justice in relation to the New Zealand Security Intelligence Service Amendment Bill emphasising the inadequacy of public reporting obligations in relation to interception warrants, 9 February 1999. <http://www.privacy.org.nz/people/nzsisab.html>.

[798] Nicky Hager, Secret Power: New Zealand's Role in the International Spy Network (Nelson, MZ: Craig Potton, 1996).

[799] Crimes (Exemption of Listening Device) Order 1997 (SR 1997/145).

The Broadcasting Amendment Act of 2000 amended the Broadcasting Act of 1989[800] to empower the Broadcasting Standards Authority (BSA) to encourage the development and observance by broadcasters of codes of broadcasting practice in relation to the privacy of the individual. This amendment came into effect on July 1, 2000. During the year there were a number of BSA privacy cases. Particular controversy surrounded several television broadcasts unreasonably intruding on the privacy of children with one program, widely publicized in advance, revealing the results of a DNA paternity test live on TV with mother, father and young child present.

During 1998/99, 2,954 blood samples were added by consent, and 748 samples by compulsion order, to the DNA databank maintained under the Criminal Investigations (Blood Samples) Act of 1995. The total number of DNA profiles stored on the DNA databank as of June 30, 1999, was 8,623.

The Official Information Act of 1982[801] and the Local Government Official Information and Meetings Act of 1987[802] are freedom of information laws governing the public sector. There are significant interconnections between this freedom of information legislation and the Privacy Act in subject matter, administration, and jurisprudence, so much so that the three enactments may be viewed, in relation to access to information, as complementary components of one overall statutory scheme. Enforcement is supervised by the Office of the Ombudsman.[803] The Ombudsman hears around 1,100 complaints each year under the Official Information Act and 170 each year under the Local Government Official Information and Meetings Act.

New Zealand is a member of the Organization for Economic Cooperation and Development and has adopted the OECD Guidelines on the Protection of Privacy and Transborder Flows of Personal Data. New Zealand is one of six countries involved in a European Commission study of methods of assessing whether laws of "third countries" meet the provisions of the EU data protection directive.[804]

---

[800] Available online at http://www.spectrum.net.nz/archive/acts.shtml

[801] Official Information Act 1982 <http://www.ombudsmen.govt.nz/official.htm>.

[802] Local Government Official Information and Meetings Act 1987 <http://www.ombudsmen.govt.nz/local.htm>.

[803] Homepage: http://www.ombudsmen.govt.nz/

[804] <http://www.knowledge-basket.co.nz/privacy/privword/eulooks.html>.

The Privacy Act does not apply to self-governing territories associated with New Zealand, the Cook Islands and Niue. Nor does it apply to the soon-to-be self-governing territory of Tokelau.

Kingdom of Norway

There is no provision in the Norwegian Constitution of 1814 dealing specifically with the protection of privacy.[805] The closest provision is section 102, which prohibits searches of private homes except in "criminal cases." More generally, section 110c of the Constitution places state authorities under an express duty to "respect and secure human rights." The Norwegian Supreme Court has held that there exists in Norwegian law a general legal protection of "personality" which embraces a right to privacy. This protection of personality exists independently of statutory authority but helps form the basis of the latter (including data protection legislation), and can be applied by the courts on a case-by-case basis. This protection was first recognized in 1952.[806]

The Personal Data Registers Act of 2000 was approved on April 14, 2000.[807] It is designed to update Norwegian law and closely follows the EU Directive, even though Norway is not a member of the EU. The new law also sets specific rules on video surveillance and biometrics. It replaces the Personal Data Registers Act of 1978.[808]

The Data Inspectorate (Datatilsynet) is an independent administration body set up under the Ministry of Justice in 1980.[809] The Inspectorate accepts applications for licenses for data registers and evaluates the licenses, enforces the privacy laws and regulations, and provides information. The Inspectorate can conduct inspections and impose sanctions. Decisions of the Inspectorate can be appealed to the Ministry of Justice. As of 1999, the Inspectorate had issued 65,000 licenses. The Inspectorate had 22 staff members in 1999.

---

[805] The Constitution of the Kingdom of Norway, <http://odin.dep.no/ud/nornytt/uda-121.html>.

[806] Supreme Court decision of 13 December 1952, reported in Rt. 1952, p. 1217.

[807] LOV 2000-04-14 nr 31: Lov om behandling av personopplysninger (personopplysningsloven). <http://www.lovdata.no/all/hl-20000414-031.html>.

[808] Personal Data Registers Act of 1978 (lov om personregistre mm av 9 juni 1978 nr 48), in force 1 January 1980. <http://www.datatilsynet.no/eksternweb/informasjon/engelsk/lov-eng.htm>.

[809] Home Page: <http://www.datatilsynet.no/>.

Wiretapping requires the permission of a tribunal and is initially limited to four weeks.[810] The total number of telephones monitored was 360 in 1990, 467 in 1991, 426 in 1992, 402 in 1993, 541 in 1994 and 534 in 1995.[811] A Supervisory Board reviews the warrants to ensure the adequacy of the protections. A Parliamentary Commission of Inquiry (The Lund Commission) was set up in 1994 to investigate the post-World War II surveillance practices of Norwegian police and security services. The Commission delivered a 600 page report in 1996, causing a great deal of public and political debate on account of its finding that much of the undercover surveillance practices, including wiretapping of left wing political groups up to 1989, had been instituted and/or conducted illegally and that the courts had not generally been strong enough in their oversight.[812] This included keeping files on children as young as 11 years old.

A new act to monitor the secret services was approved in 1995 following the Commission's recommendations.[813] It created a new Control Committee to monitor the activities of the Police Security Services, the Defense Security Services and the Defense Intelligence Services. The former Minister of Justice and the head of the Norwegian security police (POT) were forced to resign from the government in 1996 after it was revealed that the POT had placed a member of the Lund Commission under surveillance and requested a copy of her Stasi file from the German authorities four times.[814] Later it was discovered that the POT had also investigated several key members of the Storting who have oversight over the agency.[815] In 1997, the Parliament agreed to allow people who were under surveillance by the POT to review their records and to obtain compensation if the surveillance was unlawful. The POT has records on over 50,000 people.[816]

The Telecommunications Act imposes a duty of confidentiality on telecommunications providers.[817] However, the Telecommunications Authority can demand information for investigations. The Norwegian police in January

---

[810] Law of 17 December 1976., Law of 24 Juin 1915. Criminal Procedure Act, chapter 16 a, by Act No. 52 of 5 June 1992. See also Regulation No. 281 of 31 March 1995 on Telephone Monitoring in Narcotics Cases.

[811] Government of Norway report to the UN Human Rights Commission, CCPR/C/115/Add.2, 26 May 1997.

[812] "Judicial Inquiry into Norwegian Secret Surveillance," Fortress Europe, FECL 43 (April/May 1996).

[813] Act No. 7 of 3 February 1995 on the Control of the Secret Services.

[814] Minister resigns, Statewatch bulletin, November-December 1996, vol 6 no 1.

[815] FECL 49 (December 1996/January 1997).

[816] "Parliament says people can see files," Statewatch bulletin, May-June 1997, vol 7 no 3.

[817] The Telecommunications Act of 23 June 1995.

2000 called for new laws requiring telecommunications providers and Internet Service Providers to keep extensive logs of usage for six months to one year.[818]

A large number of other pieces of legislation contain provisions relevant to privacy and data protection. These include the Administrative Procedures Act of 1967,[819] and the Criminal Code of 1902.[820] The criminal code first prohibited the publication of information relating to the "personal or domestic affairs" in 1889.[821]

The Public Access to Documents in the (Public) Administration provides for public access to government records.[822] Under the Act, there is a broad right of access to records. The Act has been in effect since 1971. The Act does not apply to records held by the Storting (Parliament), the Office of the Auditor General, the Storting's Ombudsman for Public Administration or other institutions of the Storting. There are exemptions for internal documents; information that "could be detrimental to the security of the realm, national defence or relations with foreign states or international organizations"; subject to a duty of secrecy; "in the interests of proper execution of the financial, pay or personnel management"; the minutes of the Council of State, photographs of persons entered in a personal data register; complaints, reports and other documents concerning breaches of the law; answers to examinations or similar tests; and documents prepared by a ministry in connection with annual fiscal budgets. The King can make a determination that historical documents in the archive that are otherwise exempted can be publicly released. If access is denied, individuals can appeal to a higher authority under the act and then to a court.

Norway is a member of the Council of Europe and has signed and ratified the Convention for the Protection of Individuals with Regard to Automatic Processing of Personal Data (ETS No. 108).[823] It has signed and ratified the European Convention for the Protection of Human Rights and Fundamental Freedoms.[824] It is a member of the Organization for Economic Cooperation and

---

818 "Norwegian police has called for law on logging," M2 Communications, January 19, 2000.

819 Administrative Procedures Act of 1967 (lov om behandlingsmåten i forvaltningssaker av 10 februar 1967).

820 Almindelig borgerlig Straffelov 22 mai 1902 nr 10.

821 See prof. dr. juris Jon Bing, Data Protection in Norway, 1996.
<http://www.jus.uio.no/iri/rettsinfo/lib/papers/dp_norway/dp_norway.html>.

822 The Freedom of Information Act of 1970 (lov om offentlighet i forvaltningen av 19 juni 1970 nr 69). Amended by Act No. 47 of 11 June 1982 and Act no. 86 of 17 December 1982 and Act of 10 January 1997 No. 7. <http://www.ub.uio.no/ujur/ulovdata/lov-19700619-069-eng.pdf>.

823 Signed 13/03/81, Ratified 20/02/84, Entered into Force 01/10/85. <http://conventions.coe.int/>.

824 <http://conventions.coe.int/>.

Development and has adopted the OECD Guidelines on the Protection of Privacy and Transborder Flows of Personal Data. Norway is a party to the 1992 Agreement on the European Economic Area (EEA). As such, it is required to comply with the EU Directive before it is formally incorporated into the EEA.

Republic of Peru

The 1993 Constitution sets out extensive privacy, data protection and freedom of information rights.[825] Article 2 states, "Every person has the right:..To solicit information that one needs without disclosing the reason, and to receive that information from any public entity within the period specified by law, at a reasonable cost. Information that affects personal intimacy and that is expressly excluded by law or for reasons of national security is not subject to disclosure. Secret bank information or tax information can be accessed by judicial order, the National Prosecutor, or a Congressional investigative commission, in accordance with law and only insofar as it relates to a case under investigation. V. To be assured that information services, whether computerized or not, public or private, do not provide information that affects personal and family intimacy. VI. To honor and good reputation, to personal and family intimacy, both as to voice and image. Every person affected by untrue or inexact statements or aggrieved by any medium of social communication has the right to free, immediate and proportional rectification, without prejudice to responsibilities imposed by law...IX. To secrecy and the inviolability of communications and private documents. Communications, telecommunications or instruments of communication, may be opened, seized, intercepted or inspected only under judicial authorization and with the protections specified by law. All matters unconnected with the fact that motivates the examination are to be guarded from disclosure. Private documents obtained in violation of this precept have no legal effect. Books, ledgers, and accounting and administrative documents are subject to inspection or investigation by the competent authority in conformity with law. Actions taken in this respect may not include withdrawal or seizure, except by judicial order."

A Data Protection Bill was introduced in Parliament by the Partido Popular Cristiano political party in October 1999.[826] The bill is based on the new Spanish Data Protection Act, the Italian Data Privacy Act, the Privacy Act of 1988 of

---

[825] Constitution of Peru <http://www.asesor.com.pe/teleley/5000%2Din.htm>.

[826] Proyecto No. 5233, Ley Sobre La Privacidad de los Datos Informaticos y la Creacion del Comisionado para la Proteccion de la Privacidad, presentado por miembros del grupo parlamentario del Partido Popular Cristiano, 1999.

Australia, the U.S. Restatement of Torts and the EU Data Protection Directive. The bill proposes the creation of a Data Protection Commissioner. If approved, the bill will make Peru fully compatible with the EU Directive legal system.

Article 154 of the Penal Code states that "a person who violates personal or family privacy, whether by watching, listening to or recording an act, a word, a piece of writing or an image using technical instruments or processes and other means, shall be punished with imprisonment for not more than two years."[827]

Article 151 of the Penal Code states "that a person who unlawfully opens a letter, document, telegram, radiotelegram, telephone message or other document of a similar nature that is not addressed to him, or unlawfully takes possession of any such document even if it is open, shall be liable to imprisonment of not more than 2 years and to 60 to 90 days' fine."[828] A sentence of not less than one year nor more than three years is to be given to any "person who unlawfully interferes with or listens to a telephone or similar conversation." Public servants guilty of the same crime must serve not less than three or more than five years and must be dismissed from their post. A person who unlawfully tampers with, deletes, or misdirects "the address on a letter or telegram," but does not open it, "is liable to 20 to 52 days' community service."

However, there have been constant abuses of wiretap authority by Peru's National Intelligence Service (Servicio Nacional de Inteligencia or SIN), headed by a close adviser to the president. The SIN has conducted widespread surveillance and illegal phone tapping of government ministers and judges assigned to constitutional cases, beginning in the early 1990s. Army agents used sophisticated Israeli phone-tapping equipment to monitor telephone conversations, and copies of the conversations were delivered to Montesinos.[829] The SIN maintains close ties with the U.S. Central Intelligence Agency, including a covert assistance program to combat drug trafficking.[830] The SIN has allegedly conducted a nationwide surveillance campaign with the sole purpose of intimidating political opposition figures. In 1990, an opposition congressman's house was blown up after he delivered a congressional report on domestic surveillance of opposition politicians, journalists, human rights workers and

---

[827] The United Nations High Commissioner For Human Rights. Third periodic report of Peru: 21/03/95. CCPR/C/83/Add.1.

[828] The United Nations High Commissioner For Human Rights. Third periodic report of Peru: 21/03/95. CCPR/C/83/Add.1.

[829] "Former Agent Accuses Peru Spy Chief," AP, March 17, 1998.

[830] 1998 Human Rights Watch Report, <http://www.hrw.org/hrw/worldreport/Americas.htm>.

companies suspected of tax evasion.[831] In August, 1997 former UN Secretary General Javier Perez de Cuellar filed charges against the SIN with the Peruvian Attorney General and the Inter-American Human Rights Commission for taping 1,000 conversations he made from his home telephone between October 1994 and August 1995 while he ran for President against Alberto Fujimori.[832] President Fujimori absolved the SIN of the accusations against it, asserting that private individuals with commercial scanners had carried out the wiretapping.[833] The allegations prompted the resignation of the Defense Minister and a special prosecutor was appointed to investigate the incident.[834] The Defense Commission's three-month inquiry confirmed accusations of the widespread wiretapping but concluded that there was no evidence the intelligence services carried out the spying.[835] A member of Congress and several journalists filed a suit on grounds that their constitutional rights had been violated (an *acción de amparo*), and to put an end to the tapping of their telephone calls.[836]

The Organic Law of the National Identification Registry and Civil Society (1995) created an autonomous agency which may "collaborate with the exercise of the functions of pertinent political and judicial authorities in order to identify persons" but is "vigilant regarding restrictions with respect to the privacy and identity of the person" and "guarantees the privacy of data relative to the persons who are registered." The Law also requires all persons to carry a National Identity Document featuring a corresponding number, photograph and fingerprint.[837] The court must provide all personal data kept on file at the Public Registry upon request within 15 days.[838] In July 2000, a computer crimes act was enacted.

Freedom of information is constitutionally protected under the right of habeas data. The first case to test the habeas data clause, which reviewed clause 7 of Article 2, was brought in the criminal court system in January 1994. The

---

[831] "As Lima Talks Hit Snag, Some Ex-Hostages Are Complaining,," The New York Times, January 13, 1997.

[832] "Former U.N. chief charges Peru tapped his phone," Reuters, Aug 4, 1997.

[833] "President Fujimori denies intelligence services behind phone-tapping," America Television, Lima, BBC Summary of World Broadcasts, July 19, 1997.

[834] "Peru defense head resigns in crisis," Reuters, July 17, 1997.

[835] "Peru Congress probe fails to catch phonetappers," Reuters World Report, May 29, 1998.

[836] International Freedom of Expression eXchange (IFEX) Clearing House (Toronto), July 21, 1997 <http://www.ifex.org/alert/00002190.html>.

[837] Ley Organica Del Registro Nacional De Identificacion Y Estado Civil, Ley No. 26497, July 11, 1995. <http://www.congreso.gob.pe/ccd/leyes/cronos/1995/ley26497.htm>.

[838] Ley de aplicación de la acción constitucional del habeas data, Ley No. 26301, Nov. 13, 1995, <http://www.asesor.com.pe/teleley/bull505.htm>.

Supreme Court ruled in March 1994 that the case should not have been brought in the criminal courts, nullified all previous decisions on the case, and ordered it resubmitted to the civil court system.[839] Several cases have allowed the courts to establish their jurisdiction over, and support for, habeas data. In 1996 the Supreme Court, citing clause 5 of Article 2 of the Constitution, ordered the Ministry of Energy and Mines to release environmental surveys of a private mining operation to the Peruvian Society of Environmental Rights.[840] Also in 1996, the Supreme Court sided with the Civil Labor Association against the General Director of Mining and ordered the release of an environmental impact study submitted by the Southern Perú Cooper Corporation.[841]

In May, 1994, Law N° 26301 was passed in order to set temporary legal standards for the legal application of habeas data.[842] The Law requires that all habeas data actions be notarized, although reasons for the requested action need not be given, and filed with the legal authority from which information or an action is desired. The Law sets out the time periods and procedures for taking actions under clauses 5, 6 and/or 7 of Article 2 of the Constitution. The Law was updated in June 1995 to give a right of action, provide greater access to records, and to limit its use as a means of censorship.[843]

Peru signed the American Convention on Human Rights on July 28, 1978, but withdrew from the jurisdiction of the American Court of Human Rights in July 1999.

Republic of the Philippines

Article III of the 1987 Constitution protects the right of privacy. Section 2 states, "The right of the people to be secure in their persons, houses, papers, and effects against unreasonable searches and seizures of whatever nature and for any purpose shall be inviolable, and no search warrant or warrant of arrest shall issue

---

[839] "AUTOS & VISTOS: Comentarios jurisprudenciales". Colegio de Abogados de Lima y Gaceta Juridica, January, 1996. pp. 41-53.

[840] VerExp. N° 1658-95. published in the Diario Oficial El Peruano. "Jurisprudencia". September 4, 1996. pp. 2297.

[841] VerExp. N° 263-96. published in the Diario Oficial El Peruano. December 28, 1996. pp. 2698: repeated December 29, 1996. pp. 2748-2749.

[842] Ley N° 26301, Aprueban Ley Referida a la Aplicacio de la Accion Constitucional de Habeas Data, May 2, 1994. <http://www.asesor.com.pe/teleley/bull505.htm>.

[843] IFEX, "Habeas Data law modified and approved," 1995/04/25; IFEX, "President's Office promulgates reforms to Habeas Data laws," 1995/06/12.

---

except upon probable cause to be determined personally by the judge after examination under oath or affirmation of the complainant and the witnesses he may produce, and particularly describing the place to be searched and the persons or things to be seized." Section 3 states, "(1) The privacy of communication and correspondence shall be inviolable except upon lawful order of the court, or when public safety or order requires otherwise as prescribed by law. (2) Any evidence obtained in violation of this or the preceding section shall be inadmissible for any purpose in any proceeding." Section 7 states, "The right of the people to information on matters of public concern shall be recognized. Access to official records, and to documents and papers pertaining to official acts, transactions, or decisions, as well as to government research data used as basis for policy development, shall be afforded the citizen, subject to such limitations as may be provided by law."[844]

The Supreme Court ruled in July 1998 that Administrative Order No. 308, the Adoption of a National Computerized Identification Reference System, introduced by former President Ramos in 1996, was unconstitutional. The Court said that the order, "will put our people's right to privacy in clear and present danger . . . No one will refuse to get this ID for no one can avoid dealing with government. It is thus clear as daylight that without the ID, a citizen will have difficulty exercising his rights and enjoying his privileges." While stating that all laws invasive of privacy would be subject to "strict scrutiny," the Court also was careful to note that "the right to privacy does not bar all incursions to privacy."[845] President Joseph Estrada reiterated his support for the use of a national identification system in August 1998 stating that only criminals are against a national ID.[846] Justice Secretary Serafin Cuevas authorized the National Statistics Office (NSO) to proceed to use the population reference number (PRN) for the Civil Registry System-Information Technology Project (CRS-ITP) on August 14, claiming that it is not covered by the decision.[847]

There is no general data protection law but there is a recognized right of privacy in civil law.[848] The Civil Code also states that "[e]very person shall respect the dignity, personality, privacy, and peace of mind of his neighbors and other

---

[844] Constitution of the Republic of the Philippines, <http://pdx.rpnet.com/consti/index.htm>.

[845] Philippine Supreme Court Decision of the National ID System, July 23, 1998, G.R. 127685. <http://bknet.org/laws/nationalid.html>.

[846] "Erap wants nat'l ID system (Only criminals disagree with it, says the President)," Businessworld, August 12, 1998.

[847] Opinion Number 91. See Foundation laid for proposed nat'l ID, "Businessworld, August 14, 1998.

[848] Cordero v. Buigasco, 34130-R, April 17, 1972, 17 CAR (2s) 539; Jaworski v. Jadwani, CV-66405, December 15, 1983.

persons," and punishes acts that violate privacy by private citizens, public officers, or employees of private companies.[849] Bank records are protected by the Bank Secrecy Act.[850] The Senate debated a proposal in March to force three million citizens to file an annual "Statement of Assets and Liabilities (SAL)"[851]

In May 2000, the ILOVEYOU email virus was traced to a hacker in the Philippines, focusing international attention on the country's cyberlaw regime. The lack of any internet-specific laws frustrated investigation efforts, and prosecutors finally were able to gain a warrant under the 1998 Access Devices Regulation Act, a law intended to punish credit card fraud that outlaws the use of unauthorized access devices to obtain goods or services broadly.[852] On the heels of the virus attack, in May, President Joseph Estrada signed into law Republic Act 8972, the Electronic Commerce Act of 2000.[853] Sections 8,9, and 10 of the law give legal status to data messages, electronic writing, and digital signatures, making them admissible in court. Section 23 mandates a minimum fine of PP100,000 and a prison term of 6 months to 3 years for unlawful and unauthorized access to computer systems, and extends the consumer act, RA7394, to transactions using data messages. Section 21 of the Act requires the government to transact business with citizens through the web.[854] President Estrada signed the Implementing Rules and Regulations for the Act in July of 2000.[855]

The Anti-Wiretapping Law requires a court order to obtain a telephone tap.[856] The court order is to be awarded only if: 1) the wiretap is used to pursue the commission of certain crimes including treason, espionage, or sedition, 2) there are reasonable grounds to believe that evidence gained will be essential to conviction, and 3) there are no other means of obtaining the evidence. The law mandates a penalty of 6 months to 6 years for violators and limits the wiretapping authorization order to a renewable 60 days.[857] In April 1999, The

---

[849] Article 26 of the Civil Code, see Note 35 of the Philippine Supreme Court Decision of the National ID System, July 23, 1998, G.R. 127685. <http://bknet.org/laws/nationalid.html>.

[850] Republic Act 7653.

[851] House Bill 5345.

[852] Republic Act No. 8484, <http://www.chanrobles.com/republicactno8484.htm>.

[853] Republic Act No 8972, <http://www.bknet.org/laws/ecomm.html>.

[854] Republic Act No. 8792, the Electronic Commerce Act of 2000. <http://www.bknet.org/laws/ecomm.html>.

[855] Stephen Lawson, "Philippine leader gives e-commerce law teeth," IDG News Service, July 13, 2000.

[856] Republic Act 4200, June 19, 1965; Penal Code, Articles 290-292. <http://www.bknet.org/laws/ra4200.html>.

[857] Republic Act No. 4200. <http://www.bknet.org/laws/ra4200.html>.

National Bureau of Investigation and the Ombudsman started investigations after reports that police had tapped up to 3,000 telephone lines including top government officials, politicians, religious leaders, businessmen and print and television journalists. In May 1998, Director Gen. Santiago Alino, chief of the Philippine National Police, ordered an investigation of the alleged electioneering and illegal wiretapping activities by members of the National Police's Special Project Alpha (SPA). Matillano said that his office received information that the former SPA men had been using the office as their "monitoring center" against Vice-President Estrada's political opponents. Five recorders used to monitor wiretaps were found at the offices.[858] The House and the Senate held investigations in August 1997 after officials of the telephone company admitted that their employees were being paid to conduct illegal wiretaps.[859]

The Code of Conduct and Ethical Standards for Public Officials and Employees[860] mandates the disclosure of public transactions and guarantees access to official information, records or documents. Agencies must act on a request within 15 working days from receipt of the request. Complaints against public officials and employees who fail to act on request can be filed with the Civil Service Commission or the Office of the Ombudsman.

Republic of Poland

The Polish Constitution recognizes the rights of privacy and data protection. Article 47 states, "Everyone shall have the right to legal protection of his private and family life, of his honor and good reputation and to make decisions about his personal life." Article 51 states, "(1) No one may be obliged, except on the basis of statute, to disclose information concerning his person. (2) Public authorities shall not acquire, collect nor make accessible information on citizens other than that which is necessary in a democratic state ruled by law. (3) Everyone shall have a right of access to official documents and data collections concerning himself. Limitations upon such rights may be established by statute. (4) Everyone shall have the right to demand the correction or deletion of untrue or incomplete information, or information acquired by means contrary to statute. (5) Principles and procedures for collection of and access to information shall be specified by statute."[861]

---

[858] Balita News Service, May 7, 1998.

[859] "Wiretapping probe," BusinessWorld (Manila), August 26, 1997.

[860] Republic Act 6713 of 1987 <http://www.bknet.org/laws/ra6713.html>.

[861] The Constitutional Act of 1997. <http://www.sejm.gov.pl/eng/konst/kon1.htm>.

The Law on the Protection of Personal Data Protection was approved in October 1997 and took effect in April 1998.[862] The law is based on the European Union Data Protection Directive. Under the Law, personal information may only be processed with the consent of the individual. Everyone has the right to verify his or her personal records held by government agencies or private companies. Every citizen has the right to be informed whether such databases exist and who administers them; queries should be answered within 30 days. Upon finding out that data is incorrect, inaccurate, outdated or collected in a way that constitutes a violation of the Act, citizens have the right to request that the data be corrected, filled in or withheld from processing.[863] Personal information cannot generally be transferred outside of Poland unless the country has "comparable" protections. A 1998 regulation from the Minister of Internal Affairs and Administration sets out standards for the security of information systems that contain personal information.[864]

The Act is enforced by the Bureau of Inspector General for the Protection of Personal Data.[865] The Bureau maintains a register of data files and can make checks on the basis of a complaint or by random inspections. The Bureau is also responsible for registering databases. An inspector has the right to access data, check data transfer and security systems, and determine whether the information gathered is appropriate for the purpose that it is supposed to serve.[866] The office monitors the activities of all central government, local government and private institutions, individuals and corporations. Between April 1998 and April 1999, the Bureau received 3,150 written inquiries, 4,500 phone calls, and 402 complaints. The Inspector General expressed her opinion in 92 cases and notified many government agencies on the legality of their activities. She also referred one case to the Public Prosecutors Office. The Bureau had 51 staff as of April 1999. It said in July 1999 that estimates that it will register between 100,000 and 150,000 databases.[867]

---

[862] Law on Protection of Personal Data, Dz.U. nr 133, poz. 833, 29 October 1997.

[863] "The Info Boom's Murky Side," Warsaw Voice, November 9, 1997.

[864] The Regulation of June 3, 1998 By the Minister of Internal Affairs and Administration As regards establishing basic, technical and organisational conditions which should be fulfilled by devices and information systems used for the personal data processing (Journal of Laws of June 30, 1998, No. 80, item 521).

[865] Homepage: http://www.giodo.gov.pl

[866] "A One-Woman Orchestra," Warsaw Voice, June 21, 1998.

[867] Letter from the Bureau of Inspector General, July 1, 1999.

There are two separate schemes for the regulation of interception of communications. Under the Code of Penal Procedure that took effect in September 1998, telephones can be tapped only after the person in charge of the investigation has obtained permission from a court. In special instances, the prosecutor has the right to authorize a wiretap, but the decision must be confirmed by a court within five days.[868] The law specifies for which cases the interception of communications may be authorized.[869] There is also the system of administratively authorized interception, which applies to pre-emptive activities of the police, the Office of State Security (UOP), the Office of Revenue Control and the Border Guard. The police must obtain an order which is issued by the Ministry of Interior and accepted by the Prosecutor General. The UOP can tap for cases involving state sovereignty; illegal trafficking in arms and explosives, drugs and psychotropic substances as well as radioactive materials which are international nature or terrorist character; grave corruption of public officials endengaring the interests of the state.

According to official data released by the Internal Affairs Ministry in 1995, 3,000 wiretaps and mail intercepts were ordered in 1995.[870] In April 1999, Minister Janusz Palubicki admitted that the Office of State Security (UOP) had conducted surveillance of left and right political parties from 1992 until 1997.[871] An inquiry into the surveillance is ongoing. The Ministry of Justice has asked former Prime Ministers Waldemar Pawlak, Jozef Oleksy and Wlodzimierz Cimoszewicz to give testimony in the case.[872] The Sejm Committee on Special Services rejected the Military Information Services (WSI) bill in March 1999 saying that it failed to adequately restrict surveillance by military agencies.[873] The Ministry of Internal Affairs and Administration announced in January 2000 that it was setting up a new unit of 1,500 officers based on the US FBI to combat organized crime. The new unit will have the power to conduct electronic surveillance and create extensive databases.[874]

The United Nations Human Rights Committee in July 1999 was critical of the legal controls noting, "the Committee is concerned that the Prosecutor (without judicial consent) may permit telephone tapping and that there is no independent

---

[868] "Bugged About Wiretapping," Warsaw Voice, May 26, 1996.

[869] Article 237.

[870] Ibid Warsaw Voice, May 26, 1996.

[871] "UOP Head Confirms Political Surveillance," Polish News Bulletin, April 8, 1999.

[872] "Former Prime Ministers to Testify in Surveillance Case," Polish News Bulletin, April 8, 1999.

[873] "Military Intelligence Bill Criticised," Polish News Bulletin, February 17, 1999.

[874] "New Police Unit to Combat Organised Crime," Polish News Bulletin, January 4, 2000.

monitoring of the use of the entire system of tapping telephones. The State party should review these matters so as to ensure compatibility with article 17, introduce a system of independent monitoring."[875] The International Helsinki Federation for Human Rights stated in its 1999 report that "there was a clear tendency of increased inference in individuals' privacy. In addition to the police, the State Security Office, Military Information Service, customs inspectors, fiscal control agencies, and others were allowed to use various operational techniques such as tapping phones and monitoring correspondence."[876]

Controversy still surrounds efforts to create an expanded national id system. The Electronic Census System (PESEL) number, which has been issued since the mid-1970s, is the biggest collection of personal data in Poland. Every identity card contains a PESEL number, which is a confirmation of the owner's date of birth and sex. The system is fully computerized. A Tax Identification Number (NIP) is also being developed. This system will be fully computerized in the near future.

The Constitutional Tribunal ruled in March 1998 that requiring doctors to identify, on sick leave certificates, the disease of the patient violated the patients' right to privacy.

There is a governmental proposal to give the Polish police the right to set up personal data bases that include 'sensitive' information such as sexual orientation, DNA fingerprints, health status, religious and political beliefs on crime suspects. This initiative was stopped by the opposition (SLD) during the ballot after the first reading of the bill. However, the provisions relating to access to bank records and traffic data of telecom providers are likely to be reviewed again by the Parliament.

There is no general freedom of information act in Poland. The Polish Journalists' Union (SDP) and the Adam Smith Centre developed a bill and presented it to Parliament in June 2000. They urged the government to adopt the bill in the current session of Parliament. In May, the two groups met with Prime Minister Jerzy Buzek, who agreed that the law should be adopted.[877] Poland enacted the Classified Information Protection Act in January 1999 as a condition to entering

---

[875] United Nations, Report of the Human Rights Committee, A/54/40, 21 October 1999.

[876] International Helsinki Federation for Human Rights. ANNUAL REPORT 1999: Poland. <http://www.ihf-hr.org/reports/ar99/ar99pol.htm>.

[877] "Journalists, Adam Smith Centre present freedom of information," PAP news agency, June 12, 2000.

NATO.[878] The act covers classified information or information collected by government agencies that disclosure "might damage interests of the state, public interests, or lawfully protected interests of citizens or of an organization."

There have also been efforts to deal with the files of former employees of the communist era secret police. A law creating a National Remembrance Institute (IPN) to allow victims of this secret police agency access to records was approved by the Parliament in October 1998. President Aleksander Kwasniewski vetoed the bill saying that it should allow all Poles access to the records but his veto was overridden and he later signed the bill.[879] A new director was finally approved for the institute in June 2000. The IPN will now take control of all archives of the communist-era security service and those of courts, prosecutors' offices, the former communist party and other institutions. "It will take several months before the opening of the first file," said the new director. [880] Poles will be allowed to see their personal files compiled by the authorities before 1989 and learn if they suffered from discrimination and possibly who informed on them.

The Screening Act, which allows a special commission to examine the records of government officials who might have collaborated with the secret police, was approved in June 1997. In November 1998, the Constitutional Tribunal ruled that the act was constitutional except for two provisions. As of January 1999, the Screening Department of the Appellate Court had received 23,460 screening statements from public officials.[881] There are continuing concerns about the accuracy of the records and their use for political reasons. In July 2000, the Parliamentary Commission for Special Services determined that the State Protection Office had not violated the Act when it gave the lustration court documents on President Aleksander Kwasniewski. However, it said that the UOP improperly concluded that Kwasniewski was a secret agent and had delayed providing documents which prevented the court from investigating. The Democratic Left Alliance (SLD) said that the UOP had done this deliberately to influence the election.[882] In August 2000, the court found that the secret police had attempted to frame Nobel Prize winner Lech Walesa, who is running for President, by falsifying documents alleging that he was an informer. Prime Minister Jerzy Buzek called the accusations "a dismal joke of history."[883]

---

[878] The Classified Information Protection Act of 22 January 1999.

[879] "Veto Overridden, President Signs Secret Files Bill," Polish News Bulletin, December 21, 1998.

[880] Reuters, June 8, 2000.

[881] "Appellate Court Receives Over 23,000 Screening Statements," Polish News Bulletin, January 5, 1999.

[882] RFE/RL NEWSLINE Vol. 4, No. 146, Part II, 1 August 2000

[883] "Walesa Cleared as Informer," Washington Post, August 12, 2000.

Poland is a member of the Council of Europe and signed the Convention for the Protection of Individuals with Regard to Automatic Processing of Personal Data (ETS No. 108) in April 1999 but has not yet ratified it.[884] Poland has signed and ratified the European Convention for the Protection of Human Rights and Fundamental Freedoms.[885] Poland is a member of the Organization for Economic Cooperation and Development and has adopted the OECD Guidelines on the Protection of Privacy and Transborder Flows of Personal Data.

Republic of Portugal

The Portuguese Constitution has extensive provisions on protecting privacy, secrecy of communications and data protection.[886] Article 26 states, "(1) Everyone's right to his or her personal identity, civil capacity, citizenship, good name and reputation, image, the right to speak out, and the right to the protection of the intimacy of his or her private and family life is recognized. (2) The law establishes effective safeguards against the abusive use, or any use that is contrary to human dignity, of information concerning persons and families. (3) A person may be deprived of citizenship or subjected to restrictions on his or her civil capacity only in cases and under conditions laid down by law, and never on political grounds." Article 34 states, "(1) The individual's home and the privacy of his correspondence and other means of private communication are inviolable. (2) A citizen's home may not be entered against his will, except by order of the competent judicial authority and in the cases and according to the forms laid down by law. (3) No one may enter the home of any person at night without his consent. (4) Any interference by public authority with correspondence or telecommunications, apart from the cases laid down by law in connection with criminal procedure, are prohibited."

In 1997, Article 35 of the Constitution was amended to give citizens a right to data protection. The new Article 35 states, "1. All citizens have the right of access to any computerised data relating to them and the right to be informed of the use for which the data is intended, under the law; they are entitled to require that the contents of the files and records be corrected and brought up to date. 2. The law shall determine what is personal data as well as the conditions applicable

---

[884] <http://conventions.coe.int/>.

[885] <http://conventions.coe.int/>.

[886] Constitution of the Portuguese Republic,
<http://www.parlamento.pt/leis/constituicao_ingles/IND_CRP_ING.htm>.

to automatic processing, connection, transmission and use thereof, and shall guarantee its protection by means of an independent administrative body. 3. Computerised storage shall not be used for information concerning a person's ideological or political convictions, party or trade union affiliations, religious beliefs, private life or ethnic origin, except where there is express consent from the data subject, authorisation provided for under the law with guarantees of non-discrimination or, in the case of data, for statistical purposes, that does not identify individuals. 4. Access to personal data of third parties is prohibited, except in exceptional cases as prescribed by law. 5. Citizens shall not be given an all-purpose national identity number. 6. Everyone shall be guaranteed free access to public information networks and the law shall define the regulations applicable to the transnational data flows and the adequate norms of protection for personal data and for data that should be safeguarded in the national interest. 7. Personal data kept on manual files shall benefit from protection identical to that provided for in the above articles, in accordance with the law.."

The 1998 Act on the Protection of Personal Data adopts the EU Data Protection requirements into Portuguese law.[887] It limits the collection, use and dissemination of personal information in manual or electronic form. It also applies to video surveillance or "other forms of capture, processing and dissemination of sound and images." It replaces the 1991 Act on the Protection of Personal Data with Regard to Automatic Processing.[888]

The Act is enforced by the National Data Protection Commission (Comissão Nacional de Protecção de Dados - CNPD).[889] The Commission is an independent Parliament-based agency that registers databases, authorizes and controls databases, issues directives, and oversees the Schengen information system.[890] In 1998, the commission conducted 78 investigations, double of the 42 investigations handled in 1997 and referred 14 cases for criminal prosecution to the Public Prosecution Service. It also authorized 553 databases for a total of 3000 approvals since 1994. The Commission also handled 100 inspections in

---

[887] Act nº 67/98 of 26 October. Act on the Protection of Personal Data (transposing into the Portuguese legal system Directive 95/46/EC of the European Parliament and of the Council of 24 October 1995 on the protection of individuals with regard to the processing of personal data and on the free movement of such data). <http://www.cnpd.pt/Leis/lei_6798en.htm>.

[888] Lei nº 10/91 - Lei da Protecção de Dados Pessoais face à Informática, <http://www.cnpdpi.pt/Leis/lei_1091.htm>. Amended by Lei n.º 28/94, de 29 de Agosto. Aprova medidas de reforço da protecção de dados pessoais <http://www.cnpdpi.pt/>.

[889] Web Site: <http://www.cnpd.pt/>.

[890] <http://www.cnpdpi.pt/bin/competencias.htm>.

1998, mostly relating to financial services.[891] It issued opinions on obtaining subscriber information from telecommunications providers, access to marketing databases by the Criminal Investigation Police, denied access by the Information and Security Service to the information system of the Aliens and Frontiers Department and approved transborder dataflows to the United States when the parent company promised to protect the information under European law. In June 1997, the Supreme Administrative Tribunal upheld the Commission in a case against a shoe company that used smart cards to control employees' bathroom visits.

The penal code has provisions against unlawful surveillance and interference with privacy.[892] Evidence obtained by any violation of privacy, the home, correspondence or telecommunications without the consent of the interested party is null and void.[893] An inquiry was opened in October 1994 on illegal surveillance of politicians after microphones were discovered in the offices of a state prosecutor and several ministers.[894] The Portuguese government ordered cellular telephone companies to assist with surveillance in October 1996.[895] Law 69/98 implements the EU Telecommunications Directive 97/66/EC.[896]

There are also specific laws on the Schengen Information System,[897] computer crime,[898] and counseling centers.[899]

Law n° 65/93, of 26 August 1993 provides for access to government records in any form by any person.[900] Documents can be withheld for "internal or external

---

[891] National Commission for the Protection of Computerised Personal Data (NCPCPD), 1998 Report <http://www.cnpd.pt/bin/rel98ing.htm>.

[892] Chapter VI, Penal Code, Section 179-183.

[893] Article 126 of the Code of Penal Procedure paragraph 3. See United Nations, "Committee Against Torture Consideration of Reports Submitted by States Parties Under Article 19 of the Convention," Addendum, Portugal, 10 June 1997.

[894] "Bug Found in Portuguese State Prosecutor's Office," The Reuters European Business Report, April 27, 1994.

[895] "Portugal to tap mobile phones in drugs war," Reuters World Service, October 9, 1996.

[896] Regula o tratamento dos dados pessoais e a protecÇÃo da privacidade no sector das telecomunicaçoes (transpoe a directiva 97/66/ce, do parlamento europeu e do conselho, de 15 de dezembro de 1997) <http://www.cnpd.pt/Leis/lei_6998.htm>.

[897] Lei n.º 2/94, de 19 de Fevereiro Estabelece os mecanismos de controlo e fiscalização do Sistema de Informação Schengen, <http://www.cnpdpi.pt/Leis/lei_294.htm>.

[898] Lei n° 109/91 - Sobre a criminalidade informática, <http://www.cnpdpi.pt/Leis/lei_10991.htm>.

[899] Act No. 3/84 of 24 March.

[900] Lei n° 65/93, de 26 de Agosto, com as alterações constantes da Lei n° 8/95, de 29 de Março e pela Lei n°94/99, de 16 de Julho <http://www.cada.pt/paginas/lada.html>.

---

security," secrecy of justice, and personal privacy. It is overseen by the Commission for Access to Administrative Documents (CADA), an independent Parliamentary agency.[901] The CADA can examine complaints, provide opinions on access, and decide on classification of systems. CADA issued 177 opinions in 1998.

Portugal is a member of the Council of Europe and has signed and ratified the Convention for the Protection of Individuals with Regard to Automatic Processing of Personal Data (ETS No. 108).[902] It has signed and ratified the European Convention for the Protection of Human Rights and Fundamental Freedoms.[903] It is a member of the Organization for Economic Cooperation and Development and has adopted the OECD Guidelines on the Protection of Privacy and Transborder Flows of Personal Data.

Russian Federation

The Constitution of the Russian Federation recognizes rights of privacy, data protection and secrecy of communications. Article 23 states, "1. Everyone shall have the right to privacy, to personal and family secrets, and to protection of one's honor and good name. 2. Everyone shall have the right to privacy of correspondence, telephone communications, mail, cables and other communications. Any restriction of this right shall be allowed only under an order of a court of law." Article 24 states, "1. It shall be forbidden to gather, store, use and disseminate information on the private life of any person without his/her consent. 2. The bodies of state authority and the bodies of local self-government and the officials thereof shall provide to each citizen access to any documents and materials directly affecting his/her rights and liberties unless otherwise stipulated under the law." Article 25 states, "The home shall be inviolable. No one shall have the right to enter the home against the will of persons residing in it except in cases stipulated by the federal law or under an order of a court of law."[904] The Russian Supreme Court ruled in 1998 that regulations requiring individuals to register and obtain permission from local officials before they could live in Moscow violated the Constitution.[905]

---

[901] Home Page: <http://www.cada.pt/>.

[902] Signed 14/05/81, Ratified 02/09/93, Entered into force 01/01/94, <http://conventions.coe.int/>.

[903] Signed 22/09/76, Ratified 09/11/78, Entered into force 09/11/78, <http://conventions.coe.int/>.

[904] Constitution of the Russian Federation, 1993. <http://www.friends-partners.org/oldfriends/constitution/russian-const-ch2.html>. (English).

[905] RFE/RL, March 11, 12, 1998.

The Duma approved the Law of the Russian Federation on Information, Informatization, and Information Protection in January 1995.[906] The law covers both the government and private sectors and licenses the processing of personal information by the private sector. It imposes a code of fair information practices on the processing of personal information. It prohibits the use of personal information to "inflict economic or moral damage on citizens." The use of sensitive information (social origin, race, nationality, language, religion or party membership) is also prohibited. Citizens and organizations have the right of access to the documented information about them, to correct it and supplement it.

The Russian law does not establish a central regulatory body for data protection and it is not clear that it has been effective. It application to the Internet has also been limited. The law specifies that responsibility for data protection rests with the data controllers. The law is overseen by the Committee of the State Duma on Information and Informatization and the State Committee on Information and Informatization under the Russian President Authority.

The Duma is reviewing the Law on Information of Personal Character bill to update the 1995 act to make it more compliant with the Council of Europe's Convention 108 and the E.U. Directive. The bill has been pending for several years.

Secrecy of communications is protected by the 1995 Communications Act. The tapping of telephone conversations, scrutiny of electric-communications messages, delay, inspection and seizure of postal mailings and documentary correspondence, receipt of information therein, and other restriction of communications secrets are allowed only on the basis of a court order.[907] The Law on Operational Investigation Activity regulates surveillance methods of the secret services and requires a warrant.[908] This law was amended in December 1998 by the State Duma. Guarantees for the protection of privacy were stressed and additional controls imposed on prosecutors. In December 1999, the law was expanded to allow surveillance by the tax police, Interior Ministry, Border Guards, the Kremlin security service, the presidential security service, the

---

[906] Russian Federation Federal Act No. 24-FZ, Law of the Russian Federation on Information, Informatization and Information Protection, 25th January 1995. <http://www.datenschutz-berlin.de/gesetze/internat/fen.htm>. (extracts).

[907] Russian Federation Federal Act No. 15-FZ. Adopted by the State Duma on January 20, 1995.

[908] "Yeltsin Signs Law Regulating Criminal Investigations, " OMRI, August 16, 1995.

parliamentary security services and the Foreign Intelligence Service.[909] It is widely accepted that the Federal Security Service (FBS) still conducts widespread illegal wiretapping. In July 2000, a tabloid newspaper posted files on hundred of prominent Russians including politicians, bankers, and journalists showing that they were under surveillance.[910]

In 1998, the FSB issued a secret ministerial act named the System for Operational Research Actions on the Documentary Telecommunication Networks (SORM-2) that would require Internet Service Providers to install surveillance devices and high speed links to the FSB which would allow the FSB direct access to the communications of Internet users without a warrant.[911] ISPs would be required to pay for the costs of installing and maintaining the devices. Most ISPs have not publicly resisted the FSB demands to install the devices but one ISP in Volgograd, Bayard Slavia Communication, challenged the FSB demands to install the system. The local FSB and Ministry of Communication attempted to have their license revoked but backed off after the ISP challenged their decision in court. A lawyer in Irkutsk sued, challenging the legality of the declaration and the Supreme Court ruled in May 2000 that the SORM-2 was not a valid ministerial act because it failed several procedural requirements. The case is now pending before a trial court.

There are also privacy protections in the Civil Code[912] and the Criminal Code.[913] The United Nations Human Rights Committee expressed concerns over the state of privacy in Russia in 1995 and recommended the enactment of additional privacy laws. It noted: "The Committee is concerned that actions may continue which violate the right to protection from unlawful or arbitrary interference with privacy, family, home or correspondence. It is concerned that the mechanisms to intrude into private telephone communication continue to exist, without a clear legislation setting out the conditions of legitimate interference with privacy and providing for safeguards against unlawful interference.....The Committee urges that legislation be passed on the protection of privacy, as well as strict and positive action be taken to prevent violations of the right to protection from

---

[909] "Police Get Window Of Access To E-mail," The Moscow Times, January 13, 2000.

[910] "Alleged Russian Spy Files Posted," Associated Press, July 7, 2000.

[911] "Russia Prepares To Police Internet," The Moscow Times, July 29, 1998. More information in English and Russian is available from the Moscow Libertarium Forum <http://www.libertarium.ru/libertarium/sorm/>.

[912] Civil Code, Article 19. RF Act No. 51-FZ. Adopted By The State Duma on October 21, 1994.

[913] The Criminal Code of the Russian Federation No. 63-FZ of June 13, 1996.

unlawful or arbitrary interference with privacy, family, home or correspondence."[914]

The Christian Orthodox Church issued an official protest about the new national Tax ID card in March 2000. The card, issued for tax collection, contained the series of numbers 666. Government officials have also proposed that the ID card be used as a social security card and eventually replace passports.[915]

Law of the Russian Federation on Information, Informatization, and Information Protection also serves as a Freedom of Information law. The scope of the law in generally limited. A more broad FOIA bill entitled "Federal Law on the Right to Access Information" is currently pending in the Duma. The bill creates a presumption that information is "available and open," "reliable and complete" and "must be timely disclosed." Agencies must respond within 30 days. Information can be withheld if it is a "national, commercial, official, professional or banking secret" or related to a "valid investigation and fact-finding proceedings." If information is withheld, the person can appeal to the agency, then to a court and the Human Rights Ombudsman.

Russia is a member of the Council of Europe but has not signed and ratified the Convention for the Protection of Individuals with Regard to Automatic Processing of Personal Data (ETS No. 108).[916] It has signed and ratified the European Convention for the Protection of Human Rights and Fundamental Freedoms.[917]

Autonomous Russian Republics

Some of the twenty-two autonomous republics of the Russian Federation have constitutional provisions on privacy. In some cases, these republics claim that their constitutions take precedence within their territories over that of the Russian Federation.

---

[914] United Nations Human Rights Committee, Comments on Russian Federation, U.N. Dcc. CCPR/C/79/Add.54 (1995), <http://www.law.wits.ac.za//humanrts/hrcommittee/RUSSIA.htm>.

[915] "Devil in the numbers for russian tax id card plan," Reuters, March 23, 2000.

[916] <http://conventions.coe.int/>.

[917] Signed 28/02/96, Ratified 05/05/98, Entered into force 05/05/98, <http://conventions.coe.int/>.

Republic of San Marino

The Act on Collection, Elaboration and Use of computerized personal data was enacted in 1983 and amended in 1995.[918] The Act applies to any computerized filing system or data bank, both private and public. It prohibits the collection of personal and confidential data through fraudulent, illegal or unfair means. It requires that information is accurate, relevant and complete. Any individual is entitled both to inquire whether his or her personal data have been collected or processed, to obtain a copy, and to require that inaccurate, outdated, incomplete or ambiguous data, or data whose collection, processing, transmission or preservation is forbidden, be rectified, integrated, clarified, updated or canceled. The creation of a data bank requires the prior authorization of both the State Congress (the Government) and the Guarantor for the Safeguard of Confidential and Personal Data. There are additional rules for sensitive information. Infringements can be punished by means of administrative sanctions or penalties. There were a number of Regency's Decrees issued under the 1983 Act that remained in force after the 1995 revisions.[919] The Regulation on Statistical Data Collection and Public Competence in Data Processing[920] regulates data processing within the Public Administration.

The Act is enforced by the Guarantor for the Safeguard of Confidential and Personal Data, a judge of the Administrative Court. The Guarantor can examine any claim or petition relating to the application of the above-mentioned law and pass judgment whenever the confidentiality of personal data is violated. His judgment can be appealed to a higher court. The release of information to other countries is conditioned on the prior authorization of the Guarantor, who must verify that the country to which confidential information is being transmitted ensures the same level of protection of personal data as that established in Sammarinese legislation.

San Marino is a member of the Council of Europe but has not signed or ratified the Convention for the Protection of Individuals with Regard to Automatic

---

[918] Regulating the Computerized Collection of Personal Data, Law N. 70 of 23 May 1995 revising Law N. 27 of 1 March 1983. Amended by law 70/95. See
<http://www.hri.ca/fortherecord1997/documentation/commission/e-cn4-1997-67.htm>.

[919] Decree N. 7 of 13 March 1984, "Establishment of a State Data Bank as provided for by Article 5 of Law N. 27 of 1 March 1983"; Decree N. 7 of 3 June 1986, "Integration to Decree N. 7 of 13 March 1984, Establishing a State Data Bank"; Decree N. 140 of 26 November 1987, "Procedures for the Establishment of Private Data Banks."

[920] Regulation on Statistical Data Collection and Public Competence in Data Processing, Law N. 71 of 23 May 1995.

Processing of Personal Data (ETS No. 108).[921] It has signed and ratified the European Convention for the Protection of Human Rights and Fundamental Freedoms.[922]

Republic of Singapore

The Singapore Constitution is based on the British system and does not contain any explicit right to privacy.[923] The High Court has ruled that personal information may be protected from disclosure under a duty of confidences.[924]

There is no general data protection or privacy law in Singapore. The government has been aggressive in using surveillance to promote social control and limit domestic opposition.[925] In 1986, then-Prime Minister and founder of modern Singapore Lee Kwan Yew proudly described his stance on privacy:

> I am often accused of interfering in the private lives of citizens. Yet, if I did not, had I not done that, we wouldn't be here today. And I say without the slightest remorse, that we wouldn't be here, we would not have made economic progress, if we had not intervened on very personal matters – who your neighbor is, how you live, the noise you make, how you spit, or what language you use. We decide what is right, never mind what the people think. That's another problem.[926]

In September 1998, the National Internet Advisory Board released an industry-based self-regulatory "E-Commerce Code for the Protection of Personal Information and Communications of Consumers of Internet Commerce."[927] The code encourages providers to ensure the confidentiality of business records and personal information of users, including details of usage or transactions, would prohibit the disclosure of personal information, and would require providers not

---

921 <http://conventions.coe.int/>.

922 Signed 16/11/88, Ratified 22/03/89, Entered into force 22/03/89, <http://conventions.coe.int/>.

923 Constitution of the Republic of Singapore, 16 September 1963. <http://www.uni-wuerzburg.de/law/sn00t___.html>.

924 X v CDE1992 2 SLR 996

925 See Christophen Tremewan, The Political Economy of Social Control in Singapore (St. Martin's Press, 1994)

926 Lee Kwan Yew's speech at National Day Rally, 1996, Straights Times, 20 April 1987, Cited in The Political Economy of Social Control in Singapore.

927 Report of the National Internet Advisory Board 1997/1998, September 1998. <http://www.sba.gov.sg/work/sba/internet.nsf/>.

---

to intercept communications unless required by law. The code would also limit collection and prohibit disclosure of personal information without informing the consumer and giving them an option to stop the transfer, ensure accuracy of records and provide a right to correct or delete data. According to the Singapore Broadcast Authority, in 1999, the Code was adopted by CaseTrust and incorporated into its Code of Practice as part of an accreditation scheme promoting good business practices among store-based and web-based retailers. CaseTrust is a joint project operated by the Consumers Association of Singapore, CommerceNet Singapore Limited and the Retail Promotion Centre in Singapore. The Infocomm Development Authority announced in March 2000 that it would endorse the TRUSTe system as "an industry 'trustmark' seal."[928]

The Singapore Broadcasting Authority is the regulatory authority for the electronic medium in Singapore. It is a statutory board under the Ministry of Information and the Arts (MITA). The IDA is also developing a "Model Code for the Protection of Personal Information."

In July 1998, the Singapore government enacted three major bills concerning computer networks. They are the Computer Misuse (Amendment) Act, the Electronic Transactions Act and the National Computer Board (Amendment) Act. The CMA prohibits the unauthorized interception of computer communications.[929] The CMA also provides the police with additional powers of investigations. Under the amended Act, it is now an offense to refuse to assist the police in an investigation. Amendments also widened the provisions allowing the police lawful access to data and encrypted material in their investigations of offenses under the CMA as well as other offenses disclosed in the course of their investigations. Such power of access requires the consent of the Public Prosecutor. The Electronic Transactions Act imposes a duty of confidentiality on records obtained under the act and imposes a maximum SG$10,000 fine and 12 month jail sentence for disclosing those records without authorization. Police have broad powers to search any computer and to require disclosure of documents for an offence related to the act without a warrant.[930]

Electronic surveillance of communications is governed by the Telecommunications Authority of Singapore (TAS). The government has extensive powers under the Internal Security Act and other acts to monitor

---

[928] Infocomm Development Authority, Helping Singaporeans Go Online, March 2000. <http://www.ida.gov.sg>.

[929] Computer Misuse Act (Chapter 50A), <http://www.lawnet.com.sg/freeaccess/CMA.htm>.

[930] Electronic Transactions Act (Act 25 of 1998) <http://www.lawnet.com.sg/freeaccess/ETA.htm>.

---

anything that is considered a threat to "national security." The U.S. State Department in 1998 stated, "Divisions of the Government's law enforcement agencies, including the Internal Security Department and the Corrupt Practices Investigation Board, have wide networks for gathering information. It is believed that the authorities routinely monitor citizens' telephone conversations and use of the Internet. While there were no proven allegations that they did so in 1997, it is widely believed that the authorities routinely conduct surveillance on some opposition politicians and other critics of the Government."[931] All of the Internet Services Providers are operated by government-owned or government-controlled companies.[932] Each person in Singapore wishing to obtain an Internet account must show their national ID card to the provider to obtain an account.[933] ISPs reportedly provide information on users to government officials without legal requirements on a regular basis. In 1994, Technet – then the only Internet provider in the country serving the academic and technical community – scanned through the email of its members looking for pornographic files. According to Technet, they scanned the files without opening the mails, looking for clues like large file sizes. In September 1996, a man was fined US$43,000 for downloading sex films from the Internet. It was the first enforcement of Singapore's Internet regulation. The raid followed a tip-off from Interpol, which was investigating people exchanging pornography online. Afterwards, the SBA assured citizens that it does not monitor e-mail messages, chat groups, what sites people access, or what they download.[934]

In 1999, the Home Affairs Ministry scanned 200,000 users of SingNet ISP at the request of the company looking for the "Back Orifice" program without telling the subscribers. The Telecommunications Authority of Singapore said that the ISP had violated no law but SingNet apologized for the scans and the National Information Technology Committee announced that it would create new guidelines.[935] The Infocomm Development Authority released guidelines in January 2000.[936] Under the guidelines, a subscriber's explicit consent must be obtained before scanning can occur. The scanning must be minimally intrusive and must not intercept web browsing or electronic communications. A November

---

[931] U.S. Department of State Singapore Country Report on Human Rights Practices for 1997, January 30, 1998.

[932] Garry Roday, "The Internet and Social Control in Singapore," Pol. Sci. Q. Vol. 113, No. 1, Spring 1998.

[933] Ibid.

[934] The Straits Times, September 27, 1996.

[935] "ISPs to get guidelines on scanning," The Straits Times, May 12, 1999.

[936] Infocomm Development Authority of Singapore, Guidelines for IASPs on Scanning of Subscribers' Computers, January 6, 2000. <http://www.ida.gov.sg>.

1999 study by the Singapore Polytechnic's business administration revealed 60 percent of consumers who stated they were unready for virtual shopping cited privacy concerns.[937]

The Minister for Home Affairs announced in March 2000 that it was creating a "Speakers Corner" based on the one in London. However, speakers will be required to register with the local police station and show their national ID card or passport. The personal information will be held for five years.[938] Home Affairs Minister Wong Kan Seng said that the records will be kept for investigative purposes to ensure that the speaker had registered.[939]

The Ministry of Health announced in August 1999 that it was creating a central medical database.[940] The database will hold all patients' records from all hospitals and clinics in Singapore and be available to government and private doctors.

An extensive Electronic Road Pricing system for monitoring road usage went into effect in 1998. The system collects information on an automobile's travel from smart cards plugged into transmitters in every car and in video surveillance cameras.[941] The service claims that the data will only be kept for 24 hours and does not maintain a central accounting system. Video surveillance cameras are also commonly used for monitoring roads and preventing littering in many areas.[942] It was proposed in Tampines in 1995 that cameras be placed in all public spaces including corridors, lifts, and open areas such as public parks, car parks and neighborhood centers and broadcast on the public cable television channel.[943] A man was prosecuted under the Films Act in May 1999 for filming women in bathrooms.[944]

The Banking Act prohibits disclosure of financial information without the permission of the customer.[945] Numbered accounts can also be opened with the

---

[937] "Not many ready to cyber-shop, says poll," The Straits Times, November 18, 1999.

[938] "Singapore To Get `Speakers' Corner'," Asian Wall Street Journal, April 25, 2000.

[939] "Keeping records of speakers," The Straits Times, May 9, 2000.

[940] "Patients' database planned," The Straits Times, August 17, 1999.

[941] "You're on candid camera," The Straits Times, September 2, 1998.

[942] "Video cameras to monitor traffic at 15 junctions," The Straits Times, March 12, 1995; "Surveillance system set up in Jurong East," The Straits Times, July 16, 1996.

[943] "Do we really want an all-seeing camera?," The Straits Times, July 13, 1995.

[944] "Peeping Tom used hidden camera to spy," The Straits Times, May 29, 1999.

[945] Banking Act, Chapter 19, <http://www.mas.gov.sg/statutes/BankingAct-c.html>.

---

permission of the authority. The High Court can require disclosure of records to investigate drug trafficking and other serious crimes. The Monetary Authority of Singapore issued new "Know Your Customer" guidelines to banks in May 1998 on money laundering. Banks are required to "clarify the economic background and purpose of any transactions of which the form or amount appear unusual in relation to the customer, finance company or branch office concerned, or whenever the economic purpose and the legality of the transaction are not immediately evident.[946] Banks must report suspicious transactions to the MAS.

Slovak Republic

The 1992 Constitution provides for protections for privacy, data protection and secrecy of communications. Article 16 states, "(1) The inviolability of the person and its privacy is guaranteed. It can be limited only in cases defined by law." Article 19 states, "(1) Everyone has the right to the preservation of his human dignity and personal honor, and the protection of his good name. (2) Everyone has the right to protection against unwarranted interference in his private and family life. (3) Everyone has the right to protection against the unwarranted collection, publication, or other illicit use of his personal data." Article 22 states "(1) The privacy of correspondence and secrecy of mailed messages and other written documents and the protection of personal data are guaranteed. (2) No one must violate the privacy of correspondence and the secrecy of other written documents and records, whether they are kept in private or sent by mail or in another way, with the exception of cases to be set out in a law. Equally guaranteed is the secrecy of messages conveyed by telephone, telegraph, or other similar means."[947]

The Act on Protection of Personal Data in Information Systems was approved in February 1998 and went into effect in March 1998.[948] The Act replaces the previous 1992 Czechoslovakian legislation.[949] The new act closely tracks the EU Data Protection Directive and limits the collection, disclosure and use of personal information by government agencies and private enterprises either in electronic or manual form. It creates duties of access, accuracy and correction, security, and

---

[946] Monetary Authority of Singapore, Guidelines On Prevention Of Money Laundering," May 26, 1999 <http://www.mas.gov.sg/regulations/notices_MAS824-c.html>.

[947] Constitution of the Slovak Republic, 3 September 1992. <http://www.sanet.sk/Slovakia/Court/const.html>.

948 Act No. 52 of February 3, 1998 on Protection of Personal Data in Information Systems. <http://www.statistics.sk/webdata/english/acts/act5298/act5298.htm>. Decree of the Statistical Office of the Slovak Republic of 11 May 1998 <http://www.statistics.sk/webdata/english/acts/155decre/155decre.htm>.

[949] Act of April 29, 1992 on Protection of Personal Data in Information Systems (No. 256/92).

confidentiality on the data processor. Processing of information on racial, ethnic, political opinions, religion, philosophical beliefs, trade union membership, health, and sexuality is forbidden. Transfers to other countries are limited unless the country has "adequate" protection. All systems are required to be registered with the Statistical Office of the Slovak Republic.[950]

The Act creates a new office for a Commissioner for the Protection of Personal Data in Information Systems who will supervise and enforce the Act. The Commission monitors the protection of personal data in information systems and their registration, inspects the processing of personal data in information systems, receives and handles complaints concerning the violation of personal data protection in information systems, and initiates corrective actions whenever a breach of legal obligations is ascertained. The Commission has an Inspection Unit for Personal Data Protection which carries out supervision of tasks. The unit has 12 staff. The Office has conducted 20 investigations in the past year.[951]

Under the Code of Criminal Procedure, the police are required to obtain permission from a court or prosecutor before undertaking any telephone tapping.[952] However, the communist-era secret police still remain in positions of power and there have been many public revelations of illegal wiretapping of opposition politicians, reporters and dissidents.[953] In 1997, the UN Human Rights Committee recommended that the government: "ensure control, by an independent judicial authority, of the interception of confidential communications – related to, for example, wire-tapping and protection of the right to privacy."[954]

There are also other legal protections. Article 11 of the Civil Code states "everyone shall have the right to be free from unjustified interference in his or her privacy and family life." There are also computer-related offenses linked with the protection of a person (unjustified treatment of a personal data).[955] The

---

[950] Web Page: <http://www.statistics.sk/webdata/english/index2.htm>.

[951] Letter from Mr. Pavol Husar, Commissioner for the Protection of Personal Data in Information Systems to EPIC, August 1, 2000.

[952] Code of Criminal Procedure, sections 86 to 88.

[953] "Hungarian Politicians in Slovakia are Being Bugged," CTK National News Wire, February 21, 1995, "Deputy Brings Charges Against Slovak Secret Services Spokesman," CTK National News Wire, August 21, 1997.

[954] United Nations Human Rights Committee, July/August 1997 Session. <http://www.hri.ca/fortherecord1997/vol5/slovakia.htm>.

[955] European Commission, Agenda 2000 - Commission Opinion on Slovakia's Application for Membership of the European Union, Doc 97/20, July 15, 1997.

Slovak Constitutional Court ruled in March 1998 that the law allowing public prosecutors to demand to see the files or private correspondence of political parties, private citizens, trade union organizations and churches, even when not necessary for prosecution, was unconstitutional. Court chairman Milan Cic said this was "not only not usual, but opens the door to widespread violation of peoples' basic rights and their right to privacy."[956]

The Act on Free Access to Information was approved by the Parliament in May 2000. It sets broad rules on disclosure of information held by the government. There are limitation on information that is classified, a trade secret, would violate privacy, was obtained "from a person not required by law to provide information, who upon notification of the Obligee instructed the Obligee in writing not to disclose information," or "concerns the decision-making power of the courts and law enforcement bodies." Appeals are made to higher agencies and can be reviewed by a court. There are separate requirements for disclosure of environmental information that covers private organizations. It will become effective January 1, 2001.[957] Act 171/1998 of the National Council on Free Access to Environmental Information is revoked.

Slovakia is a member of the Council of Europe and signed the Convention for the Protection of Individuals with Regard to Automatic Processing of Personal Data (ETS No. 108) in April 2000.[958] It has signed and ratified the European Convention for the Protection of Human Rights and Fundamental Freedoms.[959]

Republic of Slovenia

The 1991 Constitution recognizes many privacy rights. Article 35 on the Protection of the Right to Privacy and of Personal Rights states, "The physical and mental integrity of each person shall be guaranteed, as shall be his right to privacy and his other personal rights." Article 37 on the Protection of Privacy of Post and Other Means of Communication states, "The privacy of the post and of other means of communication shall be guaranteed. In accordance with statute, a court may authorize action infringing on the privacy of the post or of other means of communication, or on the inviolability of individual privacy, where such actions are deemed necessary for the institution or continuance of criminal

---

[956] "Court Rules Law on Public Prosecutors Unconstitutional," CTK National News Wire, March 4, 1998.

[957] Act on Free Access to Information <http://www.infozakon.sk/zakon-schvalenyvnrsr.htm> (In Slovakian).

[958] See <http://conventions.coe.int/>.

[959] Signed 21/02/91, Ratified 18/03/92, Entered into force 01/01/93. <http://conventions.coe.int/>.

proceedings or for reasons of national security." Article 38 on the Protection of Personal Data states, "The protection of personal data relating to an individual shall be guaranteed. Any use of personal data shall be forbidden where that use conflicts with the original purpose for which it was collected. The collection, processing and the end-use of such data, as well as the supervision and protection of the confidentiality of such data, shall be regulated by statute. Each person has the right to be informed of the personal data relating to him which has been collected and has the right to legal remedy in the event of any misuse of same."[960]

A new Law on Personal Data Protection went into effect in August 1999.[961] The new law is based on the EU Data Protection Directive and the COE Convention No 108. It replaces the 1990 act.[962] The new act will create an 'Inspectorate' to supervise and enforce. The previous law had a limited oversight of personal data protection practices. However, the Human Rights Ombudsman had issued numerous decisions on data protection.[963]

A judge's warrant must be issued prior to a house search or telephone tapping. A new Law on the Police was adopted in 1998 allows for surveillance to be authorized under special circumstances by a General Police Director.[964] In 1994, Parliament fired the country's defense minister, Janez Jansa, following claims that he tapped journalists' phones.[965] Defense Minister Tit Turnsek resigned in February 1998 after two military intelligence officers were arrested by Croatian authorities while driving a vehicle filled with electronic surveillance equipment.[966]

The Law on National Statistics regulates the privacy of information collected for statistical purposes.[967] The Law on Telecommunications requires telecommunications service providers to "guarantee the confidentiality of transmitted messages and of personal and non-personal data known only to

---

[960] Constitution of the Republic of Slovenia, 1991. <http://www.sigov.si/us/eus-usta.html>.

[961] ESIS, Regulatory Developments: Slovenia, April 2000. <http://www.eu-esis.org/esis2reg/SIreg4.htm>.

[962] Law on Personal Data Protection, March 7, 1990 (The Official Journal of the Republic of Slovenia, No. 8/90, 38/90 and 19/91).

[963] Home Page: http://www.varuh-rs.si/cgi/teksti-eng.cgi/Index?vsebina=/cgi/teksti-eng.cgi?pozdrav

[964] Law on the Police, 18 July 1998.

[965] United Press International March 28, 1994.

[966] Deutsche Presse-Agentur, February 25, 1998.

[967] Law on National Statistics, 25 July 1995. <http://www.sigov.si/zrs/eng/szakoni.html>.

---

them."[968] The Electronic Commerce and Electronic Signature Act was approved in June 2000.[969]

Slovenia is a member of the Council of Europe and has signed and ratified the Convention for the Protection of Individuals with Regard to Automatic Processing of Personal Data (ETS No. 108).[970] It has also signed and ratified the European Convention for the Protection of Human Rights and Fundamental Freedoms.[971]

Republic of South Africa

Section 14 of the South African Constitution of 1996 states, "Everyone has the right to privacy, which includes the right not to have – (a) their person or home searched; (b) their property searched; (c) their possessions seized; or (d) the privacy of their communications infringed." Section 32 states, "(1) Everyone has the right of access to – (a) any information held by the state, and; (b) any information that is held by another person and that is required for the exercise or protection of any rights; (2) National legislation must be enacted to give effect to this right, and may provide for reasonable measures to alleviate the administrative and financial burden on the state."[972] The interim Constitution contained an essentially similar provision to Section 14, in Section 13.[973] It is clear that both sections are written in a way that directly responds to the experiences during the apartheid era of gross interferences with peoples' right to privacy.

The South African Constitutional Court has delivered a number of judgments on the right to privacy relating to the possession of indecent or obscene photographs,[974] the scope of privacy in society,[975] and searches.[976] All the

---

[968] Law on Telecommunications, <http://www.gov.si/urst/angl/docum/decr/a35_97.htm>.

[969] The Electronic Commerce and Electronic Signature Act <http://www.gov.si/ep/ecaes.doc>.

[970] Signed 23/11/93, Ratified 27/05/94, Entered into force 01/09/94. <http://conventions.coe.int/>.

[971] Signed 14/05/93, Ratified 28/06/94, Entered into force 28/06/94. <http://conventions.coe.int/>.

[972] The Constitution of the Republic of South Africa, Act 108 of 1996.
<http://www.parliament.gov.za/legislation/1996/saconst.html>.

[973] The interim Constitution (Act 200 of 1993).

[974] Case and Another v Minister of Safety and Security and Curtis and Another v Minister of Safety and Security 1996 (3) SA 617 (CC).

[975] Bernstein and others v Von Weilligh Bester NO and others,1996 (2) SA 751 (CC); 1996 (4) BCLR 449 (CC) - delivered 27 March 1996.

judgments were delivered under the provisions of the Interim Constitution as the causes of action arose prior to the enactment of the Final Constitution. However, as there is no substantive difference between the privacy provisions in the Interim and Final Constitutions, the principles remain authoritative for future application.

The Access to Information Act was approved in February 2000.[977] The bill covers both public and private sector entities and allows for access, rights of correction and limitations on disclosure of information. Originally introduced as the Open Democracy Bill, the proposed legislation also included comprehensive data protection provisions.[978] However, those provisions were removed by the Parliamentary committee in November 1999. The Committee wrote that, "it would be dealing with the right to privacy in section 14 of the Constitution in an ad hoc and undesirable manner...it is intended that South-Africa, in following the international trend, should enact separate privacy legislation. The Committee, therefore, requests the Minister for Justice and Constitutional Development to introduce Privacy and Data Protection legislation, after thorough research on the matter, as soon as reasonably possible."[979] The Privacy and Data Protection Bill is still in its early stages of development.

The Department of Communications is planning to release its long awaited green paper on a draft e-commerce bill in August 2000. After public discussion, a white paper is expected to be released by the end of the year and legislation will be introduced next year. A July 1999 discussion paper raised a number of questions about new legislation:

> Should South Africa adopt specific requirements for database owners and others collecting personal information, with regard to the treatment of such data?
> • To what extent should companies be allowed/encouraged to adopt self-regulation standards for privacy protection?
> • Should there be official minimum requirements for notice, choice, access and security practices concerning data collection and use?
> • What penalties should be imposed for misuse of personal data, either by collecting information without consent, selling or distributing unauthorized data, or other abuses?

---

[976] Mistry v The Interim National Medical and Dental Council of South Africa and others as yet unreported, CCT 13/97, 29 May 1998.

[977] Promotion of Access to Information Act No 2 of 2000.
<http://www.polity.org.za/govdocs/legislation/2000/index.html>.

[978] Open Democracy Bill No. 67, 1998. <http://www.parliament.gov.za/bills/1998/b67-98.pdf>.

[979] Report of the Ad hoc Committee on Open Democracy Bill [B 67-98], Parliament of the Republic of South Africa, January 24, 2000.

- If direct government regulation is to be considered, which bodies (e.g., the Human Rights Commission or a new agency) should be responsible for monitoring and enforcing privacy rules? What powers and limitations should such an agency have with regard to examining companies' databases and practices?
- What role should other consumer protection bodies (e.g. the Consumer Council) play in this regard?[980]

South Africa does not have a privacy commission but has a Human Rights Commission which was established under Chapter 9 of the Constitution and whose mandate is to investigate infringements on and to protect the fundamental rights guaranteed in the Bill of Rights, and to take steps to secure appropriate redress where human rights have been violated. The Commission has limited powers to enforce the Access to Information Act.

The Interception and Monitoring Act of 1992 regulates the interception of communications.[981] This Act prohibits the interception of certain and monitoring of communications and also provides for the interception of postal articles and communications and for the monitoring of conversations in the case of a serious offense, or if the security of the country is threatened. In November 1998, the South African Law Commission recommended changes to the Interception and Monitoring Act to facilitate monitoring of cellular phones and Internet Service Providers.[982] The Ministry of Justice is now working on a draft bill to implement the recommendations of the SALC. The bill would require that all telecommunications services including ISPs make their services capable or being intercepted before they could offer the service to the public. Providers would be required to pay for the costs of making their systems wiretap-enabled. The National Intelligence Agency announced in February 2000 that it was creating a signals intelligence service based on the model of the UK's GCHQ.[983]

In 1996, it was revealed that the South African Police Service was monitoring thousands of international and domestic phone calls without a warrant.[984] In February 2000, the government apologized to the German Government after it was found that an intelligence operative had placed spy cameras outside the

---

[980] Discussion Paper on E-Commerce, July 1999 <http://www.ecomm-debate.co.za/docs/discuss-contents.html>.

[981] Interception and Monitoring Prohibition Act, No 77 of 1992 (amended by the Intelligence Services Act, No. 38 of 1994).

[982] Discussion Paper 78 (Project 105), Review of Security Legislation, The Interception and Monitoring Prohibition Act 127 of 1992 (November 1998) <http://www.law.wits.ac.za/salc/discussn/monitoring.pdf>.

[983] "South Africa to set up signals intelligence centre," Reuters, February 7, 2000.

[984] "Newspaper Uncovers 'Unlawful' Tapping by Intelligence Units," The Star, 21 February 1996.

Germany Embassy.[985] The opposition Democratic Party announced in November 1999 that it found surveillance devices at its parliamentary offices and national headquarters.[986]

There are no other specific pieces of legislation on general data protection law. Other than the Constitutional right to privacy, the South African common law protects rights of personality under the broad umbrella of the *actio injuriarum*. The elements of liability for an action based on invasion of privacy are the same as any other injury to the personality, namely an unlawful and intentional interference with another's right to seclusion and to private life. The Law Commission is currently drafting a new computer crimes law.

Financial privacy is covered by a weak code of conduct for banks issued by the Banking Council in March 2000. Credit bureau Experian accidentally made available on its web site the records on 1.5 million clients in July 1999.[987] The information was from cell phone company Vodac and banks Nedcor, Standard Bank, Mercantile, Teljoy and Homechoice and included names, addresses and identity, telephone and cellphone numbers, and bank account details. In February 2000, it was discovered that First National Bank's (FNB) telephone banking service allowed callers to obtain a balance statement and available credit level for the accounts of any client. The service was reported to get 170,000 calls a month.[988]

The Cabinet approved a plan in March 1998 to issue a multi-purpose smart card that combines access to all government departments and services with banking facilities. This is part of the information technology strategy formulated by the Department of Communications to provide kiosks for access to government services.[989] In the long term, the smart card is intended to function as passport, driver's license, identity document and bank card. The driver's license will include fingerprints. The new ID cards are to be issued in the second half of 2001.[990]

---

[985] "S.Africa admits to spying on German embassy," Reuters, February 6, 2000.

[986] "Democratic Party Outraged By Bugging Of Its Offices," Africa News, November 23, 1999.

[987] "Fears That Website Listed Confidential Bank Data," Africa News, July 12, 1999.

[988] "FNB allows access to account balance data," Business Day, February 21, 2000.

[989] David Shapshak, "SA services get 'smart'," Mail & Guardian, April 24, 1998.

[990] "Smart Cards To Replace ID Books In SA In 2001," Africa News, February 1, 2000.

The Access to Information Act is a comprehensive Freedom of Information Act.[991] It was reported that the apartheid-era security police maintained 314,000 files on individuals and 9,400 on organizations.[992] Many documents were reported destroyed in 1993 by military intelligence.

Kingdom of Spain

The Constitution recognizes the right to privacy, secrecy of communications and data protection. Article 18 states, "(1). The right of honor, personal, and family privacy and identity is guaranteed. (2) The home is inviolable. No entry or search may be made without legal authority except with the express consent of the owners or in the case of a flagrante delicto. (3) Secrecy of communications, particularly regarding postal, telegraphic, and telephone communication, is guaranteed, except for infractions by judicial order. (4) The law shall limit the use of information, to guarantee personal and family honor, the privacy of citizens, and the full exercise of their rights."[993]

The Spanish Data Protection Act (LORTAD) was enacted in 1992 and amended in December 1999 to implement the EU Data Protection Directive.[994] It covers files held by the public and private sector. The law establishes the right of citizens to know what personal data is contained in computer files and the right to correct or delete incorrect or false data. Personal information may only be used or disclosed to a third party with the consent of the individual and only for the purpose for which it was collected. Questions still remain about citizens who do not wish to be included in the "promotional census." Consumer groups are also concerned about the law provisions allowing use of information without consent unless the consumer has opted out of the use.

The Agencia de Protección de Datos is charged with enforcing the LORTAD.[995] The Agency maintains the registry and can investigate violations of the law. The agency has issued a number of decrees setting out in more detail the legal

---

[991] Access to Information Act,
<http://www.privacyinternational.org/countries/south_africa/access_info_bill.pdf>.

[992] Gavin Evans, "South Africa: Home truths," The Independent, October 31, 1998.

[993] Constitution of Spain, Amendment 27 Aug 1992. <http://www.uni-wuerzburg.de/law/sp00t___.html>.

[994] Ley Organica 5/1992 de 29 de Octubre de Regulación del Tratamiento Automatizado de los Datos de Caracter Personal (LORTAD). Ley Orgánica 15/99 de 13 de Diciembre de Protección de Datos de Carácter Personal. <https://www.agenciaproteccciondatos.org/datd1.htm>.

[995] Agencia de Protección de Datos. <https://www.agenciaproteccciondatos.org>.

---

requirements for different types of information.[996] It can also impose penalties. In June 1997, it fined Telefonica, the Spanish telephone company, 110 million pesetas for providing information from their subscriber database to banks, direct marketing companies and Reader's Digest.[997] The agency issued a total ES1.5 billion in fines in 1999.[998] The Agency fined Microsoft ES10 million (US $60,000) in May 1999 for misusing personal information. It fined the General Council of Official Medical Colleges US$333,000 and Banco Espanol de Credito Banesto $67,000 for using confidential information about doctors to offer mortgage and pension services.[999] The agency in 1997 registered 3,312 new databases, received 682 complaints, conducted over 10,000 telephone consultations, and issued 20 reports.[1000] As of December 1997, 229,000 databases were listed in the Register.

Interception of communications requires a court order.[1001] The 1997 Telecommunications Act amended the law and restricts the use of cryptography but that provision has not been enforced.[1002] There have been a number of scandals in Spain over illegal wiretapping by the intelligence services. In 1995, Deputy Prime Minister Narcis Serra, Defense Minister Julian Garcia Vargas and military intelligence chief Gen. Emilio Alonso Manglano were forced to quit following revelations that they had monitored the conversations of hundreds of people, including King Juan Carlos.[1003] In May 1999, Gen. Manglano, the former director of the CESID, and Col. Juan Alberto Perote, a former operations chief were convicted and sentenced to six months jail time for their role in the wiretappings. Five other ex-agents who did the actual surveillance were given four-month terms.[1004] Defence Minister Eduardo Serra was called before Parliament in April 2000 after an illegal CESID bugging operation was revealed above the offices of Herri Batasuna (HB) coalition.[1005]

---

[996] See <https://www.agenciaprotecciondatos.org/datd.htm>.

[997] "Telefonica De Espana Appeals Fine For Sharing Database," Dow Jones, June 19, 1997.

[998] Protección de Datos multa a Microsoft Ibérica por tratar información personal sin permiso, El País Digital, 16 de Junio de 2000.

[999] Spain's medical council fined for selling members' private data, The Lancet, November 20, 1999.

[1000] Working Party on the Protection of Individuals with Regard to the Processing of Personal Data, Second Annual Report, 30 November 1998.

[1001] Ley Organica 11/1980 de 1 de Dec 1980. Penal Code, Sections 196-199.

[1002] See Global Internet Liberty Campaign, New Spanish telecommunications law opens a door to mandatory key recovery systems, July 1998. <http://www.gilc.org/crypto/spain/gilc-crypto-spain-798.html>.

[1003] "Spain Socialists seek opposition apology on bugging," Reuters, February 6, 1996.

[1004] "Ex-Spy Chief Sentenced in Spain, Associated Press," May 26, 1999.

[1005] "Spies Caught Between the 'Dirty War' and Botched Jobs," IPS, April 20, 2000.

There are also additional laws in the penal code,[1006] and relating to credit information[1007] video surveillance,[1008] and automatic tellers.[1009] The government issued a decree on digital signatures in September 1999.[1010] The Spanish Supreme Court ruled in March 1999 that a Spanish reporter who disclosed the initials of two AIDS-infected inmates working in a prison kitchen would be given a one-year suspended sentence, fined $26,000 and be barred from journalism for a year.[1011] The Minister of Justice is expected to submit a bill on DNA databases and testing to the Parliament.

The law of 30/26/11/1992 provides for access to government information.[1012] The law was amended in 1998 by Ley 29/1998, de 13 de julio. Under Article 37.2, the right of access and correction can be denied if reasons of public interest prevail.

Spain is a member of the Council of Europe and has signed and ratified the Convention for the Protection of Individuals with Regard to Automatic Processing of Personal Data (ETS No. 108).[1013] It has signed and ratified the European Convention for the Protection of Human Rights and Fundamental Freedoms.[1014] It is a member of the Organization for Economic Cooperation and Development and has adopted the OECD Guidelines on the Protection of Privacy and Transborder Flows of Personal Data.

Kingdom of Sweden

Sweden's Constitution, which consists of several different legal documents, contains several provisions which are relevant to data protection. Section 2 of the

---

[1006] See <http://www.onnet.es/ley0009.htm>.

[1007] INSTRUCCION 1/1995, de 1 de marzo, de la Agencia de Protección de Datos, relativa a prestación de servicios de información sobre solvencia patrimonial y crédito. <http://www.onnet.es/ley0029.htm>.

[1008] Ley Organica 4/1997, de 4 de agosto por la que se regula la utilización de videocámaras por las Fuerzas y Cuerpos de Seguridad en lugares públicos. <http://www.onnet.es/ley0064.htm>.

[1009] Seguridad en cajeros automáticos y otros servicios. ORDEN de 23 de abril de 1997. <http://www.onnet.es/ley0060.htm>.

[1010] See http://www.el-mundo.es/nacional/consejoministros/1999/09/1990917.html

[1011] Spanish Court Convicts Reporter, Associated Press, March 4, 1999.

[1012] Ley 30/1992, de 26 de Noviembre, de Régimen Jurídico de las Administraciones Públicas y del Procedimiento Administrativo Común. <http://www.um.es/siu/marco/30-92.htm>.

[1013] Signed 28/01/82, Ratified 31/04/84, Entered into Force 01/10/85. <http://conventions.coe.int/>.

[1014] Signed 24/11/77, Ratified 04/10/79, Entered into Force 04/10/79. <http://conventions.coe.int/>.

Instrument of Government Act of 1974[1015] provides, *inter alia*, for the protection of individual privacy. Section 13 of Chapter 2 of the same instrument states also that freedom of expression and information – which are constitutionally protected pursuant to the Freedom of the Press Act of 1949[1016] – can be limited with respect to the "sanctity of private life." Moreover, Section 3 of the same chapter provides for a right to protection of personal integrity in relation to automatic data processing. The same article also prohibits non-consensual registration of persons purely on the basis of their political opinion. It is also important to note that the European Convention on Human Rights has been incorporated into Swedish law as of 1994. The ECHR is not formally part of the Swedish Constitution but has, in effect, similar status.

Sweden enacted the Personal Data Act of 1998 to bring Swedish law into conformity with the requirements of the EC Directive on data protection.[1017] The new Act essentially adopts the EU Data Protection Directive into Swedish law. It regulates the establishment and use, in both public and private sectors, of automated data files on physical/natural persons. The Act replaced the Data Act of 1973, which was the first comprehensive national act on privacy in the world.[1018] The 1973 Act shall continue to apply until October 2001 with respect to processing of personal data which is initiated prior to October 24, 1998. Section 33 of the Act was amended in 1999 to adopt the EU Directive standards on the transfer of personal data to a third country. According to the Data Inspection Board, the amendment will facilitate transfer of data through international communication networks, such as the Internet. There may be situations where a third country - despite not having any data protection rules at all - still can be considered having an adequate level of protection. This would be depending on the other circumstances. It is also possible that the level of protection in a third country may be assessed as adequate in some areas but not in others. The amendment entered into force in January 2000

The Data Inspection Board (Datainspektionen) is an independent board that oversees the enforcement of the Data Act.[1019] In 1999, under the new act, the board received 409 complaints and conducted 298 investigations. In 1998, the board received 269 complaints according and conducted 199 investigations. In 1997, it received 250 complaints and made 302 investigations. There are 29,464

[1015] Regeringsformen, SFS 1974:152.

[1016] Tryckfrihetsförordningen, SFS 1949:105.

[1017] Personuppgiftslagen, SFS 1998:204, <http://www.datainspektionen.se/in_english/legislation/data.shtml>.

[1018] Datalagen, SFS 1973:289.

[1019] Web Site: http://www.din.se/.

registered databases and 855 processings under section 36 of the Act.[1020] The Board has been active in trying to limit the use of the personal identity number.[1021] One of their most publicized cases was against SABRE, the airline reservation system, for transferring medical information of passengers without adequate controls. The Supreme Administrative Court recently declined to hear the case following decisions by lower courts upholding the Board's ruling.

Numerous other statutes also contain provisions relating to data protection. These include the Secrecy Act of 1980,[1022] Credit Information Act of 1973,[1023] Debt Recovery Act of 1974,[1024] and Administrative Procedure Act of 1986.[1025]

A court order is required to obtain a wiretap.[1026] The law was amended in 1996 to facilitate surveillance of new technologies.[1027] According to the Office of the Prosecutor-General, wiretapping has declined in the last several years from 397 court orders in 1996, to 339 in 1997 and 312 in 1998. At the same time, court orders for "monitoring of electronic traffic" has increased substantially from 99 in 1996 to 165 in 1997 to 333 in 1998. Court orders for video surveillance has remained constant, from 40 in 1996, 43 in 1997 to 45 in 1998.[1028] Swedish press reported in September 1999 that the Swedish Minister of Justice Laila Freivalds was planning to ask for the power to use hidden microphones and expand surveillance.[1029] The International Helsinki Federation for Human Rights noted, "State interference in the private lives of its citizens lacked in legal rights and transparency."[1030]

[1020] Email communications from The Data Inspection Board, June 23, 1999.

[1021] Anitha Bondestam, "Identity Numbers," Presentation at the XVth International Conference of Data Protection and Privacy Commissioners, September 1993.

[1022] Sekretesslagen, SFS 1980:100. For information on the background to the new Act, see the report,Integritet-Offentlighet-InformationsteknikIntegrity-Publicity–Information Technology, SOU 1997:39.

[1023] Kreditupplysningslag, SFS 1973:1173.
<http://www.datainspektionen.se/in_english/legislation/credit.shtml>.

[1024] Inkassolag, SFS 1974:182. <http://www.datainspektionen.se/in_english/legislation/debt.shtml>.

[1025] Förvaltningslagen, SFS 1986:223.

[1026] Law 1974/203 amended by Law 1989/529/. Telecommunications Act (1993:597).
<http://www.pts.se/infoeng/telecomact.pdf>.

[1027] Law of 8 May 1996.

[1028] Email from Rune Björk, Librarian, Office of the Prosecutor-General, July 7, 2000.

[1029] "Bugging may become legal in Sweden," Nordic Business Report, September 6, 1999.

[1030] International Helsinki Federation for Human Rights, Human Rights in the OSCE Region: the Balkans, the Caucasus, Europe, Central Asia and North America, Report 2000.

The DIB released a report in December 1998 revealing that Sweden's police/security services carried out, over a long period, covert surveillance of thousands of Swedish citizens, mostly politically leftists, often on highly tenuous or trivial grounds from 1969 until 1998. The surveillance had been repeatedly denied to exist by high government officials such as the Justice Chancellor, who at the same time wrote secret reports about the investigations.[1031] The Lund/McDonald commission was set up in early 1999 in order to investigate these surveillance practices, which were demanded by the United States as a condition to receiving military technology. The intelligence agency also used their files to attempt to prevent journalists critical of them from being hired by the national television and radio networks. Observers are skeptical that the commission will be effective because of a lack of expertise in intelligence matters.

Previously, it was also discovered that the Swedish statistical agency, Statistika, was monitoring 15,000 Stockholm residents born in 1953 in intimate detail. The information included statistics on drinking habits, religious beliefs, and sexual orientation. The DIB subsequently ordered the destruction of the master tape containing the data.[1032]

Sweden is a country that has traditionally adhered to the Nordic tradition of open access to government files. The world's first freedom of information act was the Riksdag's (Swedish Parliament) "Freedom of the Press Act of 1766." The Act required that official documents should "upon request immediately be made available to anyone making a request" at no charge. The Freedom of the Press Act is now part of the Constitution and decrees that "every Swedish citizen shall have free access to official documents." Decisions by public authorities to deny access to official documents may be appealed to general administrative courts and ultimately, to the Supreme Administrative Court. The Parliamentary Ombudsman has some oversight functions for freedom of information.

Sweden is a member of the Council of Europe and has signed and ratified the Convention for the Protection of Individuals with Regard to Automatic Processing of Personal Data (ETS No. 108).[1033] It has signed and ratified the European Convention for the Protection of Human Rights and Fundamental

---

[1031] "Sweden: The personnel control system 1969-1996," Statewatch Bulletin, vol 9 no 1 (January-February 1999).

[1032] Wayne Madsen, Handbook of Personal Data Protection, (New York: Stockton Press, 1992).

[1033] Signed 28/01/81, Ratified 29/09/82, Entered into Force 01/10/85. <http://conventions.coe.int/>.

Freedoms.[1034] It is a member of the Organization for Economic Cooperation and Development and has adopted the OECD Guidelines on the Protection of Privacy and Transborder Flows of Personal Data.

Swiss Confederation (Switzerland)

Article 36(4) of the 1874 Constitution guaranteed, "[t]he inviolability of the secrecy of letters and telegrams."[1035] This Constitution was repealed and replaced by public referendum in April 1999. The new constitution, which entered into force on January 1, 2000, greatly expanded the older privacy protection provision. Article 13 of the Constitution now states: "All persons have the right to receive respect for their private and family life, home, mail and telecommunications. All persons have the right to be protected against abuse of their personal data." [1036]

The Federal Act of Data Protection of 1992 regulates personal information held by government and private bodies.[1037] The Act requires that information must be legally and fairly collected and places limits on its use and disclosure to third parties. Private companies must register if they regularly process sensitive data or transfer the data to third parties. Transfers to other nations must be registered and the recipient nation must have equivalent laws. Individuals have a right of access to correct inaccurate information. Federal agencies must register their databases. There are criminal penalties for violations. There are also separate data protection acts for the Cantons (states).

In June 1999, the E.U. Data Protection Working Party determined that Swiss law was adequate under the E.U. Directive.[1038] In July 2000, the European Commission formally adopted this position, thereby approving all future transfers of all personal data transfers to Switzerland. [1039]

[1034] Signed 28/11/50, Ratified 04/02/52, Entered into Force 03/09/53. <http://conventions.coe.int/>.

[1035] Constitution of Switzerland, 1874. <http://www.uni-wuerzburg.de/law/sz01000_.html>.

[1036] Constitution of Switzerland, 1999. <http://www.uni-wuerzburg.de/law/sz00000_.html>.

[1037] Loi fédérale sur la protection des données (LPD) du 19 juin 1992. <http://www.admin.ch/ch/f/rs/235_1/index.html>.

[1038] Working Party on the Protection of Individuals with Regard to the Processing of Personal Data, Opinion 5/99 on the level of protection of personal data in Switzerland, 7 June 1999. <http://europa.eu.int/comm/dg15/en/media/dataprot/wpdocs/wp22fr.pdf>

[1039] "Commission adopts decisions recognising adequacy of regimes in US, Switzerland and Hungary," July 27, 2000. <http://europa.eu.int/comm/internal_market/en/media/dataprot/news/safeharbor.htm>.

The 1992 Act created a Federal Data Protection Commission.[1040] The commission maintains and publishes the Register for Data Files, supervises federal government and private bodies, provides advice, issues recommendations and reports, and conducts investigations. The commissioner also consults with the private sector. Its most recent report recommended improvements in telecommunications privacy, controls on workplace monitoring, legal limitations on DNA databases, the development of strong privacy enhancing technologies and greater consumer protections in the areas of unwanted telemarketing, Caller-ID, spam, on-line profiling and data mining. It also recommended increased co-operation at international level to protect privacy and the introduction of legislation, similar to that in Germany, providing an explicit right to anonymity.[1041] There are currently 20 people employed by the Commission.

Telephone tapping is governed by the Penal Code and Penal Procedure Code amended by the 1997 Telecommunication Act that came into effect on January 1, 1998.[1042] This Act established a specialized agency, Le Service des Taches Speciales (STS), within the Department of the Environment, Transport, Energy and Communications to administer wiretaps. A court order is required for every wiretap. There were 2,138 wiretaps requested by the federal and cantonal authorities in 1996.[1043] A Department of Justice working group has been developing revisions for the wiretap legislation for several years. A proposal to modify wiretapping and mail interception was introduced in July 1998.[1044] In 1999, the Privacy Commission withdrew its support after the working group expanded the number of offenses to include many minor offenses.[1045] In December 1999, the Conseil National approved the draft law by a majority vote of 128 to 3, but laid down certain restrictions on the categories of crimes for which surveillance may be authorized and the use of surveillance as a preventative measure.[1046] In the Spring of 2000, the Conseil des Etats amended

---

[1040] Home Page: http://www.edsb.ch/.

[1041] Préposé fédéral de la protection des données, Rapport d'activités 1999/2000. <http://www.edsb.ch/framesf.html>.

[1042] Art 66-73, Procédure pénal fédérale. Loi de 23 Mars 1979 sue la protection de la vie priveé. Telecommunications Law (LTC) of 30 April 1997. Ordinance du 1er décembre 1997 sur le service de surveillance de la correspondance postale et des télécommunications. <http://www.admin.ch/ch/f/rs/c780_11.html>.

[1043] Conseil National, Heures de Questions: Session d'hiver 1999. Reponse du Conseil federal concernant les ecoutes telephoniques, 20 Decembre 1999. <http://www.parlament.ch/afs/data/f/gesch/1999/f_gesch_19993427.htm>.

[1044] Departement Federal de Justice et Police, Ecoutes téléphoniques: Communiqué de presse, 1er juillet 1998. <http://www.admin.ch/cp/f/359B36DB.3BB3@mbox.gsejpd.admin.ch.html>.

[1045] Préposé fédéral de la protection des données, Rapport d'activités 1998/99.

[1046] "Le Conseil national emet de nombreuses restrictions," Service de base francaise, December 21, 2000.

---

the proposal to directly include surveillance of cellular telephone and prepaid calling card users.[1047] The law will now return to the Conseil National for reconsideration. In February 2000, the Department of the Environment Transport, Energy and Communications introduced a project to create a national security agency.[1048] The agency is intended to update surveillance concerning technical security issues arising solely within the activities of the Department itself.

There have been numerous public revelations of illegal wiretapping. A 1993 inquiry found that phones used by journalists and ministers in the Swiss Parliament were tapped.[1049] The Data Protection Commissioner also accused the Telecom PTT, the state telephone company, of illegally wiretapping telephones. There were considerable protests in 1996 when it was revealed that the federal government was wiretapping journalists to discover their sources after which Swiss President Arnold Koller described the taps as "excessive."[1050] In December 1997, the newspaper Sonntags Zeitung reported that Swisscom, (formerly PTT), was tracking the location of cellular phone users and maintaining those records for an extended period.[1051] The Data Protection Commissioner issued a report on this subject in July 1998.[1052] In February 1998, an agent for Israel's Mossad Secret Service was arrested by the Swiss authorities for attempting to tap the phone of a Lebanese immigrant whom he believed had links to the Hizbollah. On July 7, the Swiss court handed down a one year sentence to be suspended for two-years.[1053]

Besides the Data Protection Act, there are also legal protections for privacy in the Civil Code[1054] and Penal Code,[1055] and special rules relating to workers' privacy from surveillance,[1056] telecommunications information,[1057] health care

---

[1047] "Les utilisateurs de portables devront etre identifiable," Service de base francaise June 20, 2000.

[1048] Departement federal de L'Environment, des Transport, de l'Energie et de la Communication, Communique de Presse, le 24 fevrier, 2000. <http://www.uvek.admin.ch/doku/presse/2000/f/000222404.htm>.

[1049] Statewatch bulletin, vol. 3 no 1, January-February 1993.

[1050] "Phone Taps Raise Ire Of Swiss Public, Media," Christian Science Monitor, March 14, 1997.

[1051] Digital Cellular Report, January 15, 1998.

[1052] See <http://cryptome.com/swisscom-nix.htm>.

[1053] "Swiss court hands Mossad spy a suspended one-year sentence," Associated Press, July 10, 2000.

[1054] Section 28 of the Civil Code, 10 December 1907.

[1055] Code pénal, Titre troisiéme: Infractions contre l'honneur et contre le domaine secret ou le domaine privé, Art 173-179.

[1056] Section 328 of the Code of Obligations. See International Labour Organization, Conditions of Work Digest, Vol. 12, 1/1993.

[1057] Telecommunications Law (LTC) of 30 April 1997. <http://www.admin.ch/ch/f/rs/c784_10.html>.

---

statistics,[1058] professional confidentiality including medical and legal information,[1059] medical research,[1060] police files,[1061] and identity cards.[1062] In 1989, a Parliamentary inquiry revealed that the Federal Police had collected files on about 900,000 people, most of whom were not suspected of having committed any offence. Banking records are protected by the Swiss Federal Banking Act 1934. This Act was passed to guarantee strong protections for the privacy and confidentiality of bank customers, especially those subject to persecution for racial, political or religious reasons.[1063] Switzerland has come under increasing pressure from the EU and OECD to weaken these laws and provide greater access to bank records for the purposes of tax collection. Swiss Finance Minister, Kaspar Villiger, has so far rejected these calls, maintaining that the banking secrecy laws are essential for Switzerland's role as an important financial center.[1064]

Switzerland is a member of the Council of Europe and signed and ratified the Convention for the Protection of Individuals with Regard to Automatic Processing of Personal Data (ETS No. 108) in 1997.[1065] Switzerland has signed and ratified the European Convention for the Protection of Human Rights and Fundamental Freedoms.[1066] Switzerland is a member of the Organization for Economic Cooperation and Development and has adopted the OECD Guidelines on the Protection of Privacy and Transborder Flows of Personal Data. Switzerland is not an EU member state but has been granted associate status.

[1058] Office fédéral de la statistique, La protection des données dans la statistique médicale, 1997. <http://www.admin.ch/bfs/stat_ch/ber14/statsant/ff1403c.htm>.

[1059] Code pénal, Art 320-322.

[1060] O du 14 juin 1993 concernant les autorisations de lever le secret professionnel en matière de recherche médicale (OALSP), 14 juin 1993. <http://www.admin.ch/ch/f/rs/c235_154.html>.

[1061] Ordinance du 31 août 1992 sur le système provisoire de traitement des données relatives à la protection de l'Etat (Ordonnance ISIS), 31 août 1992. <http://www.admin.ch/ch/f/rs/c172_213_60.html>. Ordonnance du 14 juin 1993 relative à la loi fédérale sur la protection des données (OLPD) < http://www.admin.ch/ch/f/rs/c235_11.html>. Ordinance du 19 juin 1995 sur le système de recherches informatisées de police (RIPOL), <http://www.admin.ch/ch/f/rs/c172_213_61.html>.

[1062] Ordinance du 18 mai 1994 relative à la carte d'identité suisse. <http://www.admin.ch/ch/f/rs/c143_3.html>.

[1063] 'Swiss News', Information Access Company, November 1, 1999. See also, 7 Pace Int'l L. Rev. 329 on effects of money laundering legislation on limiting banking privacy.

[1064] "Switzerland's Villiger says bank secrecy still needed," AFX News Limited, June 7, 2000.

[1065] Signed 02/10/97, Ratified 02/10/97, Entered into force 01/02/98. <http://conventions.coe.int/>.

[1066] <http://conventions.coe.int/>.

Republic of China (Taiwan)

Article 12 of the 1994 Taiwanese Constitution states, "The people shall have freedom of privacy of correspondence."[1067]

The Computer-Processed Personal Data Protection Law was enacted in August 1995.[1068] The Act governs the collection and use of personally identifiable information by government agencies and many areas of the private sector. The Act requires that "The collection or utilization of personal data shall respect the rights and interests of the principal and such personal data shall be handled in accordance with the principles of honesty and credibility so as not to exceed the scope of the specific purpose." Individuals have a right of access and correction, the ability to request cessation of computerized processing and use, and the ability to request deletion of data. Data flows to countries without privacy laws can be prohibited.[1069] Damages can be assessed for violations. The Act also establishes separate principles for eight categories of private institutions: credit information organizations, hospitals, schools, telecommunication businesses, financial businesses, securities businesses, insurance businesses, mass media, and "other enterprises, organizations, or individuals designated by the Ministry of Justice and the central government authorities in charge of concerned end enterprises."

There is no single privacy oversight body to enforce the Act. The Ministry of Justice enforces the Act for government agencies. For the private sector, the relevant government agency for that sector enforces compliance. The Criminal Investigation Bureau (CIB) arrested several people in November 1998 for selling lists of more than 15 million voters and personal data of up to 40 million individuals in violation of the Act.[1070]

The Parliament approved the Communication Protection and Surveillance Act in June 1999 to impose stricter guideline on when and how wiretaps can be used. However taps can still be approved for broad reasons such as "national security"

[1067] Constitution of the Republic of China, Adopted by the National Assembly on December 25, 1946, promulgated by the National Government on January 1, 1947, and effective from December 25, 1947. <http://www.oop.gov.tw/roc/charter/echarter.htm>.

[1068] Computer-Processed Personal Data Protection Law of August 11, 1995. <http://virtualtaiwan.com/members/guide/legal/cpdpl.htm>. Enforcement rules, 1 May 1996, <http://virtualtaiwan.com/members/guide/legal/cpdpl2.htm>.

[1069] <http://jcmc.huji.ac.il/vol2/issue1/asiapac.html>.

[1070] "Police arrest data thieves," China News, November 10, 1998.

---

and "social order." It also requires telecommunications providers to assist law enforcement and sets technical requirements for interception, which is being opposed by mobile phone providers.[1071] The Act replaces the martial law-era Telecommunications Surveillance Act. Article 315 of Taiwan's Criminal Code states that a person who, without reason, opens or conceals a sealed letter or other sealed document belonging to another will be punishable under the law. The 1996 Telecommunications Law states "Unauthorized third parties shall not receive, record or use other illegal means to infringe upon the secrets of telecommunications enterprises and telecommunications messages. A telecommunications enterprise should take proper and necessary measures to protect its telecommunications security."[1072] The Act was amended in October 1999 to increase penalties for illegal telephone taps to NT1.5 million and up to five years in prison. In 1998, the Supreme Court ruled that evidence obtained through illegal wiretaps was not admissible in a criminal trial.

The Prosecutor General's Office revealed in 1999 that over 15,000 people were subject to wiretapping in the just the first half of 1999 including for "political intelligence."[1073] In January 2000, a wiretap was found at the campaign office of presidential candidate Chen Shui-bian.[1074] Independent presidential candidate James Soong alleged in November 1999 that the government was tapping his campaign and home phones.[1075] The U.S. State Department was also critical of the government stating "Wiretapping of telephones also is a serious problem. The Telecommunication Law and the Code of Criminal Procedure provide that judicial and security authorities may file a written request to a prosecutor's office to monitor telephone calls to collect evidence against a suspect involved in a major crime. According to media reports this practice is commonplace, with more than 106,000 successful applications for wiretapping in 1997. Moreover, the intelligence services have their own wiretapping capabilities, which are not subject to supervision by the judicial branch. Ministry of Justice authorities have stated that such steps are required in view of the threat Taiwan faces from Mainland China."[1076]

[1071] Private cellular firms feel threatened by wiretap law, Taipei Times, November 13, 1999.

[1072] Telecommunications Law 1996, February 5, 1996.
<http://virtualtaiwan.com/members/guide/legal/telecom_law.html>.

[1073] "Surveillance must not be abused," China News, November 7, 1999.

[1074] "'Taiwan's Watergate,' says Chen after wiretap found," Taipei Times, January 26, 2000.

[1075] "Soong aides make wiretapping claim," China News, November 4, 1999.

[1076] U.S. Department of State, Taiwan Country Report on Human Rights Practices for 1998, February 26, 1999.

Under the HIV Prevention Law, the government can demand that foreigners who have been in Taiwan for over three months provide an HIV test.[1077] If they are found to have HIV, they are immediately deported. The legislature amended the law in July 2000 to allow for a change for debate their cases.[1078]

In May 2000, the Ministry of Justice proposed that all banks link their customer databases to a central database at the Ministry of Finance. The proposal is being opposed by the Ministry of Finance. Deputy Finance Minster Chen Chung said at a hearing in May, "This proposal takes aim at the vast majority of people, who are not criminals, before a crime has even taken place. Is this really necessary? Shouldn't there be more serious consideration."[1079]

In 1997, the Taiwanese government proposed a new national ID card called the "National Integrated Circuit (IC) Card." The plan called for a smartcard based system with over 100 uses for the card including ID, health insurance, driver's license, taxation and possibly small-value payments. The card would be issued and operated by Rebar Corporation, a private company which would have set up and paid for the system on its own but would have kept any profits from its creation. The entire system was estimated to cost NTD 10 billion (USD 357 million). There were hearings to evaluate privacy concerns after protests about the plan arose.[1080] The government dropped the plan and is now creating a paper-based card, which may include a fingerprint. A smartcard-based system just for health information is also being developed which will use the national ID number.

Kingdom of Thailand

Section 34 of the 1997 Constitution states, "A persons family rights, dignity, reputation or the right of privacy shall be protected. The assertion or circulation of a statement or picture in any manner whatsoever to the public, which violates or affects a person's family rights, dignity, reputation or the right of privacy, shall not be made except for the case which is beneficial to the public." Section 37 states, "Persons have the freedom to communication with one another by

---

[1077] An Enforcement Ordinance of the HIV Prevention Law,
<http://www.undphiv.apdip.net/subreg/east/korealaw.htm>.

[1078] "Legislature revises HIV Prevention Law regarding foreigners found to be positive," Taipei Times, July 1, 2000.

[1079] "Sparks fly over bank database," Taipei Times, June 21, 2000.

[1080] "When Smart Cards Get Too Smart," The Industry Standard, September 7, 1998.

lawful means. Search, detention or exposure of lawful communication materials between and among persons, as well as actions by other means so as to snoop into the contents of the communications materials between and among persons, is prohibited unless it is done by virtue of the power vested in a provision of the law specifically for the purpose of maintaining national security or for the purpose of maintaining peace and order or good public morality." Section 58 states, "A person shall have the right to get access to public information in possession of a State agency, State enterprise or local government organization, unless the disclosure of such information shall affect the security of the State, public safety or interests of other persons which shall be protected as provided by law." [1081]

The National Information Technology Committee (NITC) approved plans in February 1998 for a series of information technology (IT) laws. Six sub-committees under the National Electronics and Computer Technology Centre (Nectec) were set up to draft the following bills: E-Commerce Law, EDI Law, Privacy Data Protection Law, Computer Crime Law, Electronics Digital Signature Law, Electronics Fund Transfer Law and Universal Access Law. All six bills were reportedly submitted to the Cabinet in January 2000.[1082] A combined electronic commerce and digital signature law was approved by the Cabinet in July 2000 and is expected to be approved by the Parliament this year. The rest of the bills, including the data protection act, are still awaiting Cabinet approval. The Association of Thai Computer Industry (ATCI) called on the government in May 2000 to adopt the data protection law to promote trust in e-commerce.[1083]

The Official Information Act was approved in 1997.[1084] The Act sets a code of information practices on personal information system run by state agencies. The agency: must ensure that the system is relevant to and necessary for the achievement of the objectives of the operation of the State agency; make efforts to collect information directly from the subject; publish material about its use in the Government Gazette; provide for an appropriate security system; notify such person if information is collected about them from a third party; not disclose personal information in its control to other State agencies or other persons

---

[1081] Constitution of the Kingdom of Thailand, 1997.
<http://www.krisdika.go.th/law/text/lawpub/e11102540/text.htm>.

[1082] "IT laws will be reviewed today- Ready for Cabinet early next month," Bangkok Post, January 20, 2000.

[1083] "Industry body prods Govt on privacy issues - Laws needed to gain trust," Bangkok Post, May 10, 2000.

[1084] Official Information Act, B.E. 2540 (1997),
<http://www.krisdika.go.th/law/text/lawpub/e02092540/text.htm

without prior or immediate consent given in writing by the person except in limited circumstances; and provide rights of access, correction and deletion.

The Official Information Commission oversees the Act.[1085] The Commission is under the Office of the Prime Minister. In August 1999, Director Surasi Kosolnawin was removed from the post after fighting with Minister Supatra Masdit over his aggressive efforts to force government agencies to implement the Act.

Phone tapping is a criminal offense under the 1934 Telegraph and Telephone Act.[1086] Wiretaps can be conducted for security reasons. Violators can face up to five years in jail. The Narcotics Control Board recently proposed legislation that would authorize tapping in drug cases with a court order. Illegal wiretapping is common in Thailand. Communications Minister Suthep Thuagsuban told reporters in June 2000, "Tapping telephones is not new in Thailand, everybody knows there is telephone tapping...When you return home you should check your line."[1087] In April 1997, tapes and transcripts from wiretaps of Sanan Kachornprasart, the opposition party Democrat secretary-general, were found in the compound of Government House.[1088] The Armed Forces Security Centre was accused of being behind the tapping.[1089] Wiretaps were found on the telephone of the chairperson of the Civil Rights and Freedom Protection Group, an anti corruption group in June 2000. After a technician from the Telephone Organisation of Thailand (TOT) was charged with the tap, the president of the TOT resigned. The National Counter Corruption Commission has taken over the investigation.[1090]

In 1997, Thailand began issuing a new national ID card with a magnetic strip. The computer system will be linked with other government departments including the Revenue Department, the Ministry of Foreign Affairs, the Ministry of Defense and the Office of the Narcotics Control Board. The government also plans to link the system with other governments to allow holders to travel in Asian countries without the need for a passport, using only the new card. Bank customers who carry the new ID card can use it as an ATM card as well.[1091] In

---

[1085] Home Page: http://www.oic.thaigov.go.th/

[1086] Telegraph and Telephone Act, B.E. 2476 <http://www.krisdika.go.th/law/text/lawpub/ei004/text.htm>.

[1087] Thai telecoms chief resigns amid phone tapping scandal, Agence France Presse, June 6, 2000.

[1088] "Thailand: Politics - PM Denies Chuan's Wire-tapping Claim," Bangkok Post, April 8, 1997.

[1089] "Inside Politics Infuriated by tap rap," FT Asia Intelligence Wire, July 3, 1997.

[1090] "Anti-graft agency to probe bugging case," Bankok Post, June 16, 2000.

[1091] "Thailand: Issuing Computerized National Identity Cards," Newsbytes, September 8, 1997.

1995, Control Data Systems was awarded a $11.5 million contract by the Bangkok Metropolitan Administration (BMA) project to install the Computerized National Census and Services Project. The system includes names, addresses, national ID card numbers, and census information such as birth and death records and address changes. It will be used for checking individual tax returns and compiling census statistics.[1092] It is expected to be completed by next year for elections.

The Official Information Act allows for citizens to obtain government information such as the result of a consideration or a decision which has a direct effect on a private individual, work-plan, project and annual expenditure estimates, and manuals or order relating to work procedure of State officials which affects the rights and duties of private individuals. Individuals can appeal denials to the Official Information Commission. According to the OIC, in 1999, there were 191 complaints, 80 of which were solved during the year. There were 32 cases in 1998. [1093] The OIC is currently reviewing the government's withholding of most of the official report on the 1992 bloody Black May military crackdown on political protests.

Republic of Turkey

Section Five of the 1982 Turkish Constitution is entitled, "Privacy and Protection of Private Life."[1094] Article 20 of the Turkish constitution deals with "Privacy of the Individual's Life," and it states, "Everyone has the right to demand respect for his private and family life. Privacy of individual and family life cannot be violated. Exceptions necessitated by judiciary investigation and prosecution are reserved. Unless there exists a decision duly passed by a judge in cases explicitly defined by law, and unless there exists an order of an agency authorized by law in cases where delay is deemed prejudicial, neither the person nor the private papers, nor belongings of an individual shall be searched nor shall they be seized." Article 22 states, "Secrecy of communication is fundamental. Communication shall not be impeded nor its secrecy be violated, unless there exists a decision duly passed by a judge in cases explicitly defined by law, and unless there exists an order of an agency authorized by law in cases where delay is deemed prejudicial. Public establishments or institutions where exceptions to the above may be applied will be defined by law."

[1092] "Control Data Wins Thai Census Project," Newsbytes, October 3, 1995.

[1093] Nakorn Serirak, Thailand's Information Law, March 2000.

[1094] Constitution Republic of Turkey, <http://www.mfa.gov.tr/GRUPI/Anayasa/i142.htm>.

The Turkish Ministry of Justice as of summer of 2000 has been working on draft legislation on the protection of personal data. For this purpose, yet another working party has been established but there are currently no further details available in relation to the schedule of the working party or whether this time the efforts of such a working party will result with a Turkish Data Protection law. The Ministry has been working on this for several years without success. The proposals discussed within the May 1998 E-Commerce Laws Working Party Report[1095] emphasize both the importance of facilitating the collection and processing of personal data and the protection of personal data of individuals in the information age.

Within the Turkish national legislation, the protection of personal rights is regulated in the Civil Code. Pursuant to Article 24 of the Civil Code, an individual whose personal rights are violated unjustly may request protection against the violation from the judge. Individuals can bring action for violation of their private rights. However, there is no criminal liability for such violations of personal rights and currently there is no protection for personal data (through data protection laws or any other laws) under the current Turkish Criminal Code.

Articles 195-200 of the Turkish Criminal Code on the freedom of communications govern communication through letters, parcels, telegram and telephone. Despite the existing laws and regulations, the right to privacy and to private communications seem to be rather problematic in Turkey. There is widespread illegal wiretapping by the government. According to acting Security Director Kemal Celik, all telephones in Turkey are bugged. The Turkish parliament's telephone bugging committee, set up to investigate allegations of government phone taps, confirmed allegations that the Security Directorate listens in on all telephone communications, including cellular calls, according to a secret 50-page report documenting and confirming the bugging of telephones.[1096] In December 1999, a Turkish court convicted the deputy head of Ankara's police intelligence division Zafer Aktas of abuse of office for his part in a telephone tapping scandal, in which Ankara police were accused of bugging the prime minister's telephones.[1097] In March, Chairman of the Supreme Court's 8th Department, Naci Unver, sued the Interior Ministry after finding out that his official phone is being bugged. The Interior Ministry defended the tapping saying

---

[1095] Turkish Republic Foreign Trade Office, E-Commerce Laws Working Party Report, 8 May, 1998. A summary of the report in Turkish is available at <http://kurul.ubak.gov.tr/e-ticaret.html>.

[1096] Asia Times, "No privacy on the phone lines," April 16, 1997, p 8.

[1097] "Turk policeman convicted in phone tapping scandal," Reuters, December 6, 1999.

that the claims of the suitor that the incident was a violation of personal freedom and of the independence of the juridical system were "obscure and pointless." The Ministry demanded the withdrawal of the lawsuit for compensation, saying, "Or else there would be no end to lawsuits filed." The Ministry also claimed that the police department had "just listened but not carried out a criminal recording and thus the events did not damage suitors in any concrete way. In the second report, it is also stated that if compensation were to be paid, it would result in an unnecessary wealth gain for the victim.[1098] The Interior Minister said in March 2000 that new guidelines would be issued soon and punishment for illegal wiretaps would be forthcoming.[1099]

A new bill to set up a "Council for the Security of National Information and its duties" is pending in the Parliament. The bill would set up the Council to address issues including data protection, encryption, and security of information systems. The Council will be part of the Prime Minister's office and the Ministry of Justice, Ministry of Defense, MIT (Turkish CIA), the Army and other ministries will be involved. The draft Bill was heavily criticized and received only support from the General Staff (representing the Army). According to Vice-Admiral Taner Uzunay, the Head of the Electronic Communication department within the General Staff, the US government is listening to Turkish communications which it is why it is urgent to develop policies on protection of the information and communication infrastructure in Turkey.[1100] TUBITAK-BILTEN, the Scientific and Technical Research Council Of Turkey - The Institute of Information Technologies recommended that the duties of the National Council for the Security of National Information need to be clarified.[1101] According to their report, the Council cannot be an intelligence agency, research and development unit, a standards institute, a certification authority, and a public policy making body at the same time.[1102] Industry groups and NGOs also expressed concern about the Council have control over information security.

In 1990, a parliamentary commission on human rights was established with the power to monitor the human rights situation in Turkey and abroad. Currently, the commission consists of 25 parliamentarians, three consultants and four secretaries. Since its inception, the commission has taken up some 20 cases on its own initiative. Most of these cases relate to alleged violations of physical

---

[1098] "Comedy of phone bugging," Milliyet, 16 March, 2000.

[1099] Hurriyet, 13 Mar 2000.

[1100] BThaber, "e-RTÜK yakinda," No:260, 13-26 March, 2000.

[1101] See <http://www.bilten.metu.edu.tr/>.

[1102] See <http://www.bilten.metu.edu.tr/publications/ubg.html>.

integrity[1103] and it is unknown whether the Commission has dealt with any cases of individual privacy.

Turkey is a member of the Council of Europe and has accepted the Council's monitoring mechanism.[1104] It signed the Convention for the Protection of Individuals with Regard to Automatic Processing of Personal Data (ETS No. 108) in 1981 but has not ratified the act.[1105] It has signed and ratified the European Convention for the Protection of Human Rights and Fundamental Freedoms.[1106] Turkey has also been a member of the Organization for Economic Co-operation and Development since 1961.

Republic of Ukraine

The Constitution of Ukraine guarantees the right of privacy and data protection.[1107] Article 31 states, "Everyone is guaranteed privacy of mail, telephone conversations, telegraph and other correspondence. Exceptions shall be established only by a court in cases envisaged by law, with the purpose of preventing crime or ascertaining the truth in the course of the investigation of a criminal case, if it is not possible to obtain information by other means." Article 32 states "No one shall be subject to interference in his or her personal and family life, except in cases envisaged by the Constitution of Ukraine. The collection, storage, use and dissemination of confidential information about a person without his or her consent shall not be permitted, except in cases determined by law, and only in the interests of national security, economic welfare and human rights. Every citizen has the right to examine information about himself or herself, that is not a state secret or other secret protected by law, at the bodies of state power, bodies of local self-government, institutions and organizations. Everyone is guaranteed judicial protection of the right to rectify incorrect information about himself or herself and members of his or her family, and of the right to demand that any type of information be expunged, and also the

---

[1103] See Commission On Human Rights, Question of the Human Rights of All Persons Subjected to any Form of Detention or Imprisonment: Promotion and protection of the right to freedom of opinion and expression, report of the Special Rapporteur, Mr. Abid Hussain, submitted pursuant to Commission on Human Rights resolution 1996/53 Addendum Mission to Turkey at <http://www.unhchr.ch/html/menu4/chrrep/3197a1.htm>, Distr. General E/CN.4/1997/31/Add.1 11 February 1997.

[1104] See Republic of Turkey, Ministry of Foreign Affairs paper, "Human Rights in Turkey: V. Turkey's Place and Role in the International Context," at <http://www.mfa.gov.tr/GRUPF/hrtur.htm>.

[1105] See <http://conventions.coe.int/>.

[1106] Signed 04/11/50, Ratified 18/05/54, Entered into force 18/05/54, <http://conventions.coe.int/>.

[1107] Constitution of Ukraine, Adopted at the Fifth Session of the Verkhovna Rada of Ukraine on 28 June 1996 <http://alpha.rada.kiev.ua/const/conengl.htm>.

---

right to compensation for material and moral damages inflicted by the collection, storage, use and dissemination of such incorrect information." There is also a limited right of freedom of information. Article 50 states, "Everyone is guaranteed the right of free access to information about the environmental situation, the quality of food and consumer goods, and also the right to disseminate such information. No one shall make such information secret."

There is currently an effort to enact a data protection act. The draft bill on Data Protection prepared by State Committee of Communications and Computerization was introduced to the Cabinet of Ministers for consideration in December 1999. The draft is loosely based on the Council of Europe Convention No. 108 and the State of Hesse's (Germany) 1970 data protection act and focuses on property rights for privacy control. The original drafts proposed the establishment of a Data Protection Ombudsman but the most recent draft leaves out the office because of opposition by the State Security Service and Ministry of Justice. Observers note that it is not likely to be compliant with the COE convention or the EU Directive.

The Act "On Information" defines only general principles of citizens' access to information personally related to them. Article 9 provides individuals with access to information concerning them. Exceptions are to be defined by Law. Article 23 of the Statute prohibits collection of personal data without consent of the data subject, and provides the right to know about data collection.[1108] The Constitutional Court of Ukraine ruled in October 1997 that Article 23 prohibited not only the collection of information, but also the storage, use and dissemination of confidential personal information without the consent of the individual.[1109] There are exceptions for national security, economic well-being, and information that would affect another's rights and freedoms. Confidential information includes, in particular, information about a person such as education, marital status, state of health, date and place of birth, property status and other personal details.

The Act on the Operational Investigative Activity of February 18, 1992, and the Act on organizational and legal foundations of struggle with organized crime empowers law enforcement agencies to conduct surveillance. The agencies are obliged to obtain a warrant under the court procedure as implemented by the Act

---

[1108] Statute "On information" of October 2, 1992 (# 2657-XII).

[1109] Verdict of the Constitutional Court of Ukraine Concerning the case of the official treatment of Articles 3, 23, 31, 47, 48 of the Law of Ukraine "On information" and Article 12 of the Law of Ukraine "On the Prosecutor's Office" (case of K. G. Ustimenko), October 30, 1997. <http://www2.datatestlab.com/privacy/files/ENCLOSURE.doc>.

of the Supreme Court Plenary Session of November 1, 1996.[1110] The Statute does not provide wiretapping procedure rules. Those are regulated by secret rules, adopted by the joint Ministry of Internal Affairs and State Committee as Communications Order No 745/90 of September 30, 1999. The applications are registered and include the names of officials, and the date and type of communications. Statistical data on wiretapping activity is not publicly available. Under article 11, priests, doctors, and lawyers can not be asked about information concerning their clients, and any such information cannot be used as evidence in court. However, in practice, the courts regularly use such information. The special services investigated the Kazakhstan Energy Grid Operating Company in June 2000 for the illegal tapping of employee conversations and charged one employee with a violation of the criminal code.[1111]

The Department of Special Telecommunication Systems and Information Safeguarding of the Security Service of Ukraine is authorized under an April 2000 Presidential Order to adopt regulations on the protection of information in data transmitting networks, as well as to establish the "application of the tools for the protection of state information resources."[1112] In July 2000, President Kuchma signed a decree on "development of national content of the global informational network (Internet) and wide access to this network in Ukraine." It sets rules on digital signatures, information security and protection of information "which can not be published according to the law."[1113]

In September 1999, President Leonid Kuchma proposed regulations requiring that Internet Service Providers install surveillance devices on their systems based on the Russian SORM system. The regulations had to be withdrawn because of a Constitutional issue and he proposed a bill to implement them. The bill was attacked by the Parliament and withdrawn. However, in August 1999, the security service visited a number of the large ISPs who were reported to have installed the boxes. In June 2000, several high government officials (including the deputy chair of the security service, the chair of the headquarters of the Ministry of Defense, and the chair of the Presidential Committee on informational security) held closed meetings with representatives of the major

---

[1110] Directive of the Supreme Court of Ukraine, No.9 of November 1, 1996, 'On referring to the Constitution in administering justice'.

[1111] "Power company denies involvement in telephone tapping," BBC Summary of World Broadcasts June 02, 2000.

[1112] Presidential Order No. 582/2000 of April 10, 2000.

[1113] Decree of 31.07.2000, No. 928/2000.

Ukrainian ISPs to discuss new SORM regulations. A working group released a document announcing that the group had agreed to implement surveillance capabilities based on ENFOPOL 98 and create a working group on filtering and monitoring of unlawful information.[1114] The large ISPs are expected to support the regulations to eliminate competition from smaller ISPs who will not be able to afford the new systems.

There are a number of other laws that control personal information.[1115] The cabinet approved the creation of a Single State Automated Passport System in January 1997 as a component of the State Register of Population.[1116] The system will be used as an internal ID system and hold both textual and graphical data about every Ukrainian. The text data will include: first, patronymic and last name, date of birth, sex, identification number, date of registration and residence, data of another state citizenship, data of passport and its duplicates, data of job/study, matrimonial status, data of husband/wife and children, education, military draft status, date of documents for travelling abroad, and memorandums (disability care, restriction for travelling abroad). The graphical information will include: identifier, biometrics data and signature. There are also laws relating to tax information,[1117] social insurance,[1118] domicile registration,[1119] retirement insurance,[1120] unemployment insurance,[1121] criminal investigations,[1122] juvenile records,[1123] former prisoners,[1124] military service records,[1125] medical records,[1126] and HIV and AIDS records.[1127]

[1114] See Andriy Pazyuk, Privacy Ukraine, Ukrainian ISPs demonstrate their willingness to be subservient to Big Brother, July 7, 2000. <http://www.cyber-rights.org/documents/ukrainia.htm>.

[1115] See Andriy Pazyuk, Privacy Ukraine Privacy of Data Subject in Ukraine, 1999 for more details on the laws. <http://www2.datatestlab.com/privacy/>.

[1116] The Statutory Order of the Cabinet of Ministers (CM) of 20th of January 1997 (No 40).

[1117] Law "On State Register of natural persons – taxpayers" of the 22nd of December 1994 (No320/94).

[1118] Law "The Basic legislation of Ukraine on Obligatory State Social Insurance" of the 14th of January 1998 (No.16/98).

[1119] The MIA Order of the 3rd of February 1992 (No.66).

[1120] Statutory Order of the CM of the 4th of June 1998 (No.794).

[1121] The Statutory Order of CM of the 27th of May 1998 (No.578).

[1122] The Order of Office of Public Prosecutor of the 21st of December 1995 (No.22/835); The MIA Order of 14th January 1994 (No.190).

[1123] The Law "On organs and services on juveniles and dedicated educational institution for juveniles" of the 24th of January 1995 (No.20/95); Ministry of Education Order of the 27th of December 1994 (No.362).

[1124] The Law "On Administrative Control the Former Prisoners" of the 1st of December 1994 (No.264/94).

[1125] Department of Defense Orders of 27th June 1995 No 165, 166 approved the Regulation "On military record maintained at the place of employment or study (public or private)" and the Regulation "On military domiciliary registration."

[1126] Law of the 19th of September 1992.

Religious conservatives demonstrated in opposition to the application of personal identification numbers approved by the Act On State Register of Natural Persons – Taxpayers.[1128] The Parliament approved an amendment to the statute in July 1999 allowing for an alternative system of registration to be used for persons with religious grounds for opposing identity numbers.[1129]

In October 1998, a CD "All Kyiv-2" was offered for sale at markets in the city of Kiev. The CD contained all addresses and telephone directories of the City, including the phone numbers and addresses not only of residents but also of top state management, including the former and current President of Ukraine. It is clear that the release took place as a result of a violation of the access regime of the State Information Service.

The 1992 Act on Information provides a right of access to government records.[1130] Article 21 sets out methods for making official information public, including disclosing it to interested persons orally, in writing or in other ways. Article 29 of the Statute prohibits the limitation of the right to obtain non-covert information. Article 37 sets out a long list of exceptions. The author of a rejected or postponed request has a right to appeal the decision to a higher echelon or court (Article 34). There is limited access to the files of the former secret police under the Act "on rehabilitation of victims of political repressions," which gives the rehabilitated citizen or his heirs the right to read his personal file kept in the KGB archives.

Ukraine is a member of the Council of Europe but has not signed or ratified the Convention for the Protection of Individuals with Regard to Automatic Processing of Personal Data (ETS No. 108).[1131] It has signed and ratified the European Convention for the Protection of Human Rights and Fundamental Freedoms.[1132]

[1127] Law "On prevention of AIDS contamination and social aid on civilians" (in redaction of the 3rd of March 1998) as well as Article 13 of the Discipline of medical inspection on HIV results, registration of HIV and AIDS persons and medical care (approved by the Statutory Order of the CM of the 18th of December 1998).

[1128] "On State Register of Natural Persons – Taxpayers" of December 22, 1994 (No.320/94).

[1129] Statute of July 16, 1999 (No.1003-XIV) on the alterations to the Statute "On State Register of Natural Persons – Taxpayers."

[1130] Statute "On Information" adopted by Parliament on October 2, 1992 (No.2657-XII).

[1131] See <http://conventions.coe.int/>.

[1132] Signed 9/11/95, Ratified 11/09/97, Entered into force 11/09/97, <http://conventions.coe.int/>.

United Kingdom of Great Britain and Northern Ireland

The UK does not have a written constitution. In 1998, the Parliament approved the Human Rights Act that will incorporate the European Convention on Human Rights into domestic law, a process which will establish an enforceable right of privacy.[1133] The Act will come into force on October 2, 2000.

The Parliament approved the Data Protection Act (1998) in July 1998.[1134] The legislation, which came into force on March 1, 2000, updates the 1984 Data Protection Act in accordance with the requirements of the European Union's Data Protection Directive.[1135] The Act covers records held by government agencies and private entities. It provides for limitations on the use of personal information, access to records and requires that entities that maintain records register with the Data Protection Commissioner.

The Office of the Data Protection Commissioner is an independent agency that maintains the register and enforces the Act.[1136] There are currently 237,146 data users registered with the Commission. In the 11 months prior to the end of February 2000, the agency received 4,570 complaints,[1137] an increase of 36 percent over the previous year. Of these complaints, 145 resulted in prosecutions by the Data Commission and 130 guilty verdicts were issued by the courts. The Commissioner is also responsible for enforcing the Telecommunications (Data Protection and Privacy) Regulations. These regulations came into force on March 1, 2000, and fully implement the EU Telecommunications Directive.[1138] They repeal and replace the Telecommunications (Data Protection and Privacy) (Direct Marketing) Regulations 1998 which came into effect on May 1, 1999. The Commissioner has already issued two enforcement notices against companies acting in breach of these regulations. The Commissioner issues a number of comprehensive reports for the public. She has published a Code of Practice for

---

[1133] Human Rights Bill, CM 3782, October 1997. <http://www.official-documents.co.uk/document/hoffice/rights/rights.htm>.

[1134] Data Protection Act 1998c. 29. <http://www.hmso.gov.uk/acts/acts1998/19980029.htm>.

[1135] Data Protection Act 1984 (c. 35). <http://www.hmso.gov.uk/acts/acts1984/1984035.htm>.

[1136] Home page of the Data Protection Commissioner, formerly known as the Data Protection Registrar: <http://www.dataprotection.gov.uk/>. For an overview of the Commission's powers see 'Media Summary", October 1999 <http://wood.ccta.gov.uk/dpr/dpdoc.nsf>.

[1137] This figure represents complaints received prior to 29th February 2000 inclusive. Complaints received after 1st March 2000 were handled as requests for assessment.

[1138] Directive 97/66/EC concerning the processing of personal data and the protection of privacy in the telecommunications sector.

---

the use of Closed Circuit Television (CCTV),[1139] a study of the availability and use of personal information in public registers,[1140] and guidelines concerning employer/employee relationships.[1141] A specially created internal working group of the Commission is currently preparing a comprehensive introductory paper to the new law in order to help individuals and organizations understand their new rights and obligations. An updated guidance on the Telecommunications (Data Protection and Privacy) Regulations will also be published soon.[1142]

The Regulation of Investigatory Powers Act 2000 became law in July 2000.[1143] It provides powers for the Home Secretary to warrant interception of communications and to require Communications Service Providers to provide a "reasonable interception capability" in their networks. It further allows any public authority designated by the Home Secretary to access "communications data." This data includes the source, destination and type of any communication, such as mobile phone location information. Finally, powers are provided for senior members of the civilian and military police, Customs, and members of the judiciary to require the plaintext of encrypted material, or in certain circumstances decryption keys themselves. It replaces the Interception of Communications Act of 1985.[1144] It also sets rules on other types of investigatory powers that had not been previously regulated under UK law. Many legal experts, including the Data Protection Commissioner, believe that many of the provisions violate the European Convention on Human Rights and a legal challenge is likely.

In 1998, 1,913 orders for intercepting telephone communications were approved, an increase of 25 percent from the previous year and nearly 400 percent over ten years. Telephone taps for national security purposes are authorized by the Foreign Minister. There were also 118 orders for interception of mail

---

[1139] CCTV Code of Practice, July 2000, <http://wood.ccta.gov.uk/dpr/dpdoc.nsf>.

[1140] Study of the Availability and Use of Personal Information in Public Registers. Final Report to the Office of the Data Protection Registrar J.E. Davies and C. Oppenheim, Loughborough University, September 1999. <http://wood.ccta.gov.uk/dpr/dpdoc.nsf>.

[1141] Draft report on the uses and misuses of Personal Data in employer/employee relationships, by Robin Chater - Director of the Personnel Policy Research Unit, commissioned by the Data Protection Commissioner, January 1999. A Draft code of practice and management checklist by Robin E J Chater, Director: PPRU , commissioned by the Office of the Data Protection Commissioner, February 25th 1999, <http://wood.ccta.gov.uk/dpr/dpdoc.nsf - 25/02/99>.

[1142] This will replace the interim guidance on the Telecommunications (Data Protection and Privacy)(direct Marketing) Regulations 1998, published in June 1999.

[1143] Regulation of Investigatory Powers Act 2000. <http://www.homeoffice.gov.uk/ripa/ripact.htm>. See the FIPR Regulation of Investigatory Powers Information Centre <http://www.fipr.org/rip/>.

[1144] Interception of Communications Act 1985, 1985 CHAPTER 56 <http://www.butterworths.co.uk/academic/lloyd/Statutes/communications.htm>.

---

communications. The National Criminal Intelligence Service published a series of codes of practice on interception, surveillance, use of informants, undercover operations and use of intelligence materials in May 1999 to ensure adherence with the European Convention on Human Rights incorporation into UK law.[1145]

There is a long history of illegal wiretapping of political opponents, labor unions and others in the UK.[1146] In 1985, the European Court of Human Rights ruled that police interception of individuals' communications was a violation of Article 8 of the European Convention on Human Rights.[1147] The decision resulted in the adoption of the Interception of Communications Act 1985. Most recently, the European Court of Human Rights ruled in 1997 that police eavesdropping of a policewoman violated Article 8.[1148] In the late 1970's, MI5, Britain's security service, tapped the phones of many left-leaning activists including the future Secretary of State for Trade and Industry Peter Mandelson, and kept files on Jack Straw, now Home Secretary, and Harriet Harman, former Social Security Secretary, as well as Guardian journalist Victoria Brittain. The High Court issued an injunction against the Mail on Sunday preventing the publication of further revelations. In September 1998, it was revealed that there were secret talks between the Association of Chief Police Officers (ACPO) and representatives for Internet Service Providers (ISPs) with the aim of reaching a "memorandum of understanding" to give the police access to private data held by ISPs.[1149]

In late 1997, a report commissioned by the European Parliament and prepared by the UK-based research group Omega Foundation, confirmed that Britain was a key player in a vast global signals intelligence operation controlled by the U.S. National Security Agency (NSA).[1150] According to the report, the U.S. and its UK partner, GCHQ, "routinely and indiscriminately" intercepted large amounts of sensitive data which had been identified through keyword searching. The eavesdropping was carried out from a number of spy bases in the UK, most notably the Menwith Hill base in the north of England. The European Parliament recently created a one-year temporary committee to investigate allegations that

---

[1145] National Criminal Intelligence Center, 13 May 1999, Available at <http://www.cyber-rights.org/interception/>.

[1146] See e.g., Patrick Fitzgerald & Mark Leopold, Stranger on the Line, 1987.

[1147] Malone v United Kingdom (A/95): (1991) 13 EHRR 448.

[1148] Halford v United Kingdom (Application No 20605/92), 24 EHRR 523, 25 June 1997.

[1149] "Police tighten the Net," The Guardian Online, September 17, 1998.

[1150] European Commission, Science and Technology Options Assessment Office (STOA), "Assessing the technologies of political control," Brussels, 1997.

---

the Echelon surveillance system violates individual privacy rights and is used to conduct industrial espionage.[1151]

There are also a number of other laws containing privacy components, most notably those governing medical records[1152] and consumer credit information.[1153] Other laws with privacy components include, the Rehabilitation of Offenders Act of 1974, the Telecommunications Act of 1984 (as amended by the Telecommunications Regulations of 1999), the Police Act of 1997, the Broadcasting Act of 1996, Part VI and the Protection from Harassment Act of 1997. Some of these acts are amended and may be repealed in part by the 1998 Data Protection Act. The Police and Criminal Evidence Act (1984) allows police to enter and search homes without a warrant following an arrest for any offense. And while police may not demand identification before arrest, they have the right to stop and search any person on the street on grounds of suspicion. Following arrest, a body sample will be taken for inclusion in the national DNA database.[1154] The Crime and Disorder Act of 1998 provides for information sharing and data matching among public bodies in order to reduce crime and disorder. The Data Protection Commissioner has issued a report on the privacy implications of this Act.[1155]

The privacy picture in the UK is mixed.[1156] There is, at some levels, a strong public recognition and defense of privacy. Proposals to establish a national identity card, for example, have routinely failed. On the other hand, crime and public order laws passed in recent years have placed substantial limitations on numerous rights, including freedom of assembly, privacy, freedom of movement, the right of silence and freedom of speech.[1157] There has been a proliferation of CCTV cameras in hundreds of towns and cities in Britain. The camera networks can be operated by police, local authorities or private companies, and are partly funded by a Home Office grant. Their original purpose was crime prevention and detection, though in recent years the cameras have become important tools for city center management and the control of "anti-social behavior." Between 150

[1151] 'EU to Search for Echelon', Reuters, July 5, 2000

[1152] Access to Medical Reports Act 1988 and the Access to Health Records Act 1990.

[1153] Consumer Credit Act, 1974.

[1154] Criminal Justice and Public Order Act 1994.
<http://www.hmso.gov.uk/acts/summary/01994033.htm>.

[1155] 'Crime & Disorder Act 1998: Data protection implications for information-sharing',
<http://wood.ccta.gov.uk/dpr/dpdoc.nsf>.

[1156] See Simon Davies, Big Brother (Pan Books, 1996).

[1157] See Criminal Justice and Public Order Act 1994

---

million and 300 million pounds a year is spent expanding the web of 200,000 cameras covering public spaces in Britain,[1158] but despite the ubiquity of the technology, successive governments have been reluctant to pass specific laws to govern their use. Their use has come under greater criticism recently and recent research by the Scottish Centre for Criminology found that the cameras did not reduce crime, nor improved public perception of crime problems.[1159] As mentioned above, the Data Protection Commission has also issued a code of practice for the use of these cameras.

There have been efforts for over 20 years to enact a Freedom of Information Act in the UK. A 1994 "Code of Practice on Access to Government Information" provides some access to government records but has 15 broad exemptions. Dissatisfied applicants can complain, via a Member of Parliament, to the Parliamentary Ombudsman if their request is denied.[1160]

A Freedom of Information Bill was introduced into the House of Commons in November 1999. A draft of the legislation was released for public consultation in May 1999.[1161] The Act was amended and approved by the House of Commons in April 2000. The Bill is currently pending before the House of Lords. It has received considerable criticism from by many politicians across the political spectrum and NGOs as being insufficient and weaker than the existing code of practice. Some 195 Members of Parliament signed a Parliamentary motion calling for major improvements. The law will create a new officer, the Information Commissioner, to oversee both the Freedom of Information regime and the Data Protection Act 1998. The Scottish Parliament is drafting a stronger Freedom of Information Law as one of their first actions.

The UK is a member of the Council of Europe and has signed and ratified the Convention for the Protection of Individuals with Regard to Automatic Processing of Personal Data (ETS No. 108)[1162] along with the European Convention for the Protection of Human Rights and Fundamental Freedoms.[1163] In addition to these commitments, the UK is a member of the Organization for

---

[1158] House of Lords, Science and Technology Committee, Inquiry: "Use of digital images as evidence," 3 February 1998, section 4.3.

[1159] Home Page: <http://www.scotcrim.u-net.com/researchc.htm>.

[1160] Government of the United Kingdom, Code of Practice on Access to Government Information, April 4 1994, revised in January 1997, <http://www.cfoi.org.uk/coptext.html>.

[1161] Home Office, Freedom of Information: Consultation on Draft Legislation, <http://www.homeoffice.gov.uk/foi/dfoibill.htm>.

[1162] Signed 14/05/81, Ratified 26/08/87, Entered into force 01/12/87. <http://conventions.coe.int/>.

[1163] <http://conventions.coe.int/>.

Economic Cooperation and Development and has adopted the OECD Guidelines on the Protection of Privacy and Transborder Flows of Personal Data.

Territories

The Isle of Man Data Protection Act of 1986 is based on the 1984 UK Data Protection Act. A Data Protection (Amendment) Bill is expected to be introduced in the 1999/2000 legislative programme. The Act is enforced by the Office of the Data Protection Registrar.[1164]

The Guernsey Data Protection Law of 1986 is also based on the UK Act.[1165] A committee recommended changes to the Act in June 2000 based on the revised UK Act. The Act is enforced by the Isle of Guernsey Data Protection Commissioner.[1166]

The Data Protection (Jersey) Law came into force in 1987. The law is equivalent to the 1984 UK Data Protection Act. The Act is overseen by the Data Protection Registry who registers databases and conducts investigations. It registered 1,605 databases by the end of 1998. The Registrar currently works on a part time basis.

United States of America

There is no explicit right to privacy in the U.S. Constitution. The Supreme Court has ruled that there is a limited constitutional right of privacy based on a number of provisions in the Bill of Rights. This includes a right to privacy from government surveillance into an area where a person has a "reasonable expectation of privacy"[1167] and also in matters relating to marriage, procreation, contraception, family relationships, child rearing and education.[1168] However, records held by third parties, such as financial records or telephone calling records, are generally not protected unless a legislature has enacted a specific law. The Court has also recognized a right of anonymity[1169] and the right of political groups to prevent disclosure of their members' names to government

---

1164 Home Page: http://www.gov.im/odpr/.

1165 The Data Protection (Bailiwick of Guernsey) Law 1986 <http://www.dpcommission.gov.gg/law.htm>.

1166 Home Page: http://www.dpcommission.gov.gg/

1167 Katz v. U.S., 386 U.S. 954 (1967). <http://laws.findlaw.com/US/386/954.html>.

1168 See eg Griswold v. Connecticut, 381 US 479 (1965); Whalen v. Roe, 429 US 589 (1977); Paul v. Davis, 424 U.S. 714 (1976).

1169 McIntire v. Ohio Elections Committee, April 19, 1995.

agencies.[1170] In January 2000, the Supreme Court heard *Reno v. Condon*, a case addressing the constitutionality of the Drivers Privacy Protection Act (DPPA), a 1994 law that protects drivers' records held by state motor vehicle agencies. In a unanimous decision, the Court found that the information was "an article of commerce" and can be regulated by the federal government.[1171]

The Privacy Act of 1974 protects records held by U.S. Government agencies and requires agencies to apply basic fair information practices.[1172] Its effectiveness is significantly weakened by administrative interpretations of a provision allowing for disclosure of personal information for a "routine use" compatible with the purpose for which the information was originally collected. Limits on the use of the Social Security Number have also been undercut in recent years for a number of purposes.

There is no independent privacy oversight agency in the U.S. The Office of Management and Budget plays a limited role in setting policy for federal agencies under the Privacy Act, but it has not been particularly active or effective. An office within the Office of Management and Budget to coordinate federal stances towards privacy was created in early 1999, and a Chief Counselor for Privacy was appointed. The Counselor has only a limited advisory capacity and most privacy advocates believe the position is ineffective in promoting privacy within the government. The Federal Trade Commission has oversight and enforcement powers for the laws protecting children's online privacy, consumer credit information and fair trading practices but has no general authority to enforce privacy rights.[1173] The FTC has received thousands of complaints but has issued opinions in only a few cases. It has also organized a series of workshops and surveys, which have found that industry protection of privacy on the Internet is poor, but the FTC had long said that the industry should have more time to make self-regulation work. In a shift from this historical position, the FTC recommended in this year's report to the U.S. Congress that legislation is necessary to protect consumer privacy on the Internet due to the dismal findings in a survey of online privacy policies.[1174]

[1170] NAACP v. Alabama, 357 U.S. 449 (1958). <http://laws.findlaw.com/US/357/449.html>.

[1171] RENO v. CONDON, No. 98—1464, January 12, 2000. <http://supct.law.cornell.edu/supct/html/98-1464.ZS.html>.

[1172] Privacy Act of 1974, 5 USC 552a, PL 93-579. <http://www.epic.org/privacy/laws/privacy_act.html>.

[1173] See FTC Privacy Pages, <http://www.ftc.gov/privacy/index.html>.

[1174] Privacy Online: Fair Information Practices in the Electronic Marketplace: A Federal Trade Commission Report to Congress (May 2000), <http://www.ftc.gov/os/2000/05/index.htm#22>.

The U.S. has no comprehensive privacy protection law for the private sector. A patchwork of federal laws covers some specific categories of personal information.[1175] These include financial records,[1176] credit reports,[1177] video rentals,[1178] cable television,[1179] children's (under age 13) online activities,[1180] educational records,[1181] motor vehicle registrations,[1182] and telephone records.[1183] However such activities as the selling of medical records and bank records, monitoring of workers, and video surveillance of individuals are currently not prohibited under federal law. There is also a variety of sectoral legislation on the state level that may give additional protections to citizens of individual states.[1184] The tort of privacy was first adopted in 1905 and all but two of the 50 states recognize a civil right of action for invasion of privacy in their laws.

Surveillance of wire, oral and electronic communications for criminal investigations is governed by the Omnibus Safe Streets and Crime Control Act of 1968 and the Electronic Communications Privacy Act of 1986.[1185] Police are required to obtain a court order based on a number of legal requirements. Surveillance for national security purposes is governed by the Foreign Intelligence Surveillance Act that has less rigorous requirements.[1186] There were 1,350 orders for interceptions for criminal purposes[1187] and 886 for national security purposes in 1999.[1188] The use of electronic surveillance has more than tripled in the last ten years.

[1175] See Marc Rotenberg, The Privacy Law Sourcebook, EPIC 1999. <http://www.epic.org/bookstore/pls/>.

[1176] Right to Financial Privacy Act, PL 95-630.

[1177] Fair Credit Reporting Act, PL 91-508, amended by PL 104-208 (Sept. 30, 1996). <http://www.ftc.gov/os/statutes/fcra.htm>.

[1178] Video Privacy Protection Act of 1988, 100-618, 1988.

[1179] Cable Privacy Protection Act of 1984, 98-549, 1984. <http://www.epic.org/privacy/cable_tv/ctpa.html>.

[1180] See Center for Media Education, A Parent's Guide to Online Privacy. <http://www.kidsprivacy.org/>.

[1181] Family Educational Rights and Privacy Act, Public Law 93-380, 1974. <http://www.epic.org/privacy/education/ferpa.html>.

[1182] Drivers Privacy Protection Act, PL 103-322, 1994. <http://www.epic.org/privacy/laws/drivers_privacy_bill.html>.

[1183] Telephone Consumer Protection Act, PL 102-243, 1991.

[1184] Compilation of State and Federal Privacy Laws (1997 ed.), by Robert Ellis Smith and Privacy Journal..<http://www.epic.org/privacy/consumer/states.html>.

[1185] 18 USC 2500 et sec. <http://www.law.cornell.edu:80/uscode/18/ch119.html>.

[1186] Foreign Intelligence Surveillance Act of 1978, 50 USC 1801.

[1187] Administrative Office of the US Courts, 1999 Wiretap Report. <http://www.epic.org/privacy/wiretap/stats/1999-report/default.html>.

[1188] EPIC, Chart of FISA Taps <http://www.epic.org/privacy/wiretap/stats/fisa_stats.html>.

The federal wiretap laws were amended by a controversial bill entitled the Communications Assistance to Law Enforcement Act in 1994 that required telephone companies to redesign their equipment to facilitate electronic surveillance.[1189] The Federal Communications Commission issued regulations in November 1998 implementing the law.[1190] The regulations include several additional provisions including requiring that all mobile phone companies facilitate location tracking of users. The implementation of the law is currently being challenged in federal court by privacy groups and telecommunications companies, who argue that the regulations give the government more power than authorized under the law and the Constitution.[1191]

The intelligence agencies have also pushed for more authority and funding to conduct surveillance of Internet communications, arguing that this is necessary to protect the nation's infrastructure from "information warfare." In July 2000, it was revealed that the FBI has developed a system called "Carnivore" that is placed at an Internet Service Provider's offices and can monitor all traffic about a user including email and browsing.[1192] Earthlink, a major ISP, announced that it refuses to install the system in its network.[1193] After the system was discovered, Attorney General Reno promised to conduct a review of its privacy protections.[1194] EPIC has filed suit demanding access to all information about the system.

There has been significant debate in the United States in recent years about the development of privacy laws covering the private sector. The White House and the private sector maintain that self-regulation is sufficient and that no new laws should be enacted except for a limited measure on medical information. There are currently efforts in Congress to improve financial privacy by prohibiting banks from selling personal information of customers without permission, but the proposal is strongly opposed by the banking industry. There is substantial activity

---

[1189] Communications Assistance for Law Enforcement Act of 1994, PL 103-411.
<http://www.epic.org/privacy/wiretap/calea/calea_law.html>.

[1190] Federal Communications Commission, In the Matter of the Communications Assistance for Law Enforcement Act, CC Docket No. 97-213, November 5, 1998.
<http://www.epic.org/privacy/wiretap/calea/fnprm.html>.

[1191] See EPIC Wiretap Pages, <http://www.epic.org/privacy/wiretap>.

[1192] Testimony of Robert Corn-Revere, before the Subcommittee on the Constitution of the Committee on the Judiciary, United States House of Representatives, The Fourth Amendment and the Internet, April 6, 2000. < <http://www.house.gov/judiciary/corn0406.htm>.

[1193] "EarthLink Says It Refuses to Install FBI's Carnivore Surveillance Device," Wall Street Journal, July 14, 2000.

[1194] Reno to double-check Carnivore's bite, Reuters, July 13, 2000

in the states, particularly in California, New York and Minnesota. In Massachusetts and Hawaii comprehensive privacy bills for the private sector are now under consideration.

Internet privacy has remained the hottest issue of the past year. A series of companies, including Intel and Microsoft, were discovered to have released products that secretly track the activities of Internet users. A number of lawsuits have been filed by users under the wiretap and computer crime laws. In several cases, TRUSTe, an industry-sponsored self-regulation watchdog group ruled that the practices did not violate its privacy seal program.[1195] Significant controversy arose around online profiling, the practice of advertising companies to track Internet users and compile dossiers on them in order to target banner advertisements. The largest of these advertisers, DoubleClick, set off widespread public outrage when it began attaching personal information from a marketing firm it purchased to the estimated 100 million previously anonymous profiles it had collected.[1196] The company backed down due to public opposition, a dramatic fall in its stock price and investigations from the FTC and several state attorneys general. In July 2000 the Federal Trade Commission reached an agreement with the Network Advertisers Initiative, a group consisting of the largest online advertisers including DoubleClick, which will allow for online profiling and any future merger of such databases to occur with only the opt-out consent.[1197] This agreement did not satisfy the state attorney generals and they have vowed to continue their investigation. Intel announced in May 2000 that it was dropping the incorporation of unique identifiers in its next-generation computer processors following a consumer boycott.[1198]

Several industry spokespeople, including Intel's Chairman Andrew Grove, have been supportive of federal Internet privacy legislation in order to stave off the states' recent efforts to enact such protections on their own.[1199] This year also saw the sole federal law governing information use online go into effect. The Childrens' Online Privacy Protection Act (COPPA), passed by Congress in 1998

[1195] See Big Brother Inside Campaign. <http://www.bigbrotherinside.org>.

[1196] See EPIC DoubleClick Pages, <http://www.epic.org/privacy/doubletrouble/>.

[1197] For a detailed history and critical analysis of this agreement, see Electronic Privacy Information Center (EPIC) and Junkbusters, 'Network Advertising Initiative: Principles not Privacy', July 28, 2000. <http://www.epic.org/privacy/internet/NAI_analysis.html>.

[1198] See <http://www.bigbrotherinside.org>.

[1199] "Gates, Grove Differ on Net Privacy Laws", Industry Standard, June 6, 2000.

and requiring parental consent before information is collected from children under the age of 13, went into effect in April 2000.[1200]

The end of 1999 also brought increased scrutiny on financial privacy. In 1999, the Michigan Attorney General sued several banks for revealing that they were selling information about their customers to marketers. Other banks across the country subsequently admitted that they were also selling customer records. The Gramm-Leach-Bliley Act, which eliminated traditional barriers between different financial institutions such as banks, securities firms and insurance companies, set weak protections on financial information that is likely to be shared among merged institutions. Several bills in Congress and in the states seek to increase those protections. In spite of the low level of protections conferred, the effective date of the privacy provisions were pushed back from November 2000 until July 2001.[1201] Despite pressing need, there are still no legislated federal protections covering medical records. In October 1999, the Department of Health and Human Services issued draft regulations protecting medical privacy.[1202] Public comments were solicited but the final rules have not yet been issued.

The U.S. Department of Commerce and the European Commission in June 2000 announced that they had reached an agreement on the Safe Harbor negotiations which would allow U.S. companies to continue to receive data from Europe. The European Parliament adopted a resolution in early July seeking greater privacy protections from the arrangement.[1203] The Commission announced that it was going to continue with the agreement without changes.

The Freedom of Information Act was enacted in 1966 and has been amended several times.[1204] It allows for access to federal government records by any requestor, except those held by the courts or the White House. However, there are numerous exceptions, long delays at many agencies, and little oversight unless a requestor files a lawsuit to enforce its rights. It was amended in 1996 by the Electronic Freedom of Information Act to specifically provide access to

---

[1200] FTC Privacy Pages, <http://www.ftc.gov/privacy/index.html>.

[1201] See Joint Press Release, May 10, 2000,
<http://www.bog.frb.fed.us/boarddocs/press/BoardActs/2000/20000510/default.htm>;
<http://www.ftc.gov/privacy/glbact/index.htm>.

[1202] Press Release, US Department of Health and Human Services,
<http://waisgate.hhs.gov/cgi-bin/waisgate?WAISdocID=350903248+25+0+0&WAISaction=retrieve>

[1203] European Parliament, Doubts over security personal data in US "Safe Harbors"
<http://www.europarl.eu.int/dg3/sdp/brief/en/br000703_ens.htm#9>.

[1204] Freedom of Information Act, 5 USC 552, 1966.
<http://www.epic.org/open_gov/foia/us_foia_act.html>.

records in electronic form.[1205] There are also laws in all states on providing access to government records.[1206]

The U.S. is a member of the Organization for Economic Cooperation and Development but has not implemented the OECD Guidelines on the Protection of Privacy and Transborder Flows of Personal Data in many sectors, including the financial sector and the medical sector. The 150 U.S. companies that signed the OECD Guidelines in 1981 do not appear to have kept their promises to enforce fair information practices once the threat of legislation faded in the early 1980s and many currently are actively lobbying against privacy laws.

[1205] Electronic Freedom of Information Act Amendments of 1996, <http://www.epic.org/open_gov/efoia.html>.

[1206] See Reporters Committee for Freedom of the Press. <http://www.reporters.net/nfoic/web/index.htm>.